ABOUT THIS PUBLICATION

FOR SERVICE ASSISTANCE

Customer Service
1.704.898.0770

North Carolina General Statues is published by The Muliti-Media Group of Greater Charlotte in Charlotte, North Carolina. Copyright 2015 by the Multi-Media Group of Greater Charlotte. This book or parts thereof may not be reproduced in any form, stored in a retrieval system, or transmitted in any form by any means—electronic, mechanical, photocopy, recording or otherwise—without prior written permission of the publisher, except as provided by United States of America copyright law.

The records required by U.S. Code 2257(a) through (c) and the pertinent regulations 28 C.F.R. Cli. 1, Part 75 with respect to this publication and all materials associated with such records are maintained by The Multi-Media Group of Greater Charlotte, Publisher and available for review by Attorney General.

www.visionbooks.org

Copyright © 2015 by MMGGC
All rights reserved!

TID: 5072132
ISBN (10) digit: 1502990547
ISBN (13) digit: 978-1502990549

123-4-56789-01239-Paperback
123-4-56789-01239-Hardback

First Edition

090520140547

Printed in the United States of America

2015 EDITION

North Carolina Criminal Law And Procedure-Pamphlet # 68

Printed In conjunction with the Administration of the Courts

North Carolina Criminal Law and Procedure
Pamphlet Reference Guide

Chapters	Pamphlet
Chapter 1 Civil Procedure	1
Chapter 1 Civil Procedure (Continue)	2
Chapter 1A Rules of Civil Procedure	2
Chapter 1B Contribution.	2
Chapter 1C Enforcement of Judgments.	2
Chapter 1D Punitive Damages.	2
Chapter 1E Eastern Band of Cherokee Indians.	2
Chapter 1F North Carolina Uniform Interstate Depositions and Discovery Act.	2
Chapter 2 - Clerk of Superior Court [Repealed and Transferred.]	3
Chapter 3 - Commissioners of Affidavits and Deeds [Repealed.]	3
Chapter 4 - Common Law	3
Chapter 5 - Contempt [Repealed.]	3
Chapter 5A - Contempt	3
Chapter 6 - Liability for Court Costs	3
Chapter 7 - Courts [Repealed and Transferred.]	3
Chapter 7A – Judicial Department	3
Chapter 7A – Continuation (Judicial Department)	4
Chapter 7A – Continuation (Judicial Department)	5
Chapter 7B - Juvenile Code	5
Chapter 8 - Evidence	6
Chapter 8A - Interpreters for Deaf Persons [Recodified.]	6
Chapter 8B - Interpreters for Deaf Persons	6
Chapter 8C - Evidence Code	6
Chapter 9 - Jurors	6
Chapter 10 - Notaries [Repealed.]	6
Chapter 10A - Notaries [Recodified.]	6
Chapter 10B - Notaries	6
Chapter 11 - Oaths	6
Chapter 12 - Statutory Construction	6
Chapter 13 - Citizenship Restored	6
Chapter 14 - Criminal Law	7
Chapter 14 –Criminal Law (Continuation)	8
Chapter 15 - Criminal Procedure	9
Chapter 15A - Criminal Procedure Act (Continuation)	10
Chapter 15A - Criminal Procedure Act (Continuation)	11
Chapter 15B - Victims Compensation	11
Chapter 15C - Address Confidentiality Program	11
Chapter 16 - Gaming Contracts and Futures	11
Chapter 17 - Habeas Corpus	11

Chapter 17A - Law-Enforcement Officers [Recodified.]	11
Chapter 17B - North Carolina Criminal Justice Education and Training System [Recodified.] Chapter 17C - North Carolina Criminal Justice Education and Training Standards Commission	11 11
Chapter 17D - North Carolina Justice Academy	11
Chapter 17E - North Carolina Sheriffs' Education and Training Standards Commission	11
Chapter 18 - Regulation of Intoxicating Liquors [Repealed.]	12
Chapter 18A - Regulation of Intoxicating Liquors [Repealed.]	12
Chapter 18B - Regulation of Alcoholic Beverages	12
Chapter 18C - North Carolina State Lottery	12
Chapter 19 - Offenses against Public Morals	12
Chapter 19A - Protection of Animals	12
Chapter 20 - Motor Vehicles	13
Chapter 20 - Motor Vehicles (Continuation)	14
Chapter 20 - Motor Vehicles (Continuation)	15
Chapter 20 - Motor Vehicles (Continuation)	16
Chapter 21 - Bills of Lading	17
Chapter 22 - Contracts Requiring Writing	17
Chapter 22A - Signatures	17
Chapter 22B - Contracts Against Public Policy	17
Chapter 22C - Payments to Subcontractors	17
Chapter 23 - Debtor and Creditor	17
Chapter 24 – Interest	17
Chapter 25 – Uniform Commercial Code	18
Chapter 25 – Uniform Commercial Code (Continuation)	19
Chapter 25A – Retail Installment Sales Act	20
Chapter 25B - Credit	20
Chapter 25C - Sales of Artwork	20
Chapter 26 - Suretyship	20
Chapter 27 - Warehouse Receipts [Repealed.]	20
Chapter 28 - Administration [Repealed.]	20
Chapter 28A - Administration of Decedents' Estates	20
Chapter 28B - Estates of Absentees in Military Service	20
Chapter 28C - Estates of Missing Persons	20
Chapter 29 - Intestate Succession	21
Chapter 30 - Surviving Spouses	21
Chapter 31 - Wills	21
Chapter 31A - Acts Barring Property Rights	21
Chapter 31B - Renunciation of Property and Renunciation of Fiduciary Powers Act	21
Chapter 31C - Uniform Disposition of Community Property Rights at Death Act	21
Chapter 32 - Fiduciaries	21
Chapter 32A - Powers of Attorney	21
Chapter 33 - Guardian and Ward [Repealed and Recodified.]	21

Chapter 33A - North Carolina Uniform Transfers to Minors Act	21
Chapter 33B - North Carolina Uniform Custodial Trust Act	21
Chapter 34 - Veterans' Guardianship Act	22
Chapter 35 - Sterilization Procedures	22
Chapter 35A - Incompetency and Guardianship	22
Chapter 36 - Trusts and Trustees [Repealed.]	22
Chapter 36A - Trusts and Trustees	22
Chapter 36B - Uniform Management of Institutional Funds Act [Repealed.]	22
Chapter 36C - North Carolina Uniform Trust Code	22
Chapter 36D - North Carolina Community Third Party Trusts, Pooled Trusts	23
Chapter 36E - Uniform Prudent Management of Institutional Funds Act	23
Chapter 37 - Allocation of Principal and Income [Repealed.]	23
Chapter 37A - Uniform Principal and Income Act	23
Chapter 38 - Boundaries	23
Chapter 38A - Landowner Liability	23
Chapter 39 - Conveyances	23
Chapter 39A - Transfer Fee Covenants Prohibited	23
Chapter 40 - Eminent Domain [Repealed.]	23
Chapter 40A - Eminent Domain	23
Chapter 41 - Estates	23
Chapter 41A - State Fair Housing Act	23
Chapter 42 - Landlord and Tenant	23
Chapter 42A - Vacation Rental Act	23
Chapter 43 - Land Registration	23
Chapter 44 - Liens	24
Chapter 44A - Statutory Liens and Charges	24
Chapter 45 - Mortgages and Deeds of Trust	24
Chapter 45A - Good Funds Settlement Act	24
Chapter 46 - Partition	24
Chapter 47 - Probate and Registration	25
Chapter 47A - Unit Ownership	25
Chapter 47B - Real Property Marketable Title Act	25
Chapter 47C - North Carolina Condominium Act	25
Chapter 47D - Notice of Settlement Act [Expired.]	25
Chapter 47E - Residential Property Disclosure Act	25
Chapter 47F - North Carolina Planned Community Act	25
Chapter 47G - Option to Purchase Contracts	25
Chapter 47H - Contracts for Deed	25
Chapter 48 - Adoptions +	26
Chapter 48A - Minors	26
Chapter 49 - Bastardy	26
Chapter 49A - Rights of Children	26
Chapter 50 - Divorce and Alimony	26
Chapter 50A - Uniform Child-Custody Jurisdiction and	

Enforcement Act	26
Chapter 50B - Domestic Violence	26
Chapter 50C - Civil No-Contact Orders	26
Chapter 51 - Marriage	26
Chapter 52 - Powers and Liabilities of Married Persons	27
Chapter 52A - Uniform Reciprocal Enforcement of Support Act [Repealed.]	27
Chapter 52B - Uniform Premarital Agreement Act	27
Chapter 52C - Uniform Interstate Family Support Act	27
Chapter 53 - Banks	27
Chapter 53A - Business Development Corporations and North Carolina Capital Resource Corporations	28
Chapter 53B - Financial Privacy Act	28
Chapter 54 - Cooperative Organizations	28
Chapter 54A - Capital Stock Savings and Loan Associations [Repealed.]	28
Chapter 54B - Savings and Loan Associations	29
Chapter 54C - Savings Banks	29
Chapter 55 - North Carolina Business Corporation Act	30
Chapter 55A - North Carolina Nonprofit Corporation Act	31
Chapter 55B - Professional Corporation Act	31
Chapter 55C - Foreign Trade Zones	31
Chapter 55D - Filings, Names, and Registered Agents for Corporations, Nonprofit Corporations, and Partnerships	31
Chapter 56 - Electric, Telegraph and Power Companies [Repealed.]	31
Chapter 57 - Hospital, Medical and Dental Service Corporations [Recodified.]	31
Chapter 57A - Health Maintenance Organization Act [Recodified.]	31
Chapter 57B - Health Maintenance Organization Act [Recodified.]	31
Chapter 57C - North Carolina Limited Liability Company Act.	31
Chapter 58 - Insurance.	32
Chapter 58 - Insurance (Continuation)	33
Chapter 58 - Insurance (Continuation)	34
Chapter 58 - Insurance (Continuation)	35
Chapter 58 - Insurance (Continuation)	36
Chapter 58 - Insurance (Continuation)	37
Chapter 58 - Insurance (Continuation)	38
Chapter 58A - North Carolina Health Insurance Trust Commission [Recodified.]	38
Chapter 59 - Partnership.	39
Chapter 59B - Uniform Unincorporated Nonprofit Association Act.	39
Chapter 60 - Railroads and Other Carriers [Repealed and Transferred.]	39
Chapter 61 - Religious Societies	39
Chapter 62 - Public Utilities	39

Chapter 62 - Public Utilities (Continuation)	40
Chapter 62A - Public Safety Telephone Service And Wireless Telephone Service	40
Chapter 63 - Aeronautics	40
Chapter 63A - North Carolina Global TransPark Authority	40
Chapter 64 - Aliens	40
Chapter 65 – Cemeteries	40
Chapter 66 - Commerce and Business	41
Chapter 67 - Dogs	41
Chapter 68 - Fences and Stock Law	41
Chapter 69 - Fire Protection	41
Chapter 70 - Indian Antiquities, Archaeological Resources and Unmarked Human Skeletal Remains Protection	42
Chapter 71 - Indians [Repealed.]	42
Chapter 71A - Indians	42
Chapter 72 - Inns, Hotels and Restaurants	42
Chapter 73 - Mills	42
Chapter 74 - Mines and Quarries	42
Chapter 74A - Company Police [Repealed.]	42
Chapter 74B - Private Protective Services Act [Repealed.]	42
Chapter 74C - Private Protective Services	42
Chapter 74D - Alarm Systems	42
Chapter 74E - Company Police Act	42
Chapter 74F - Locksmith Licensing Act	42
Chapter 74G - Campus Police Act	42
Chapter 75 - Monopolies, Trusts and Consumer Protection	42
Chapter 75A - Boating and Water Safety	43
Chapter 75B - Discrimination in Business	43
Chapter 75C - Motion Picture Fair Competition Act	43
Chapter 75D - Racketeer Influenced and Corrupt Organizations	43
Chapter 75E - Unlawful Activities in Connection With Certain Corporate Transactions	43
Chapter 76 - Navigation	43
Chapter 76A - Navigation and Pilotage Commissions	43
Chapter 77 - Rivers, Creeks, and Coastal Waters	43
Chapter 78 - Securities Law [Repealed.]	43
Chapter 78A - North Carolina Securities Act	43
Chapter 78B - Tender Offer Disclosure Act [Repealed.]	43
Chapter 78C - Investment Advisers	43
Chapter 78D - Commodities Act	43
Chapter 79 - Strays [Repealed.]	43
Chapter 80 - Trademarks, Brands, etc.	44
Chapter 81 - Weights and Measures [Recodified.]	44
Chapter 81A - Weights and Measures Act of 1975.	44
Chapter 82 - Wrecks [Repealed.]	44
Chapter 83 - Architects [Recodified.]	44

Chapter 83A - Architects	44
Chapter 84 - Attorneys-at-Law	44
Chapter 84A - Foreign Legal Consultants	44
Chapter 85 - Auctions and Auctioneers [Repealed.]	44
Chapter 85A - Bail Bondsmen and Runners [Recodified.]	44
Chapter 85B - Auctions and Auctioneers	44
Chapter 85C - Bail Bondsmen and Runners [Recodified.]	44
Chapter 86 - Barbers [Recodified.]	44
Chapter 86A - Barbers	44
Chapter 87 - Contractors	44
Chapter 88 - Cosmetic Art [Repealed.]	44
Chapter 88A - Electrolysis Practice Act	44
Chapter 88B - Cosmetic Art	45
Chapter 89 - Engineering and Land Surveying [Recodified.]	45
Chapter 89A - Landscape Architects	45
Chapter 89B - Foresters	45
Chapter 89C - Engineering and Land Surveying	45
Chapter 89D - Landscape Contractors	45
Chapter 89E - Geologists Licensing Act	45
Chapter 89F - North Carolina Soil Scientist Licensing Act	45
Chapter 89G - Irrigation Contractors	45
Chapter 90 - Medicine and Allied Occupations	45
Chapter 90 - Medicine and Allied Occupations (Continuation)	46
Chapter 90 - Medicine and Allied Occupations (Continuation)	47
Chapter 90 - Medicine and Allied Occupations (Continuation)	48
Chapter 90A - Sanitarians and Water and Wastewater Treatment Facility Operators	48
Chapter 90B - Social Worker Certification and Licensure Act	48
Chapter 90C - North Carolina Recreational Therapy Licensure Act	48
Chapter 90D - Interpreters and Transliterators	48
Chapter 91 - Pawnbrokers [Repealed.]	48
Chapter 91A - Pawnbrokers Modernization Act of 1989	48
Chapter 92 - Photographers [Deleted.]	48
Chapter 93 - Certified Public Accountants	48
Chapter 93A - Real Estate License Law	49
Chapter 93B - Occupational Licensing Boards	49
Chapter 93C - Watchmakers [Repealed.]	49
Chapter 93D - North Carolina State Hearing Aid Dealers and Fitters Board.	49
Chapter 93E - North Carolina Appraisers Act	49
Chapter 94 - Apprenticeship	49
Chapter 95 - Department of Labor and Labor Regulations	49
Chapter 95 - Department of Labor and Labor Regulations (Continuation)	50
Chapter 96 - Employment Security	50
Chapter 97 - Workers' Compensation Act	50
Chapter 97 - Workers' Compensation Act (Continuation)	51

Chapter 98 - Burnt and Lost Records	51
Chapter 99 - Libel and Slander	51
Chapter 99A - Civil Remedies for Criminal Actions	51
Chapter 99B - Products Liability	51
Chapter 99C - Actions Relating to Winter Sports Safety and Accidents	51
Chapter 99D - Civil Rights	51
Chapter 99E - Special Liability Provisions	51
Chapter 100 - Monuments, Memorials and Parks	51
Chapter 101 - Names of Persons	51
Chapter 102 - Official Survey Base	51
Chapter 103 - Sundays, Holidays and Special Days	51
Chapter 104 - United States Lands	51
Chapter 104A - Degrees of Kinship	51
Chapter 104B - Hurricanes or Other Acts of Nature	51
Chapter 104C - Atomic Energy, Radioactivity and Ionizing Radiation [Repealed and Recodified.]	51
Chapter 104D - Southern States Energy Compact	51
Chapter 104E - North Carolina Radiation Protection Act	51
Chapter 104F - Southeast Interstate Low-Level Radioactive Waste Management Compact [Repealed]	51
Chapter 104G - North Carolina Low-Level Radioactive Waste Management Authority Act of 1987 [Repealed]	51
Chapter 105 - Taxation	51
Chapter 105 - Taxation (Continuation)	52
Chapter 105 - Taxation (Continuation)	53
Chapter 105 - Taxation (Continuation)	54
Chapter 105A - Setoff Debt Collection Act	55
Chapter 105B - Defaulted Student Loan Recovery Act	55
Chapter 106 - Agriculture	55
Chapter 106 - Agriculture (Continue)	56
Chapter 106 - Agriculture (Continue)	57
Chapter 107 - Agricultural Development Districts [Repealed.]	57
Chapter 108 - Social Services [Repealed and Recodified.]	57
Chapter 108A - Social Services	57
Chapter 108B - Community Action Programs	58
Chapter 108C Medicaid and Health Choice Provider Requirements.	58
Chapter 108D Medicaid Managed Care for Behavioral Health Services.	58
Chapter 109 - Bonds [Recodified.]	58
Chapter 110 - Child Welfare	58
Chapter 111 - Aid to the Blind	58
Chapter 112 - Confederate Homes and Pensions [Repealed.]	58
Chapter 113 - Conservation and Development	58
Chapter 113 - Conservation and Development (Continuation)	59

Chapter	Page
Chapter 113A - Pollution Control and Environment	59
Chapter 113A - Pollution Control and Environment (Continuation)	60
Chapter 113B - North Carolina Energy Policy Act of 1975	60
Chapter 114 - Department of Justice	60
Chapter 115 - Elementary and Secondary Education [Repealed.]	60
Chapter 115A - Community Colleges, Technical Institutes, and Industrial Education Centers [Repealed.]	60
Chapter 115B - Tuition and Fee Waivers	60
Chapter 115C - Elementary and Secondary Education	60
Chapter 115C - Elementary and Secondary Education (Continuation)	61
Chapter 115C - Elementary and Secondary Education (Continuation)	62
Chapter 115C - Elementary and Secondary Education (Continuation)	63
Chapter 115D - Community Colleges	63
Chapter 115E - Private Educational Facilities Finance Act [Recodified]	63
Chapter 116 - Higher Education	63
Chapter 116 - Higher Education (Continuation)	64
Chapter 116A - Escheats and Abandoned Property [Repealed.]	64
Chapter 116B - Escheats and Abandoned Property	64
Chapter 116C - Continuum of Education Programs	64
Chapter 116D - Higher Education Bonds	64
Chapter 116E - Education Longitudinal Data System	64
Chapter 117 - Electrification	64
Chapter 118 - Firemen's and Rescue Squad Workers' Relief and Pension Funds [Recodified.]	64
Chapter 118A - Firemen's Death Benefit Act [Repealed.]	64
Chapter 118B - Members of a Rescue Squad Death Benefit Act [Repealed.]	64
Chapter 119 - Gasoline and Oil Inspection and Regulation	64
Chapter 120 - General Assembly	65
Chapter 120 - General Assembly (Continuation)	66
Chapter 120 - General Assembly (Continuation)	67
Chapter 120C - Lobbying	67
Chapter 121 - Archives and History	67
Chapter 122 - Hospitals for the Mentally Disordered [Repealed.]	67
Chapter 122A - North Carolina Housing Finance Agency	67
Chapter 122B - North Carolina Agricultural Facilities Finance Act [Repealed.]	67
Chapter 122C - Mental Health, Developmental Disabilities, and Substance Abuse Act of 1985	67
Chapter 122C - Mental Health, Developmental Disabilities, and Substance Abuse Act of 1985 (Continuation)	68

Chapter 122D - North Carolina Agricultural Finance Act	68
Chapter 122E - North Carolina Housing Trust and Oil Overcharge Act	68
Chapter 123 - Impeachment	69
Chapter 123A - Industrial Development [Repealed.]	69
Chapter 124 - Internal Improvements	69
Chapter 125 - Libraries	69
Chapter 126 - State Personnel System	69
Chapter 127 - Militia [Repealed.]	69
Chapter 127A - Militia	69
Chapter 127B - Military Affairs	69
Chapter 127C - Advisory Commission on Military Affairs	69
Chapter 128 - Offices and Public Officers	69
Chapter 128 - Offices and Public Officers (Continuation)	70
Chapter 129 - Public Buildings and Grounds	70
Chapter 130 - Public Health [Repealed.]	70
Chapter 130A - Public Health	70
Chapter 130A - Public Health (Continuation)	71
Chapter 130A - Public Health (Continuation)	72
Chapter 130B - Hazardous Waste Management Commission [Repealed.]	72
Chapter 131 - Public Hospitals [Repealed.]	72
Chapter 131A - Health Care Facilities Finance Act	72
Chapter 131B - Licensing of Ambulatory Surgical Facilities [Repealed.]	72
Chapter 131C - Charitable Solicitation Licensure Act [Repealed.]	72
Chapter 131D - Inspection and Licensing of Facilities	72
Chapter 131E - Health Care Facilities and Services	72
Chapter 131E - Health Care Facilities and Services (Continuation)	73
Chapter 131F - Solicitation of Contributions	73
Chapter 132 - Public Records	73
Chapter 133 - Public Works	74
Chapter 134 - Youth Development [Recodified.]	74
Chapter 134A - Youth Services [Repealed.]	74
Chapter 135 - Retirement System for Teachers and State Employees; Social Security; Health Insurance Program for Children	74
Chapter 135 - Retirement System for Teachers and State Employees; Social Security; Health Insurance Program for Children	75
Chapter 136 - Transportation	75
Chapter 136 - Transportation (Continuation)	76
Chapter 137 - Rural Rehabilitation [Repealed.]	76
Chapter 138 - Salaries, Fees and Allowances	76
Chapter 138A - State Government Ethics Act	76

Chapter 139 - Soil and Water Conservation Districts	76
Chapter 140 - State Art Museum; Symphony and Art Societies	76
Chapter 140A - State Awards System	76
Chapter 141 - State Boundaries	76
Chapter 142 - State Debt	76
Chapter 143 - State Departments, Institutions, and Commissions	77
Chapter 143 - State Departments, Institutions, and Commissions (Continuation)	78
Chapter 143 - State Departments, Institutions, and Commissions (Continuation)	79
Chapter 143 - State Departments, Institutions, and Commissions (Continuation)	80
Chapter 143A - State Government Reorganization	80
Chapter 143B - Executive Organization Act of 1973	80
Chapter 143B - Executive Organization Act of 1973 (Continuation)	81
Chapter 143B - Executive Organization Act of 1973 (Continuation)	82
Chapter 143C - State Budget Act	83
Chapter 143D - The State Governmental Accountability and Internal Control Act	83
Chapter 144 - State Flag, Official Governmental Flags, Motto, and Colors	83
Chapter 145 - State Symbols and Other Official Adoptions.	83
Chapter 146 - State Lands	83
Chapter 147 - State Officers	83
Chapter 148 - State Prison System	84
Chapter 149 - State Song and Toast	84
Chapter 150 - Uniform Revocation of Licenses [Repealed.]	84
Chapter 150A - Administrative Procedure Act [Recodified.]	84
Chapter 150B - Administrative Procedure Act	84
Chapter 151 - Constables [Repealed.]	84
Chapter 152 - Coroners	84
Chapter 152A - County Medical Examiner [Repealed.]	84
Chapter 152A - County Medical Examiner [Repealed.] (Continuation)	85
Chapter 153 - Counties and County Commissioners [Repealed.]	85
Chapter 153A - Counties	85
Chapter 153B - Mountain Resources Planning Act	85
Chapter 153C - Uwharrie Regional Resources Act	85
Chapter 154 - County Surveyor [Repealed.]	85
Chapter 155 - County Treasurer [Repealed.]	85
Chapter 156 - Drainage	85

Chapter 156 – Drainage (Continuation)	86
Chapter 157 - Housing Authorities and Projects	86
Chapter 157A - Historic Properties Commissions [Transferred.]	86
Chapter 158 - Local Development	86
Chapter 159 - Local Government Finance	86
Chapter 159 - Local Government Finance (Continuation)	87
Chapter 159A - Pollution Abatement and Industrial Facilities Financing Act [Unconstitutional.]	87
Chapter 159B - Joint Municipal Electric Power and Energy Act	87
Chapter 159C - Industrial and Pollution Control Facilities Financing Act	87
Chapter 159D - The North Carolina Capital Facilities Financing Act	87
Chapter 159E - Registered Public Obligations Act	87
Chapter 159F - North Carolina Energy Development Authority [Repealed.]	87
Chapter 159G - Water Infrastructure	87
Chapter 159H - [Reserved.]	87
Chapter 159I - Solid Waste Management Loan Program and Local Government Special Obligation Bonds	87
Chapter 160 - Municipal Corporations [Repealed And Transferred.]	87
Chapter 160A - Cities and Towns	88
Chapter 160A - Cities and Towns (Continuation)	89
Chapter 160B - Consolidated City-County Act	89
Chapter 160C - Baseball Park Districts [Repealed.]	90
Chapter 161 - Register of Deeds	90
Chapter 162 - Sheriff	90
Chapter 162A - Water and Sewer Systems	90
Chapter 162B Continuity of Local Government in Emergency.	90
Chapter 163 Elections and Election Laws.	90
Chapter 163 Elections and Election Laws. (Continuation)	91
Chapter 164 Concerning the General Statutes of North Carolina.	92
Chapter 165 Veterans.	92
Chapter 166 Civil Preparedness Agencies [Repealed.]	92
Chapter 166A North Carolina Emergency Management Act.	92
Chapter 167 State Civil Air Patrol [Repealed.]	92
Chapter 168 Persons with Disabilities.	92
Chapter 168A Persons With Disabilities Protection Act.	92

§ 122C-23. Licensure.

(a)   No person shall establish, maintain, or operate a licensable facility for the mentally ill, developmentally disabled, or substance abusers without a current license issued by the Secretary.

(b)   Each license is issued to the person only for the premises named in the application and shall not be transferrable or assignable except with prior written approval of the Secretary.

(c)   Any person who intends to establish, maintain, or operate a licensable facility shall apply to the Secretary for a license. The Secretary shall prescribe by rule the contents of the application forms.

(d)   The Secretary shall issue a license if the Secretary finds that the person complies with this Article and the rules of the Commission and Secretary.

(e)   Initial licenses issued under the authority of this section shall be valid for not more than 15 months. Licenses shall be renewed annually thereafter and shall expire at the end of the calendar year. The expiration date of a license shall be specified on the license when issued. Renewal of a regular license is contingent upon receipt of information required by the Secretary for renewal and continued compliance with this Article and the rules of the Commission and the Secretary. Licenses for facilities that have not served any clients during the previous 12 months are not eligible for renewal.

The Secretary may issue a provisional license for a period up to six months to a person obtaining the initial license for a facility. The licensee must demonstrate substantial compliance prior to being issued a full license.

A provisional license for a period not to exceed six months may be granted by the Secretary to a person who is temporarily unable to comply with a rule when the noncompliance does not present an immediate threat to the health and safety of the individuals in the licensable facility. During this period the licensable facility shall correct the noncompliance based on a plan submitted to and approved by the Secretary. A provisional license for an additional period of time to meet the noncompliance may not be issued.

(e1)   Except as provided in subsection (e2) of this section, the Secretary shall not enroll any new provider for Medicaid Home or Community Based services or other Medicaid services, as defined in 42 C.F.R. 440.90, 42 C.F.R. 440.130(d), and 42 C.F.R. 440.180, or issue a license for a new facility or a new service to any applicant meeting any of the following criteria:

(1) The applicant was the owner, principal, or affiliate of a licensable facility under Chapter 122C, Chapter 131D, or Article 7 of Chapter 110 that had its license revoked until 60 months after the date of the revocation.

(2) The applicant is the owner, principal, or affiliate of a licensable facility that was assessed a penalty for a Type A or Type B violation under Article 3 of this Chapter, or any combination thereof, and any one of the following conditions exist:

a. A single violation has been assessed in the six months prior to the application.

b. Two violations have been assessed in the 18 months prior to the application and 18 months have not passed from the date of the most recent violation.

c. Three violations have been assessed in the 36 months prior to the application and 36 months have not passed from the date of the most recent violation.

d. Four or more violations have been assessed in the 60 months prior to application and 60 months have not passed from the date of the most recent violation.

(3) The applicant is the owner, principal, or affiliate of a licensable facility that had its license summarily suspended or downgraded to provisional status as a result of violations under G.S. 122C-24.1(a) until 60 months after the date of reinstatement or restoration of the license.

(4) The applicant is the owner, principal, or affiliate of a licensable facility that had its license summarily suspended or downgraded to provisional status as a result of violations under Article 1A of Chapter 131D until 60 months after the date of reinstatement or restoration of the license.

(e2) The Secretary may enroll a provider described in subsection (e1) of this section if any of the following circumstances apply:

(1) The applicant is an area program or county program providing services under G.S. 122C-141, and there is no other provider of the service in the catchment area.

(2) The Secretary finds that the area program or county program has shown good cause by clear and convincing evidence why the enrollment should be allowed.

(e3) For purposes of subdivision (e1)(2), fines assessed prior to October 23, 2002, are not applicable to this provision. However, licensure or enrollment shall be denied if an applicant's history as a provider under Chapter 131D, Chapter 122C, or Article 7 of Chapter 110 is such that the Secretary has concluded the applicant will likely be unable to comply with licensing or enrollment statutes, rules, or regulations. In the event the Secretary denies licensure or enrollment under this subsection, the reasons for the denial and appeal rights pursuant to Article 3 of Chapter 150B shall be given to the provider in writing.

(f) Upon written application and in accordance with rules of the Commission, the Secretary may for good cause waive any of the rules implementing this Article, provided those rules do not affect the health, safety, or welfare of the individuals within the licensable facility. Decisions made pursuant to this subsection may be appealed to the Commission for a hearing in accordance with Chapter 150B of the General Statutes.

(g) The Secretary may suspend the admission of any new clients to a facility licensed under this Article where the conditions of the facility are detrimental to the health or safety of the clients. This suspension shall be for the period determined by the Secretary and shall remain in effect until the Secretary is satisfied that conditions or circumstances merit removal of the suspension. In suspending admissions under this subsection, the Secretary shall consider the following factors:

(1) The degree of sanctions necessary to ensure compliance with this section and rules adopted to implement this subsection, and

(2) The character and degree of impact of the conditions at the facility on the health or safety of its clients.

A facility may contest a suspension of admissions under this subsection in accordance with Chapter 150B of the General Statutes. In contesting the suspension of admissions, the facility must file a petition for a contested case within 20 days after the Department mails notice of suspension of admissions to the licensee.

(h) The Department shall charge facilities licensed under this Chapter a nonrefundable annual base license fee plus a nonrefundable annual per-bed fee as follows:

Type of Facility Per-Bed Fee	Number of Beds	Base Fee
Facilities (non-ICF/MR): $0	0 beds	$215.00
1 to 6 beds	$305.00	$0
More than 6 beds	$475.00	$17.50
ICF/MR Only: $0	1 to 6 beds	$845.00
More than 6 beds	$800.00	$17.50

(i) (Applicable to social setting detoxification facilities licensed on and after August 7, 2003) A social setting detoxification facility or medical detoxification facility subject to licensure under this Chapter shall not deny admission or treatment to an individual based solely on the individual's inability to pay. (1899, c. 1, s. 60; Rev., s. 4600; C.S., s. 6219; 1945, c. 952, s. 41; 1957, c. 100, ss. 1, 4; 1963, c. 813, s. 1; c. 1166, s. 7; 1965, c. 1178, ss. 1-3; 1969, c. 954; 1973, c. 476, ss. 133, 152; 1977, c. 679, s. 7; 1981, c. 51, s. 3; 1983, c. 718, ss. 1, 4; 1985, c. 589, s. 2; 1985 (Reg. Sess., 1986), c. 863, s. 8; 1987, c. 345, ss. 3, 4; 1989, c. 625, s. 6; 2000-55, s. 3; 2002-164, s. 4.1; 2003-284, s. 34.8(a); 2003-294, s. 2; 2003-390, s. 3; 2005-276, ss. 41.2(h), 10.40A(d); 2006-66, s. 10.23; 2009-451, s. 10.76(f).)

§ 122C-23.1. Licensure of residential treatment facilities.

The General Assembly finds:

(1)   That much of the care for residential treatment facility residents is paid by the State and the counties;

(2)   That the cost to the State for care for residents of residential treatment facilities is substantial, and high vacancy rates in residential treatment facilities further increase the cost of care;

(3)   That the proliferation of residential treatment facilities results in costly duplication and underuse of facilities and may result in lower quality service;

(4)   There is currently no ongoing relationship between some applicants for licensure and local management entities (LMEs) that are responsible for the placement of children and adults in residential treatment facilities; and

(5)   That it is necessary to protect the general welfare and lives, health, and property of the people of the State for the local management entity (LME) to verify that additional beds are needed in the LME's catchment area before new residential treatment facilities are licensed. This process is established to ensure that unnecessary costs to the State do not result, residential treatment facility beds are available where needed, and that individuals who need care in residential treatment facilities may have access to quality care.

Based on these findings, the Department of Health and Human Services may license new residential treatment facilities if the applicant for licensure submits with the application a letter of support obtained from the local management entity in whose catchment area the facility will be located. The letter of support shall be submitted to the Department of Health and Human Services, Division of Health Service Regulation and Division of Mental Health, Developmental Disabilities, and Substance Abuse Services, and shall specify the number of existing beds in the same type of facility in the catchment area and the projected need for additional beds of the same type of facility. As used in this subsection, "residential treatment facility" means a "residential facility" as defined in and licensed under this Chapter, but not subject to Certificate of Need requirements under Article 9 of Chapter 131E of the General Statutes. (2005-276, s. 10.40(a); 2007-182, s. 1.)

§ 122C-24. Adverse action on a license.

(a) The Secretary may deny, suspend, amend, or revoke a license in any case in which the Secretary finds that there has been a substantial failure to comply with any provision of this Article or other applicable statutes or any applicable rule adopted pursuant to these statutes. Action[s] under this section and appeals of those actions shall be in accordance with rules of the Commission and Chapter 150B of the General Statutes.

(b) When an appeal is filed concerning the denial, suspension, amendment, or revocation of a license, a copy of the proposal for decision shall be sent to the Chairman of the Commission in addition to the parties specified in G.S. 150B-34. The Chairman or members of the Commission designated by the Chairman may submit for the Secretary's consideration written or oral comments concerning the proposal prior to the issuance of a final agency decision in accordance with G.S. 150B-36. (1983, c. 718, s. 1; 1985, c. 589, s. 2; 1985 (Reg. Sess., 1986), c. 863, ss. 8-10; 1987, c. 345, s. 5.)

§ 122C-24.1. Penalties; remedies.

(a) Violation Classification and Penalties. - The Department of Health and Human Services shall impose an administrative penalty in accordance with provisions of this Article on any facility licensed under this Article which is found to be in violation of Article 2 or 3 of this Chapter or applicable State and federal laws and regulations. Citations for violations shall be classified and penalties assessed according to the nature of the violation as follows:

(1) "Type A1 Violation" means a violation by a facility of the regulations, standards, and requirements set forth in Article 2 or 3 of this Chapter or applicable State or federal laws and regulations governing the licensure or certification of a facility which results in death or serious physical harm, abuse, neglect, or exploitation. The person making the findings shall do the following:

a. Orally and immediately inform the facility of the Type A1 Violation and the specific findings.

a1. Require a written plan of protection regarding how the facility will immediately abate the Type A1 Violation in order to protect clients from further risk or additional harm.

b. Within 15 working days of the investigation, send a report of the findings to the facility.

c. Require a plan of correction to be submitted to the Department, based on a written report of the findings, that describes steps the facility will take to achieve and maintain compliance.

The Department shall impose a civil penalty in an amount not less than five hundred dollars ($500.00) nor more than ten thousand dollars ($10,000) for each Type Al Violation in facilities or programs that serve six or fewer persons. The Department shall impose a civil penalty in an amount not less than one thousand dollars ($1,000) nor more than twenty thousand dollars ($20,000) for each Type A1 Violation in facilities or programs that serve seven or more persons. Where a facility has failed to correct a Type A1 Violation, the Department shall access the facility a civil penalty in the amount of up to one thousand dollars ($1,000) for each day that the violation continues beyond the time specified for correction. The Department or its authorized representative shall determine whether the violation has been corrected.

(1a) "Type A2 Violation" means a violation by a facility of the regulations, standards, and requirements set forth in Article 2 or 3 of this Chapter or applicable State or federal laws and regulations governing the licensure or certification of a facility which results in substantial risk that death or serious physical harm, abuse, neglect, or exploitation will occur. The person making the findings shall do the following:

a. Orally and immediately inform the facility of the Type A2 Violation and the specific findings.

b. Require a written plan of protection regarding how the facility will immediately abate the Type A2 Violation in order to protect clients or residents from further risk or additional harm.

c. Within 15 working days of the investigation, send a report of the findings to the facility.

d. Require a plan of correction to be submitted to the Department, based on the written report of the findings, that describes steps the facility will take to achieve and maintain compliance.

The violation or violations shall be corrected within the time specified for correction by the Department or its authorized representative. The Department may or may not assess a penalty taking into consideration the compliance history, preventative measures, and response to previous violations by the facility. Where a facility has failed to correct a Type A2 Violation, the Department shall assess the facility a civil penalty in the amount of up to one thousand dollars ($1,000) for each day that the deficiency continues beyond the time specified for correction by the Department or its authorized representative. The Department or its authorized representative shall determine whether the violation has been corrected.

(1b)   "Past Corrected Type A1 or Type A2 Violation" means either (i) the violation was not previously identified by the Department or its authorized representative or (ii) the violation was discovered by the facility and was self-reported, but in either case the violation has been corrected. In determining whether a penalty should be assessed under this section, the Department shall consider the following factors:

a.   Preventative measures in place prior to the violation.

b.   Whether the violation or violations were abated immediately.

c.   Whether the facility implemented corrective measures to achieve and maintain compliance.

d.   Whether the facility's system to ensure compliance is maintained and continues to be implemented.

e.   Whether the regulatory area remains in compliance.

(2)   "Type B Violation" means a violation by a facility of the regulations, standards, and requirements set forth in Article 2 or 3 of this Chapter or applicable State or federal laws and regulations governing the licensure or certification of a facility which is detrimental to the health, safety, or welfare of any client or patient, but which does not result in substantial risk that death or serious physical harm, abuse, neglect, or exploitation will occur. The person making the findings shall do the following:

a.   Orally and immediately inform the facility of the Type B Violation and the specific findings.

b. Require a written plan of protection regarding how the facility will immediately abate the Type B Violation in order to protect clients or residents from further risk or additional harm.

c. Within 15 working days of the investigation, send a report of the findings to the facility.

d. Require a plan of correction to be submitted to the Department, based on the written report of the findings, that describes steps the facility will take to achieve and maintain compliance.

Where a facility has failed to correct a Type B Violation within the time specified for correction by the Department or its authorized representative, the Department shall assess the facility a civil penalty in the amount of up to four hundred dollars ($400.00) for each day that the violation continues beyond the date specified for correction without just reason for the failure. The Department or its authorized representative shall ensure that the violation has been corrected.

(3) Repeat Violations. - The Department shall impose a civil penalty which is treble the amount assessed under this subsection when a facility under the same management or ownership has received a citation during the previous 12 months for which the appeal rights are exhausted and penalty payment is expected or has occurred, and the current violation is for the same specific provision of a statute or regulation for which it received a violation during the previous 12 months.

(b) Repealed by Session Laws 2011-249, s. 1, effective June 23, 2011.

(c) Factors to Be Considered in Determining Amount of Initial Penalty. - In determining the amount of the initial penalty to be imposed under this section, the Department shall consider the following factors:

(1) There is substantial risk that serious physical harm, abuse, neglect, or exploitation will occur, and this has not been corrected within the time specified by the Department or its authorized representative;

(2) Serious physical harm, abuse, neglect, or exploitation, without substantial risk for client death, did occur;

(3) Serious physical harm, abuse, neglect, or exploitation, with substantial risk for client death, did occur;

(3a) A client died;

(3b) A client died and there is substantial risk to others for serious physical harm, abuse, neglect, or exploitation;

(3c) A client died and there is substantial risk for further client death;

(4) The reasonable diligence exercised by the licensee to comply with G.S. 131E-256 and other applicable State and federal laws and regulations;

(5) Efforts by the licensee to correct violations;

(6) The number and type of previous violations committed by the licensee within the past 36 months; and

(7) Repealed by Session Laws 2011-249, s. 1, effective June 23, 2011.

(8) The number of clients or patients put at risk by the violation.

(d) The facts found to support the factors in subsection (c) of this section shall be the basis in determining the amount of the penalty. The Department shall document the findings in written record and shall make the written record available to all affected parties including:

(1) The licensee involved;

(2) The clients or patients affected; and

(3) The family members or guardians of the clients or patients affected.

(e) The Department shall impose a civil penalty of fifty dollars ($50.00) per day on any facility which refuses to allow an authorized representative of the Department to inspect the premises and records of the facility.

(f) Any facility wishing to contest a penalty shall be entitled to an administrative hearing as provided in Chapter 150B of the General Statutes. A petition for a contested case shall be filed within 30 days after the Department mails a notice of penalty to a licensee. At least the following specific issues shall be addressed at the administrative hearing:

(1) The reasonableness of the amount of any civil penalty assessed, and

(2) The degree to which each factor has been evaluated pursuant to subsection (c) of this section to be considered in determining the amount of an initial penalty.

If a civil penalty is found to be unreasonable or if the evaluation of each factor is found to be incomplete, the hearing officer may recommend that the penalty be adjusted accordingly.

(g) Any penalty imposed by the Department of Health and Human Services under this section shall commence on the date of the letter of notification of the penalty amount.

(h) The Secretary may bring a civil action in the superior court of the county wherein the violation occurred to recover the amount of the administrative penalty whenever a facility:

(1) Which has not requested an administrative hearing fails to pay the penalty within 60 days after being notified of the penalty, or

(2) Which has requested an administrative hearing fails to pay the penalty within 60 days after receipt of a written copy of the decision as provided in G.S. 150B-37.

(i) In lieu of assessing all or some of the administrative penalty, the Secretary may order a facility to provide staff training if the training is:

(1) Specific to the violation;

(2) Approved by the Department of Health and Human Services; and

(3) Taught by someone approved by the Department.

(j) The clear proceeds of civil penalties provided for in this section shall be remitted to the State Treasurer for deposit in accordance with State law.

(k) In considering renewal of a license, the Department shall not renew a license if outstanding fines and penalties imposed by the Department against the facility or program have not been paid. Fines and penalties for which an appeal is pending are exempt from consideration for nonrenewal under this subsection. (2000-55, s. 4; 2005-276, ss. 10.40A(e), 10.40A(f); 2011-249, s. 1; 2011-398, s. 39.)

§ 122C-25. Inspections; confidentiality.

(a) The Secretary shall make or cause to be made inspections that the Secretary considers necessary. Facilities licensed under this Article shall be subject to inspection at all times by the Secretary. All residential facilities as defined in G.S. 122C-3(14)e. shall be inspected on an annual basis.

(b) Notwithstanding G.S. 8-53, G.S. 8-53.3 or any other law relating to confidentiality of communications involving a patient or client, in the course of an inspection conducted under this section, representatives of the Secretary may review any writing or other record concerning the admission, discharge, medication, treatment, medical condition, or history of any individual who is or has been a patient, resident, or client of a licensable facility and the personnel records of those individuals employed by the licensable facility.

A licensable facility, its employees, and any other individual interviewed in the course of an inspection are immune from liability for damages resulting from disclosure of any information to the Secretary.

Except as required by law, it is unlawful for the Secretary or an employee of the Department to disclose the following information to someone not authorized to receive the information:

(1) Any confidential or privileged information obtained under this section unless the client or his legally responsible person authorizes disclosure in writing; or

(2) The name of anyone who has furnished information concerning a licensable facility without the individual's consent.

Violation of this subsection is a Class 3 misdemeanor punishable only by a fine, not to exceed five hundred dollars ($500.00).

All confidential or privileged information obtained under this section and the names of persons providing this information are exempt from Chapter 132 of the General Statutes.

(c) The Secretary shall adopt rules regarding inspections, that, at a minimum, provide for:

(1) A general administrative schedule for inspections; and

(2) An unscheduled inspection without notice, if there is a complaint alleging the violation of any licensing rule adopted under this Article.

(d) All residential facilities, as defined in G.S. 122C-3(14)e., shall ensure that the Division of Health Service Regulation complaint hotline number is posted conspicuously in a public place in the facility. (1983, c. 718, s. 1; 1985, c. 589, s. 2; 1993, c. 539, s. 918; 1994, Ex. Sess., c. 24, s. 14(c); 2005-276, ss. 10.40A(g), 10.40A(h); 2007-182, s. 1.)

§ 122C-26. Powers of the Commission.

In addition to other powers and duties, the Commission shall exercise the following powers and duties:

(1) Adopt, amend, and repeal rules consistent with the laws of this State and the laws and regulations of the federal government to implement the provisions and purposes of this Article;

(2) Issue declaratory rulings needed to implement the provisions and purposes of this Article;

(3) Adopt rules governing appeals of decisions to approve or deny licensure under this Article;

(4) Adopt rules for the waiver of rules adopted under this Article; and

(5) Adopt rules applicable to facilities licensed under this Article:

a. Establishing personnel requirements of staff employed in facilities;

b. Establishing qualifications of facility administrators or directors;

c. Establishing requirements for death reporting including confidentiality provisions related to death reporting;

d. Establishing requirements for patient advocates; and

e. Requiring facility personnel who refer clients to provider agencies to disclose any pecuniary interest the referring person has in the provider agency, or other interest that may give rise to the appearance of impropriety.

(6) Adopt rules providing for the licensure and accreditation of residential treatment facilities that provide services to persons with traumatic brain injury. (1983, c. 718, s. 1; 1985, c. 589, s. 2; 2000-55, s. 5; 2005-276, s. 10.33; 2009-361, s. 1.)

§ 122C-27. Powers of the Secretary.

The Secretary shall:

(1) Administer and enforce the provisions, rules, and decisions pursuant to this Article;

(2) Appoint hearing officers to conduct appeals under this Article;

(3) Prescribe by rule the contents of the application for licensure and renewal;

(4) Inspect facilities and records of each facility to be licensed under this Article under the rules and decisions pursuant to this Article;

(5) Issue a license upon a finding that the applicant and facility comply with the provisions of this Article and the rules of the Commission and the Secretary;

(6) Define by rule procedures for submission of periodic reports by facilities licensed under this Article;

(7) Grant, deny, suspend, or revoke a license under this Article;

(8) In accordance with rules of the Commission, make final agency decisions for appeals from the denial, suspension, or revocation of a license in accordance with G.S. 122C-24; and

(9) In accordance with rules of the Commission, grant waiver for good cause of any rules implementing this Article that do not affect the health, safety, or welfare of individuals within a licensable facility. (1983, c. 718, s. 1; 1985, c. 589, s. 2.)

§ 122C-28. Penalties.

Operating a licensable facility without a license is a Class 3 misdemeanor and is punishable only by a fine not to exceed fifty dollars ($50.00), for the first offense and a fine, not to exceed five hundred dollars ($500.00), for each subsequent offense. Each day's operation of a licensable facility without a license is a separate offense. (1983, c. 718, s. 1; 1985, c. 589, s. 2; 1993, c. 539, s. 919; 1994, Ex. Sess., c. 24, s. 14(c).)

§ 122C-29. Injunction.

(a) Notwithstanding the existence or pursuit of any other remedy, the Secretary may, in the way provided by law, maintain an action in the name of the State for injunction or other process against any person to restrain or prevent the establishment, conduct, management, or operation of a licensable facility operating without a license or in a way that threatens the health, safety, or welfare of the individuals in the licensable facility.

(b) If any individual interferes with the proper performance or duty of the Secretary in carrying out this Article, the Secretary may institute an action in the superior court of the county in which the interference occurred for injunctive relief against the continued interference, irrespective of all other remedies at law. (1983, c. 718, s. 1; 1985, c. 589, s. 2.)

§ 122C-30. Peer review committee; immunity from liability; confidentiality.

For purposes of peer review functions of a facility licensed under the provisions of this Chapter:

(1) A member of a duly appointed peer review committee or quality assurance committee who acts without malice or fraud shall not be subject to liability for damages in any civil action on account of any act, statement, or proceeding undertaken, made, or performed within the scope of the functions of the committee; and

(2) Proceedings of a peer review or quality assurance committee, the records and materials it produces, and the material it considers shall be confidential and not considered public records within the meaning of G.S. 132-1, "Public records' defined," and shall not be subject to discovery or introduction into evidence in any civil action against a facility or a provider of professional health services that results from matters which are the subject of evaluation and review by the committee. No person who was in attendance at a meeting of the committee shall be required to testify in any civil action as to any evidence or other matters produced or presented during the proceedings of the committee or as to any findings, recommendations, evaluations, opinions, or other actions of the committee or its members. However, information, documents or records otherwise available are not immune from discovery or use in a civil action merely because they were presented during proceedings of the committee, and nothing herein shall prevent a provider of professional health services from using such otherwise available information, documents or records in connection with an administrative hearing or civil suit relating to the medical staff membership, clinical privileges or employment of the provider. Documents otherwise available as public records within the meaning of G.S. 132-1 do not lose their status as public records merely because they were presented or considered during proceedings of the committee. A member of the committee or a person who testifies before the committee may be subpoenaed and be required to testify in a civil action as to events of which the person has knowledge independent of the peer review or quality assurance process, but cannot be asked about the person's testimony before the committee for impeachment or other purposes or about any opinions formed as a result of the committee hearings. (1989 (Reg. Sess., 1990), c. 1053, s. 2; 2004-149, s. 2.8.)

§ 122C-31. Report required upon death of client.

(a) A facility shall notify the Secretary immediately upon the death of any client of the facility that occurs within seven days of physical restraint or seclusion of the client, and shall notify the Secretary within three days of the death of any client of the facility resulting from violence, accident, suicide, or homicide. The Secretary may assess a civil penalty of not less than five hundred dollars ($500.00) and not more than one thousand dollars ($1,000) against a facility that fails to notify the Secretary of a death and the circumstances surrounding the death known to the facility. Chapter 150B of the General Statutes governs the assessment of a penalty under this section. A civil penalty owed under this section may be recovered in a civil action brought by the Secretary or the Attorney General. The clear proceeds of the penalty shall be remitted to the State Treasurer for deposit in accordance with State law.

(b) Upon receipt of notification from a facility in accordance with subsection (a) of this section, the Secretary shall notify the State protection and advocacy agency designated under the Developmental Disabilities Assistance and Bill of Rights Act 2000, 42 U.S.C. § 15001, et seq., that a person with a disability has died. The Secretary shall provide the agency access to the information about each death reported pursuant to subsection (a) of this section, including information resulting from any investigation of the death by the Department and from reports received from the Chief Medical Examiner pursuant to G.S. 130A-385. The agency shall use the information in accordance with its powers and duties under applicable State and federal law and regulations.

(c) If the death of a client of a facility occurs within seven days of the use of physical restraint or seclusion, then the Secretary shall initiate immediately an investigation of the death.

(d) An inpatient psychiatric unit of a hospital licensed under Chapter 131E of the General Statutes shall comply with this section.

(e) Nothing in this section abrogates State or federal law or requirements pertaining to the confidentiality, privilege, or other prohibition against disclosure of information provided to the Secretary or the agency. In carrying out the requirements of this section, the Secretary and the agency shall adhere to State and federal requirements of confidentiality, privilege, and other prohibitions against disclosure and release applicable to the information received under this section. A facility or provider that makes available confidential information in accordance with this section and with State and federal law is not liable for the release of the information.

(f) The Secretary shall establish a standard reporting format for reporting deaths pursuant to this section and shall provide to facilities subject to this section a form for the facility's use in complying with this section.

(g) In addition to the reporting requirements specified in subsections (a) through (e) of this section, and pursuant to G.S. 130A-383, every State facility shall report, without redactions other than to protect confidential personnel information, the death of any client of the facility, and, if known, the death of any former client of a facility who dies within 14 days of release from the facility, regardless of the manner of death:

(1) To the medical examiner of the county in which the body of the deceased is found; and

(2) To the State protection and advocacy agency designated under the Developmental Disabilities Assistance and Bill of Rights Act 2000, 42 U.S.C. § 15001, et seq. The State protection and advocacy agency shall use the information in accordance with its powers and duties under applicable State or federal law and regulations.

(h) Notwithstanding G.S. 122C-52, and unless otherwise prohibited by State or federal law or requirements, in order to provide for greater transparency in connection with the reporting requirements specified in subsections (a) through (g) of this section, the following information in reports made pursuant to this section shall be public records within the meaning of G.S. 132-1 when reported by a State facility:

(1) The name, sex, age, and date of birth of the deceased.

(2) The name of the facility providing the report.

(3) The date, time, and location of the death.

(4) A brief description of the circumstances of death, including the manner of death, if known.

(5) A list of all entities to whom the event was reported.

(i) Notwithstanding G.S. 122C-22, all facilities, as defined in G.S. 122C-3(14), shall comply with this section. (2000-129, s. 3(a); 2007-323, ss. 19.1(e), (f); 2008-131, s. 1; 2009-299, ss. 1-4.)

§§ 122C-32 through 122C-50. Reserved for future codification purposes.

Article 3.

Clients' Rights and Advance Instruction.

Part 1. Client's Rights.

§ 122C-51. Declaration of policy on clients' rights.

It is the policy of the State to assure basic human rights to each client of a facility. These rights include the right to dignity, privacy, humane care, and freedom from mental and physical abuse, neglect, and exploitation. Each facility shall assure to each client the right to live as normally as possible while receiving care and treatment.

It is further the policy of this State that each client who is admitted to and is receiving services from a facility has the right to treatment, including access to medical care and habilitation, regardless of age or degree of mental illness, developmental disabilities, or substance abuse. Each client has the right to an individualized written treatment or habilitation plan setting forth a program to maximize the development or restoration of his capabilities. (1973, c. 475, s. 1; c. 1436, ss. 1, 8; 1985, c. 589, s. 2; 1989, c. 625, s. 7; 1997-442, s. 1.)

§ 122C-52. Right to confidentiality.

(a) Except as provided in G.S. 132-5 and G.S. 122C-31(h), confidential information acquired in attending or treating a client is not a public record under Chapter 132 of the General Statutes.

(b) Except as authorized by G.S. 122C-53 through G.S. 122C-56, no individual having access to confidential information may disclose this information, provided, however, a HIPAA covered entity or business associate receiving confidential information that has been disclosed pursuant to G.S. 122C-53 through G.S. 122C-56 may use and disclose such information as permitted or required under 45 Code of Federal Regulations Part 164, Subpart E.

(c) Except as provided by G.S. 122C-53 through G.S. 122C-56, each client has the right that no confidential information acquired be disclosed by the facility.

(d) No provision of G.S. 122C-205 and G.S. 122C-53 through G.S. 122C-56 permitting disclosure of confidential information may apply to the records of a client when federal statutes or regulations applicable to that client prohibit the disclosure of this information.

(e) Except as required or permitted by law, disclosure of confidential information to someone not authorized to receive the information is a Class 3 misdemeanor and is punishable only by a fine, not to exceed five hundred dollars ($500.00). (1955, c. 887, s. 12; 1963, c. 1166, s. 10; 1965, c. 800, s. 4; 1973, c. 47, s. 2; c. 476, s. 133; c. 673, s. 5; c. 1408, s. 2; 1979, c. 147; 1983, c. 383, s. 10; c. 491; c. 638, s. 22; c. 864, s. 4; 1985, c. 589, s. 2; 1985 (Reg. Sess., 1986), c. 863, s. 11; 1987, c. 749, s. 2; 1993, c. 539, s. 920; 1994, Ex. Sess., c. 24, s. 14(c); 2009-299, s. 5; 2011-314, s. 2(a).)

§ 122C-53. Exceptions; client.

(a) A facility may disclose confidential information if the client or his legally responsible person consents in writing to the release of the information to a specified person. This release is valid for a specified length of time and is subject to revocation by the consenting individual.

(b) A facility may disclose the fact of admission or discharge of a client to the client's next of kin whenever the responsible professional determines that the disclosure is in the best interest of the client.

(c) Upon request a client shall have access to confidential information in his client record except information that would be injurious to the client's physical or mental well-being as determined by the attending physician or, if there is none, by the facility director or his designee. If the attending physician or, if there is none, the facility director or his designee has refused to provide confidential information to a client, the client may request that the information be sent to a physician or psychologist of the client's choice, and in this event the information shall be so provided.

(d) Except as provided by G.S. 90-21.4(b), upon request the legally responsible person of a client shall have access to confidential information in the client's record; except information that would be injurious to the client's physical or mental well-being as determined by the attending physician or, if there is none, by the facility director or his designee. If the attending physician or, if there is none, the facility director or his designee has refused to provide confidential information to the legally responsible person, the legally responsible person may request that the information be sent to a physician or psychologist of the legally responsible person's choice, and in this event the information shall be so provided.

(e) A client advocate's access to confidential information and his responsibility for safeguarding this information are as provided by subsection (g) of this section.

(f) As used in subsection (g) of this section, the following terms have the meanings specified:

(1) "Internal client advocate" means a client advocate who is employed by the facility or has a written contractual agreement with the Department or with the facility to provide monitoring and advocacy services to clients in the facility in which the client is receiving services; and

(2) "External client advocate" means a client advocate acting on behalf of a particular client with the written consent and authorization;

a. In the case of a client who is an adult and who has not been adjudicated incompetent under Chapter 35A or former Chapters 33 or 35 of the General Statutes, of the client; or

b. In the case of any other client, of the client and his legally responsible person.

(g) An internal client advocate shall be granted, without the consent of the client or his legally responsible person, access to routine reports and other confidential information necessary to fulfill his monitoring and advocacy functions. In this role, the internal client advocate may disclose confidential information received to the client involved, to his legally responsible person, to the director of the facility or his designee, to other individuals within the facility who are involved in the treatment or habilitation of the client, or to the Secretary in accordance with the rules of the Commission. Any further disclosure shall require the written consent of the client and his legally responsible person. An external client advocate shall have access to confidential information only upon the written consent of the client and his legally responsible person. In this role, the external client advocate may use the information only as authorized by the client and his legally responsible person.

(h)   In accordance with G.S. 122C-205, the facility shall notify the appropriate individuals upon the escape from and subsequent return of clients to a 24-hour facility.

(i)   Upon the request of (i) a client who is an adult and who has not been adjudicated incompetent under Chapter 35A or former Chapters 33 or 35 of the General Statutes, or (ii) the legally responsible person for any other client, a facility shall disclose to an attorney confidential information relating to that client. (1973, c. 475, s. 1; c. 1436, ss. 2-5; 1985, c. 589, s. 2; 1989 (Reg. Sess., 1990), c. 1024, s. 26(d); 1995, c. 507, s. 23.4.)

§ 122C-54. Exceptions; abuse reports and court proceedings.

(a)   A facility shall disclose confidential information if a court of competent jurisdiction issues an order compelling disclosure.

(a1)   Upon a determination by the facility director or his designee that disclosure is in the best interests of the client, a facility may disclose confidential information for purposes of filing a petition for involuntary commitment of a client pursuant to Article 5 of this Chapter or for purposes of filing a petition for the adjudication of incompetency of the client and the appointment of a guardian or an interim guardian under Chapter 35A of the General Statutes.

(b)   If an individual is a defendant in a criminal case and a mental examination of the defendant has been ordered by the court as provided in G.S. 15A-1002, the facility shall send the results or the report of the mental examination to the clerk of court, to the district attorney or prosecuting officer, and to the attorney of record for the defendant as provided in G.S. 15A-1002(d). The report shall contain a treatment recommendation, if any, and an opinion as to whether there is a likelihood that the defendant will gain the capacity to proceed.

(c) Certified copies of written results of examinations by physicians and records in the cases of clients voluntarily admitted or involuntarily committed and facing district court hearings and rehearings pursuant to Article 5 of this Chapter shall be furnished by the facility to the client's counsel, the attorney representing the State's interest, and the court. The confidentiality of client information shall be preserved in all matters except those pertaining to the necessity for admission or continued stay in the facility or commitment under review. The relevance of confidential information for which disclosure is sought in a particular case shall be determined by the court with jurisdiction over the matter.

(d) Any individual seeking confidential information contained in the court files or the court records of a proceeding made pursuant to Article 5 of this Chapter may file a written motion in the cause setting out why the information is needed. A district court judge may issue an order to disclose the confidential information sought if he finds the order is appropriate under the circumstances and if he finds that it is in the best interest of the individual admitted or committed or of the public to have the information disclosed.

(d1) Excluding Saturdays, Sundays, and holidays, not later than 48 hours after receiving notice of any of the following judicial determinations or findings, the clerk of superior court in the county where the determination or finding was made shall cause a record of the determination or finding to be transmitted to the National Instant Criminal Background Check System (NICS):

(1) A determination that an individual shall be involuntarily committed to a facility for inpatient mental health treatment upon a finding that the individual is mentally ill and a danger to self or others.

(2) A determination that an individual shall be involuntarily committed to a facility for outpatient mental health treatment upon a finding that the individual is mentally ill and, based on the individual's treatment history, in need of treatment in order to prevent further disability or deterioration that would predictably result in a danger to self or others.

(3) A determination that an individual shall be involuntarily committed to a facility for substance abuse treatment upon a finding that the individual is a substance abuser and a danger to self or others.

(4) A finding that an individual is not guilty by reason of insanity.

(5) A finding that an individual is mentally incompetent to proceed to criminal trial.

(6) A finding that an individual lacks the capacity to manage the individual's own affairs due to marked subnormal intelligence or mental illness, incompetency, condition, or disease.

(7) A determination to grant a petition to an individual for the removal of disabilities pursuant to G.S. 122C-54.1 or any applicable federal law.

The 48-hour period for transmitting a record of a judicial determination or finding to the NICS under this subsection begins upon receipt by the clerk of a copy of the judicial determination or finding.

(d2) The record of involuntary commitment for inpatient or outpatient mental health treatment or for substance abuse treatment required by subsection (d1) of this section shall be accessible only by an entity having proper access to NICS and shall remain otherwise confidential as provided by this Article. The Administrative Office of the Courts shall adopt rules to require clerks of court to transmit information to the NICS as required by subsection (d1) of this section in a uniform manner.

(e) Upon the request of the legally responsible person or the minor admitted or committed, and after that minor has both been released and reached adulthood, the court records of that minor made in proceedings pursuant to Article 5 of this Chapter may be expunged from the files of the court. The minor and his legally responsible person shall be informed in writing by the court of the right provided by this subsection at the time that the application for admission is filed with the court.

(f) A State facility and the psychiatric service of the University of North Carolina Hospitals at Chapel Hill may disclose confidential information to staff attorneys of the Attorney General's office whenever the information is necessary to the performance of the statutory responsibilities of the Attorney General's office or to its performance when acting as attorney for a State facility or the psychiatric service of the University of North Carolina Hospitals at Chapel Hill.

(g) A facility may disclose confidential information to an attorney who represents either the facility or an employee of the facility, if such information is relevant to litigation, to the operations of the facility, or to the provision of services by the facility. An employee may discuss confidential information with his attorney or with an attorney representing the facility in which he is employed.

(h) A facility shall disclose confidential information for purposes of complying with Article 3 of Chapter 7B of the General Statutes and Article 6 of Chapter 108A of the General Statutes, or as required by other State or federal law.

(i) G.S. 132-1.4 shall apply to the records of criminal investigations conducted by any law enforcement unit of a State facility, and information described in G.S. 132-1.4(c) that is collected by the State facility law enforcement unit shall be public records within the meaning of G.S. 132-1.

(j) Notwithstanding any other provision of this Chapter, the Secretary may inform any person of any incident or event involving the welfare of a client or former client when the Secretary determines that the release of the information is essential to maintaining the integrity of the Department. However, the release shall not include information that identifies the client directly, or information for which disclosure is prohibited by State or federal law or requirements, or information for which, in the Secretary's judgment, by reference to publicly known or available information, there is a reasonable basis to believe the client will be identified. (1955, c. 887, s. 12; 1963, c. 1166, s. 10; 1973, c. 47, s. 2; c. 476, s. 133; c. 673, s. 5; c. 1408, s. 2; 1977, c. 696, s. 1; 1979, c. 147; c. 915, s. 20; 1983, c. 383, s. 10; c. 491; c. 638, s. 22; c. 864, s. 4; 1985, c. 589, s. 2; 1987, c. 638, ss. 1, 3.1; 1989, c. 141, s. 9; 1993, c. 516, s. 12; 1998-202, s. 13(dd); 2003-313, s. 2; 2008-210, s. 1; 2009-299, s. 6; 2013-18, s. 7; 2013-369, ss. 7, 8.)

§ 122C-54.1. Restoration process to remove mental commitment bar.

(a) Any individual over the age of 18 may petition for the removal of the disabilities pursuant to 18 U.S.C. § 922(d)(4) and (g)(4), G.S. 14-415.3, and G.S. 14-415.12 arising out of a determination or finding required to be transmitted to the National Instant Criminal Background Check System by subdivisions (1) through (6) of subsection (d1) of G.S. 122C-54. The individual may file the petition with a district court judge upon the expiration of any current inpatient or outpatient commitment.

(b) The petition must be filed in the district court of the county where the respondent was the subject of the most recent judicial determination or finding or in the district court of the county of the petitioner's residence. The clerk of court upon receipt of the petition shall schedule a hearing using the regularly scheduled commitment court time and provide notice of the hearing to the petitioner and the attorney who represented the State in the underlying case, or that attorney's successor. Copies of the petition must be served on the director of the relevant inpatient or outpatient treatment facility and the district attorney in the petitioner's current county of residence.

(c) The burden is on the petitioner to establish by a preponderance of the evidence that the petitioner will not be likely to act in a manner dangerous to public safety and that the granting of the relief would not be contrary to the public interest. The district attorney shall present any and all relevant information to the contrary. For these purposes, the district attorney may access and use any and all mental health records, juvenile records, and criminal history of the petitioner wherever maintained. The applicant must sign a release for the district attorney to receive any mental health records of the applicant. This hearing shall be closed to the public, unless the court finds that the public interest would be better served by conducting the hearing in public. If the court determines the hearing should be open to the public, upon motion by the petitioner, the court may allow for the in camera inspection of any mental health records. The court may allow the use of the record but shall restrict it from public disclosure, unless it finds that the public interest would be better served by making the record public. The district court shall enter an order that the petitioner is or is not likely to act in a manner dangerous to public safety and that the granting of the relief would or would not be contrary to the public interest. The court shall include in its order the specific findings of fact on which it bases its decision. In making its determination, the court shall consider the circumstances regarding the firearm disabilities from which relief is sought, the petitioner's mental health and criminal history records, the petitioner's reputation, developed at a minimum through character witness statements, testimony, or other character evidence, and any changes in the petitioner's condition or circumstances since the original determination or finding relevant to the relief sought. The decision of the district court may be appealed to the superior court for a hearing de novo. After a denial by the superior court, the applicant must wait a minimum of one year before reapplying. Attorneys designated by the Attorney General shall be available to represent the State, or assist in the representation of the State, in a restoration proceeding when requested to do so by a district attorney and approved by the Attorney General.

An attorney so designated shall have all the powers of the district attorney under this section.

(d) Upon a judicial determination to grant a petition under this section, the clerk of superior court in the county where the petition was granted shall forward the order to the National Instant Criminal Background Check System (NICS) for updating of the respondent's record. (2008-210, s. 2; 2013-369, s. 9.)

§ 122C-55. Exceptions; care and treatment.

(a) Any facility may share confidential information regarding any client of that facility with any other facility when necessary to coordinate appropriate and effective care, treatment or habilitation of the client. For the purposes of this section, coordinate means the provision, coordination, or management of mental health, developmental disabilities, and substance abuse services and other health or related services by one or more facilities and includes the referral of a client from one facility to another.

(a1) Any facility may share confidential information regarding any client of that facility with the Secretary, and the Secretary may share confidential information regarding any client with a facility when necessary to conduct quality assessment and improvement activities or to coordinate appropriate and effective care, treatment or habilitation of the client. For purposes of this subsection, subsection (a6), and subsection (a7) of this section, the purposes or activities for which confidential information may be disclosed include, but are not limited to, case management and care coordination, disease management, outcomes evaluation, the development of clinical guidelines and protocols, the development of care management plans and systems, population-based activities relating to improving or reducing health care costs, and the provision, coordination, or management of mental health, developmental disabilities, and substance abuse services and other health or related services. As used in this section, "facility" includes an LME and "Secretary" includes the Community Care of North Carolina Program, or other primary care case management programs that contract with the Department to provide a primary care case management program for recipients of publicly funded health and related services.

(a2) Any area or State facility or the psychiatric service of the University of North Carolina Hospitals at Chapel Hill may share confidential information regarding any client of that facility with any other area facility or State facility or the psychiatric service of the University of North Carolina Hospitals at Chapel Hill when necessary to conduct payment activities relating to an individual served by the facility. Payment activities are activities undertaken by a facility to obtain or provide reimbursement for the provision of services and may include, but are not limited to, determinations of eligibility or coverage, coordination of benefits, determinations of cost-sharing amounts, claims management, claims processing, claims adjudication, claims appeals, billing and collection activities, medical necessity reviews, utilization management and review, precertification and preauthorization of services, concurrent and retrospective review of services, and appeals related to utilization management and review.

(a3)   Whenever there is reason to believe that a client is eligible for benefits through a Department program, any State or area facility or the psychiatric service of the University of North Carolina Hospitals at Chapel Hill may share confidential information regarding any client of that facility with the Secretary, and the Secretary may share confidential information regarding any client with an area facility or State facility or the psychiatric services of the University of North Carolina Hospitals at Chapel Hill. Disclosure is limited to that information necessary to establish initial eligibility for benefits, determine continued eligibility over time, and obtain reimbursement for the costs of services provided to the client.

(a4)   An area authority or county program may share confidential information regarding any client with any area facility, and any area facility may share confidential information regarding any client of that facility with the area authority or county program, when the area authority or county program determines the disclosure is necessary to develop, manage, monitor, or evaluate the area authority's or county program's network of qualified providers as provided in G.S. 122C-115.2(b)(1)b., G.S. 122C-141(a), the State Plan, and rules of the Secretary. For the purposes of this subsection, the purposes or activities for which confidential information may be disclosed include, but are not limited to, quality assessment and improvement activities, provider accreditation and staff credentialing, developing contracts and negotiating rates, investigating and responding to client grievances and complaints, evaluating practitioner and provider performance, auditing functions, on-site monitoring, conducting consumer satisfaction studies, and collecting and analyzing performance data.

(a5)   Any area facility may share confidential information with any other area facility regarding an applicant when necessary to determine whether the applicant is eligible for area facility services. For the purpose of this subsection, the term "applicant" means an individual who contacts an area facility for services.

(a6)   When necessary to conduct quality assessment and improvement activities or to coordinate appropriate and effective care, treatment, or habilitation of the client, the Department's Community Care of North Carolina Program, or other primary care case management program, may disclose confidential information acquired pursuant to subsection (a1) of this section to a health care provider or other entity that has entered into a written agreement with the Community Care of North Carolina Program, or other primary care case management program, to participate in the care management support network and systems developed and maintained by the primary care case manager for the purpose of coordinating and improving the quality of care for recipients of publicly funded health and related services. Health care providers and other entities receiving confidential information that has been disclosed pursuant to this subsection may use and disclose the information as permitted or required under 45 Code of Federal Regulations Part 164, Subpart E.

(a7)   A facility may share confidential information with one or more HIPAA covered entities or business associates for the same purposes set forth in subsection (a1) of this section. Before making disclosures under this subsection, the facility shall inform the client or his legally responsible person that the facility may make such disclosures unless the client or his legally responsible person objects in writing or signs a non-disclosure form that shall be supplied by the facility. If the client or his legally responsible person objects in writing or signs a non-disclosure form, the disclosures otherwise permitted by this subsection are prohibited. A covered entity or business associate receiving confidential information that has been disclosed by a facility pursuant to this subsection may use and disclose the information as permitted or required under 45 Code of Federal Regulations Part 164, Subpart E; provided however, that such confidential information shall not be used or disclosed for discriminatory purposes including, without limitation, employment discrimination, medical insurance coverage or rate discrimination, or discrimination by law enforcement officers.

(b)   A facility, physician, or other individual responsible for evaluation, management, supervision, or treatment of respondents examined or committed for outpatient treatment under the provisions of Article 5 of this Chapter may request, receive, and disclose confidential information to the extent necessary to enable them to fulfill their responsibilities.

(c) A facility may furnish confidential information in its possession to the Division of Adult Correction of the Department of Public Safety when requested by that department regarding any client of that facility when the inmate has been determined by the Division of Adult Correction of the Department of Public Safety to be in need of treatment for mental illness, developmental disabilities, or substance abuse. The Division of Adult Correction of the Department of Public Safety may furnish to a facility confidential information in its possession about treatment for mental illness, developmental disabilities, or substance abuse that the Division of Adult Correction of the Department of Public Safety has provided to any present or former inmate if the inmate is presently seeking treatment from the requesting facility or if the inmate has been involuntarily committed to the requesting facility for inpatient or outpatient treatment. Under the circumstances described in this subsection, the consent of the client or inmate shall not be required in order for this information to be furnished and the information shall be furnished despite objection by the client or inmate. Confidential information disclosed pursuant to this subsection is restricted from further disclosure.

(d) A responsible professional may disclose confidential information when in his opinion there is an imminent danger to the health or safety of the client or another individual or there is a likelihood of the commission of a felony or violent misdemeanor.

(e) A responsible professional may exchange confidential information with a physician or other health care provider who is providing emergency medical services to a client. Disclosure of the information is limited to that necessary to meet the emergency as determined by the responsible professional.

(e1) A State facility may furnish client identifying information to the Department for the purpose of maintaining an index of clients served in State facilities which may be used by State facilities only if that information is necessary for the appropriate and effective evaluation, care and treatment of the client.

(e2) A responsible professional may disclose an advance instruction for mental health treatment or confidential information from an advance instruction to a physician, psychologist, or other qualified professional when the responsible professional determines that disclosure is necessary to give effect to or provide treatment in accordance with the advance instruction.

(f) A facility may disclose confidential information to a provider of support services whenever the facility has entered into a written agreement with a person to provide support services and the agreement includes a provision in which the provider of support services acknowledges that in receiving, storing, processing, or otherwise dealing with any confidential information, he will safeguard and not further disclose the information.

(g) Whenever there is reason to believe that the client is eligible for financial benefits through a governmental agency, a facility may disclose confidential information to State, local, or federal government agencies. Except as provided in subsections (a3) and (g1) of this section, disclosure is limited to that confidential information necessary to establish financial benefits for a client. Except as provided in subsection (g1) of this section, after establishment of these benefits, the consent of the client or his legally responsible person is required for further release of confidential information under this subsection.

(g1) A State facility operated under the authority of G.S. 122C-181 may disclose confidential information for the purpose of collecting payment due the facility for the cost of care, treatment, or habilitation.

(h) Within a facility, employees, students, consultants or volunteers involved in the care, treatment, or habilitation of a client may exchange confidential information as needed for the purpose of carrying out their responsibility in serving the client.

(i) Upon specific request, a responsible professional may release confidential information to a physician or psychologist who referred the client to the facility.

(j) Upon request of the next of kin or other family member who has a legitimate role in the therapeutic services offered, or other person designated by the client or his legally responsible person, the responsible professional shall provide the next of kin or other family member or the designee with notification of the client's diagnosis, the prognosis, the medications prescribed, the dosage of the medications prescribed, the side effects of the medications prescribed, if any, and the progress of the client, provided that the client or his legally responsible person has consented in writing, or the client has consented orally in the presence of a witness selected by the client, prior to the release of this information. Both the client's or the legally responsible person's consent and the release of this information shall be documented in the client's medical record.

This consent shall be valid for a specified length of time only and is subject to revocation by the consenting individual.

(k)   Notwithstanding the provisions of G.S. 122C-53(b) or G.S. 122C-206, upon request of the next of kin or other family member who has a legitimate role in the therapeutic services offered, or other person designated by the client or his legally responsible person, the responsible professional shall provide the next of kin, or family member, or the designee, notification of the client's admission to the facility, transfer to another facility, decision to leave the facility against medical advice, discharge from the facility, and referrals and appointment information for treatment after discharge, after notification to the client that this information has been requested.

(l)   In response to a written request of the next of kin or other family member who has a legitimate role in the therapeutic services offered, or other person designated by the client, for additional information not provided for in subsections (j) and (k) of this section, and when such written request identifies the intended use for this information, the responsible professional shall, in a timely manner:

(1)   Provide the information requested based upon the responsible professional's determination that providing this information will be to the client's therapeutic benefit, and provided that the client or his legally responsible person has consented in writing to the release of the information requested; or

(2)   Refuse to provide the information requested based upon the responsible professional's determination that providing this information will be detrimental to the therapeutic relationship between client and professional; or

(3)   Refuse to provide the information requested based upon the responsible professional's determination that the next of kin or family member or designee does not have a legitimate need for the information requested.

(m)   The Commission for Mental Health, Developmental Disabilities, and Substance Abuse Services shall adopt rules specifically to define the legitimate role referred to in subsections (j), (k), and (l) of this section. (1955, c. 887, s. 12; 1963, c. 1166, s. 10; 1973, c. 47, s. 2; c. 476, s. 133; c. 673, s. 5; c. 1408, s. 2; 1979, c. 147; 1983, c. 383, s. 10; c. 491; c. 638, s. 22; c. 864, s. 4; 1985, c. 589, s. 2; c. 695, s. 15; 1987, c. 638, ss. 2, 3; 1989, c. 141, s. 10; c. 438; c. 625, s. 8; 1989 (Reg. Sess., 1990), c. 1024, s. 27; 1991, c. 359, s. 1; c. 544, s. 1; 1998-198, s. 4; 2003-313, s. 3; 2009-65, s. 1(a), (b); 2009-487, s. 5; 2009-570, s. 43;

2011-102, ss. 3, 4; 2011-145, ss. 10.14, 19.1(h); 2011-314, s. 2(b); 2011-391, s. 23.)

§ 122C-56. Exceptions; research and planning.

(a) The Secretary may require information that does not identify clients from State and area facilities for purposes of preparing statistical reports of activities and services and for planning and study. The Secretary may also receive confidential information from State and area facilities when specifically required by other State or federal law.

(b) The Secretary may have access to confidential information from private or public agencies or agents for purposes of research and evaluation in the areas of mental health, developmental disabilities, and substance abuse. No confidential information shall be further disclosed.

(c) A facility may disclose confidential information to persons responsible for conducting general research or clinical, financial, or administrative audits if there is a justifiable documented need for this information. A person receiving the information may not directly or indirectly identify any client in any report of the research or audit or otherwise disclose client identity in any way. (1965, c. 800, s. 4; 1973, c. 476, s. 133; 1985, c. 589, s. 2; 1989, c. 625, s. 9.)

§ 122C-57. Right to treatment and consent to treatment.

(a) Each client who is admitted to and is receiving services from a facility has the right to receive age-appropriate treatment for mental health, mental retardation, and substance abuse illness or disability. Each client within 30 days of admission to a facility shall have an individual written treatment or habilitation plan implemented by the facility. The client and the client's legally responsible person shall be informed in advance of the potential risks and alleged benefits of the treatment choices.

(b) Each client has the right to be free from unnecessary or excessive medication. Medication shall not be used for punishment, discipline, or staff convenience.

(c)   Medication shall be administered in accordance with accepted medical standards and only upon the order of a physician as documented in the client's record.

(d)   Each voluntarily admitted client or the client's legally responsible person (including a health care agent named pursuant to a valid health care power of attorney) has the right to consent to or refuse any treatment offered by the facility. Consent may be withdrawn at any time by the person who gave the consent. If treatment is refused, the qualified professional shall determine whether treatment in some other modality is possible. If all appropriate treatment modalities are refused, the voluntarily admitted client may be discharged. In an emergency, a voluntarily admitted client may be administered treatment or medication, other than those specified in subsection (f) of this section, despite the refusal of the client or the client's legally responsible person, even if the client's refusal is expressed in a valid advance instruction for mental health treatment. The Commission may adopt rules to provide a procedure to be followed when a voluntarily admitted client refuses treatment.

(d1)   Except as provided in G.S. 90-21.4, discharge of a voluntarily admitted minor from treatment shall include notice to and consultation with the minor's legally responsible person and in no event shall a minor be discharged from treatment upon the minor's request alone.

(e)   In the case of an involuntarily committed client, treatment measures other than those requiring express written consent as specified in subsection (f) of this section may be given despite the refusal of the client, the client's legally responsible person, a health care agent named pursuant to a valid health care power of attorney, or the client's refusal expressed in a valid advance instruction for mental health treatment in the event of an emergency or when consideration of side effects related to the specific treatment measure is given and in the professional judgment, as documented in the client's record, of the treating physician and a second physician, who is either the director of clinical services of the facility, or the director's designee, either:

(1)   The client, without the benefit of the specific treatment measure, is incapable of participating in any available treatment plan which will give the client a realistic opportunity of improving the client's condition;

(2)   There is, without the benefit of the specific treatment measure, a significant possibility that the client will harm self or others before improvement of the client's condition is realized.

(f) Treatment involving electroshock therapy, the use of experimental drugs or procedures, or surgery other than emergency surgery may not be given without the express and informed written consent of the client, the client's legally responsible person, a health care agent named pursuant to a valid health care power of attorney, or the client's consent expressed in a valid advance instruction for mental health treatment. This consent may be withdrawn at any time by the person who gave the consent. The Commission may adopt rules specifying other therapeutic and diagnostic procedures that require the express and informed written consent of the client, the client's legally responsible person, or a health care agent named pursuant to a valid health care power of attorney. (1973, c. 475, s. 1; c. 1436, ss. 6, 7; 1981, c. 328, ss. 1, 2; 1985, c. 589, s. 2; 1995, c. 336, s. 1; 1997-442, s. 3; 1998-198, s. 5; 1998-217, s. 53(a)(4); 1999-456, s. 4; 2007-502, s. 15(b).)

§ 122C-58. Civil rights and civil remedies.

Except as otherwise provided in this Chapter, each adult client of a facility keeps the same right as any other citizen of North Carolina to exercise all civil rights, including the right to dispose of property, execute instruments, make purchases, enter into contractual relationships, register and vote, bring civil actions, and marry and get a divorce, unless the exercise of a civil right has been precluded by an unrevoked adjudication of incompetency. This section shall not be construed as validating the act of any client who was in fact incompetent at the time he performed the act. (1973, c. 475, s. 1; c. 1436, ss. 2-5; 1985, c. 589, s. 2.)

§ 122C-59. Use of corporal punishment.

Corporal punishment may not be inflicted upon any client. (1973, c. 475, s. 1; 1985, c. 589, s. 2.)

§ 122C-60. Use of physical restraints or seclusion.

(a) Physical restraint or seclusion of a client shall be employed only when there is imminent danger of abuse or injury to the client or others, when substantial property damage is occurring, or when the restraint or seclusion is necessary as a measure of therapeutic treatment. For purposes of this section, a technique to reenact the birthing process as defined by G.S. 14-401.21 is not a measure of therapeutic treatment. All instances of restraint or seclusion and the detailed reasons for such action shall be documented in the client's record. Each client who is restrained or secluded shall be observed frequently, and a written notation of the observation shall be made in the client's record.

(a1)   A facility that employs physical restraint or seclusion of a client shall collect data on the use of the restraints and seclusion. The data shall reflect for each incidence, the type of procedure used, the length of time employed, alternatives considered or employed, and the effectiveness of the procedure or alternative employed. The facility shall analyze the data on at least a quarterly basis to monitor effectiveness, determine trends, and take corrective action where necessary. The facility shall make the data available to the Secretary upon request. Nothing in this subsection abrogates State or federal law or requirements pertaining to the confidentiality, privilege, or other prohibition against disclosure of information provided to the Secretary under this subsection. In reviewing data requested under this subsection, the Secretary shall adhere to State and federal requirements of confidentiality, privilege, and other prohibitions against disclosure and release applicable to the information received under this subsection.

(a2)   Facilities shall implement policies and practices that emphasize the use of alternatives to physical restraint and seclusion. Physical restraint and seclusion may be employed only by staff who have been trained and have demonstrated competence in the proper use of and alternatives to these procedures. Facilities shall ensure that staff authorized to employ and terminate these procedures are retrained and have demonstrated competence at least annually.

(b)   The Commission shall adopt rules to implement this section. In adopting rules, the Commission shall take into consideration federal regulations and national accreditation standards. Rules adopted by the Commission shall include:

(1)   Staff training and competence in:

a.   The use of positive behavioral supports.

b. Communication strategies for defusing and deescalating potentially dangerous behavior.

c. Monitoring vital indicators.

d. Administration of CPR.

e. Debriefing with client and staff.

f. Methods for determining staff competence, including qualifications of trainers and training curricula.

g. Other areas to ensure the safe and appropriate use of restraints and seclusion.

(2) Other matters relating to the use of physical restraint or seclusion of clients necessary to ensure the safety of clients and others.

The Department may investigate complaints and inspect a facility at any time to ensure compliance with this section. (1973, c. 475, s. 1; 1985, c. 589, s. 2; 2000-129, s. 1; 2003-205, s. 2.)

§ 122C-61. Treatment rights in 24-hour facilities.

In addition to the rights set forth in G.S. 122C-57, each client who is receiving services at a 24-hour facility has the following rights:

(1) The right to receive necessary treatment for and prevention of physical ailments based upon the client's condition and projected length of stay. The facility may seek to collect appropriate reimbursement for its costs in providing the treatment and prevention; and

(2) The right to have, as soon as practical during treatment or habilitation but not later than the time of discharge, an individualized written discharge plan containing recommendations for further services designed to enable the client to live as normally as possible. A discharge plan may not be required when it is not feasible because of an unanticipated discontinuation of a client's treatment. With the consent of the client or his legally responsible person, the professionals responsible for the plans shall contact appropriate agencies at the client's

destination or in his home community before formulating the recommendations. A copy of the plan shall be furnished to the client or to his legally responsible person and, with the consent of the client, to the client's next of kin. (1973, c. 475, s. 1; c. 1436, ss. 6, 7; 1981, c. 328, ss. 1, 2; 1985, c. 589, s. 2.)

§ 122C-62. Additional rights in 24-hour facilities.

(a)   In addition to the rights enumerated in G.S. 122C-51 through G.S. 122C-61, each adult client who is receiving treatment or habilitation in a 24-hour facility keeps the right to:

(1)   Send and receive sealed mail and have access to writing material, postage, and staff assistance when necessary;

(2)   Contact and consult with, at his own expense and at no cost to the facility, legal counsel, private physicians, and private mental health, developmental disabilities, or substance abuse professionals of his choice; and

(3)   Contact and consult with a client advocate if there is a client advocate.

The rights specified in this subsection may not be restricted by the facility and each adult client may exercise these rights at all reasonable times.

(b)   Except as provided in subsections (e) and (h) of this section, each adult client who is receiving treatment or habilitation in a 24-hour facility at all times keeps the right to:

(1)   Make and receive confidential telephone calls. All long distance calls shall be paid for by the client at the time of making the call or made collect to the receiving party;

(2)   Receive visitors between the hours of 8:00 a.m. and 9:00 p.m. for a period of at least six hours daily, two hours of which shall be after 6:00 p.m.; however visiting shall not take precedence over therapies;

(3)   Communicate and meet under appropriate supervision with individuals of his own choice upon the consent of the individuals;

(4)   Make visits outside the custody of the facility unless:

a. Commitment proceedings were initiated as the result of the client's being charged with a violent crime, including a crime involving an assault with a deadly weapon, and the respondent was found not guilty by reason of insanity or incapable of proceeding;

b. The client was voluntarily admitted or committed to the facility while under order of commitment to a correctional facility of the Division of Adult Correction of the Department of Public Safety; or

c. The client is being held to determine capacity to proceed pursuant to G.S. 15A-1002;

A court order may expressly authorize visits otherwise prohibited by the existence of the conditions prescribed by this subdivision;

(5) Be out of doors daily and have access to facilities and equipment for physical exercise several times a week;

(6) Except as prohibited by law, keep and use personal clothing and possessions, unless the client is being held to determine capacity to proceed pursuant to G.S. 15A-1002;

(7) Participate in religious worship;

(8) Keep and spend a reasonable sum of his own money;

(9) Retain a driver's license, unless otherwise prohibited by Chapter 20 of the General Statutes; and

(10) Have access to individual storage space for his private use.

(c) In addition to the rights enumerated in G.S. 122C-51 through G.S. 122C-57 and G.S. 122C-59 through G.S. 122C-61, each minor client who is receiving treatment or habilitation in a 24-hour facility has the right to have access to proper adult supervision and guidance. In recognition of the minor's status as a developing individual, the minor shall be provided opportunities to enable him to mature physically, emotionally, intellectually, socially, and vocationally. In view of the physical, emotional, and intellectual immaturity of the minor, the 24-hour facility shall provide appropriate structure, supervision and control consistent with the rights given to the minor pursuant to this Part. The facility shall also, where practical, make reasonable efforts to ensure that each minor client receives treatment apart and separate from adult clients unless the treatment needs of the minor client dictate otherwise.

Each minor client who is receiving treatment or habilitation from a 24-hour facility has the right to:

(1) Communicate and consult with his parents or guardian or the agency or individual having legal custody of him;

(2) Contact and consult with, at his own expense or that of his legally responsible person and at no cost to the facility, legal counsel, private physicians, private mental health, developmental disabilities, or substance abuse professionals, of his or his legally responsible person's choice; and

(3) Contact and consult with a client advocate, if there is a client advocate.

The rights specified in this subsection may not be restricted by the facility and each minor client may exercise these rights at all reasonable times.

(d) Except as provided in subsections (e) and (h) of this section, each minor client who is receiving treatment or habilitation in a 24-hour facility has the right to:

(1) Make and receive telephone calls. All long distance calls shall be paid for by the client at the time of making the call or made collect to the receiving party;

(2) Send and receive mail and have access to writing materials, postage, and staff assistance when necessary;

(3) Under appropriate supervision, receive visitors between the hours of 8:00 a.m. and 9:00 p.m. for a period of at least six hours daily, two hours of which shall be after 6:00 p.m.; however visiting shall not take precedence over school or therapies;

(4) Receive special education and vocational training in accordance with federal and State law;

(5) Be out of doors daily and participate in play, recreation, and physical exercise on a regular basis in accordance with his needs;

(6) Except as prohibited by law, keep and use personal clothing and possessions under appropriate supervision, unless the client is being held to determine capacity to proceed pursuant to G.S. 15A-1002;

(7) Participate in religious worship;

(8) Have access to individual storage space for the safekeeping of personal belongings;

(9) Have access to and spend a reasonable sum of his own money; and

(10) Retain a driver's license, unless otherwise prohibited by Chapter 20 of the General Statutes.

(e) No right enumerated in subsections (b) or (d) of this section may be limited or restricted except by the qualified professional responsible for the formulation of the client's treatment or habilitation plan. A written statement shall be placed in the client's record that indicates the detailed reason for the restriction. The restriction shall be reasonable and related to the client's treatment or habilitation needs. A restriction is effective for a period not to exceed 30 days. An evaluation of each restriction shall be conducted by the qualified professional at least every seven days, at which time the restriction may be removed. Each evaluation of a restriction shall be documented in the client's record. Restrictions on rights may be renewed only by a written statement entered by the qualified professional in the client's record that states the reason for the renewal of the restriction. In the case of an adult client who has not been adjudicated incompetent, in each instance of an initial restriction or renewal of a restriction of rights, an individual designated by the client shall, upon the consent of the client, be notified of the restriction and of the reason for it. In the case of a minor client or an incompetent adult client, the legally responsible person shall be notified of each instance of an initial restriction or renewal of a restriction of rights and of the reason for it. Notification of the designated individual or legally responsible person shall be documented in writing in the client's record.

(f) The Commission may adopt rules to implement subsection (e) of this section.

(g) With regard to clients being held to determine capacity to proceed pursuant to G.S. 15A-1002 or clients in a facility for substance abuse, and notwithstanding the prior provisions of this section, the Commission may adopt rules restricting the rights set forth under (b)(2), (b)(3), and (d)(3) of this section if restrictions are necessary and reasonable in order to protect the health, safety, and welfare of the client involved or other clients.

(h)   The rights stated in subdivisions (b)(2), (b)(4), (b)(5), (b)(10), (d)(3), (d)(5) and (d)(8) may be modified in a general hospital by that hospital to be the same as for other patients in that hospital; provided that any restriction of a specific client's rights shall be done in accordance with the provisions of subsection (e) of this section. (1973, c. 475, s. 1; c. 1436, ss. 2-5, 8; 1985, c. 589, s. 2; 1989, c. 625, s. 10; 1995, c. 299, s. 2; 1997-456, s. 27; 2011-145, s. 19.1(h).)

§ 122C-63. Assurance for continuity of care for individuals with mental retardation.

(a)   Any individual with mental retardation admitted for residential care or treatment for other than respite or emergency care to any residential facility operated under the authority of this Chapter and supported all or in part by state-appropriated funds has the right to residential placement in an alternative facility if the client is in need of placement and if the original facility can no longer provide the necessary care or treatment.

(b)   The operator of a residential facility providing residential care or treatment, for other than respite or emergency care, for individuals with mental retardation shall notify the area authority serving the client's county of residence of his intent to close a facility or to discharge a client who may be in need of continuing care at least 60 days prior to the closing or discharge.

The operator's notification to the area authority of intent to close a facility or to discharge a client who may be in need of continuing care constitutes the operator's acknowledgement of the obligation to continue to serve the client until:

(1)   The area authority determines that the client is not in need of continuing care;

(2)   The client is moved to an alternative residential placement; or

(3)   Sixty days have elapsed;

whichever occurs first.

In cases in which the safety of the client who may be in need of continuing care, of other clients, of the staff of the residential facility, or of the general public, is concerned, this 60-day notification period may be waived by securing an emergency placement in a more secure and safe facility. The operator of the residential facility shall notify the area authority that an emergency placement has been arranged within 24 hours of the placement. The area authority and the Secretary shall retain their respective responsibilities upon receipt of this notice.

(c)   An individual who may be in need of continuing care may be discharged from a residential facility without further claim for continuing care against the area authority or the State if:

(1)   After the parent or guardian, if the client is a minor or an adjudicated incompetent adult, or the client, if an adult not adjudicated incompetent, has entered into a contract with the operator upon the client's admission to the original residential facility the parent, guardian, or client who entered into the contract refuses to carry out the contract, or

(2)   After an alternative placement for a client in need of continuing care is located, the parent or guardian who admitted the client to the residential facility, if the client is a minor or an adjudicated incompetent adult, or the client if an adult not adjudicated incompetent, refuses the alternative placement.

(d)   Decisions made by the area authority regarding the need for continued placement or regarding the availability of an alternative placement of a client may be appealed pursuant to the appeals process of the area authority and subsequently to the Secretary or the Commission under their rules. If the appeal process extends beyond the operator's 60-day obligation to continue to serve the client, the Secretary shall arrange a temporary placement in a State facility for the mentally retarded pending the outcome of the appeal.

(e)   The area authority that serves the county of residence of the client is responsible for assessing the need for continuity of care and for the coordination of the placement among available public and private facilities whenever the authority is notified that a client may be in need of continuing care. If an alternative placement is not available beyond the operator's 60-day obligation to continue to serve the client, the Secretary shall arrange for a temporary placement in a State facility for the mentally retarded. The area authority shall retain responsibility for coordination of placement during a temporary placement in a State facility.

(f) The Secretary is responsible for coordinative and financial assistance to the area authority in the performing of its duties to coordinate placement so as to assure continuity of care and for assuring a continuity of care placement beyond the operator's 60-day obligation period.

(g) The area authority's financial responsibility, through local and allocated State resources, is limited to:

(1) Costs relating to the identification and coordination of alternative placements;

(2) If the original facility is an area facility, maintenance of the client in the original facility for up to 60 days; and

(3) Release of allocated categorical State funds used to support the care or treatment of the specific client at the time of alternative placement if the Secretary requires the release.

(h) In accordance with G.S. 143B-147(a)(1) the Commission shall develop programmatic rules to implement this section, and, in accordance with G.S. 122C-112(a)(6), the Secretary shall adopt budgetary rules to implement this section. (1981, c. 1012; 1985, c. 589, s. 2.)

§ 122C-64. Client rights and human rights committees.

Client rights and human rights committees responsible for protecting the rights of clients shall be established at each State facility, for each local management entity, and provider agency. The Commission shall adopt rules for the establishment, composition, and duties of the committees and procedures for appointment and coordination with the State and Local Consumer Advocacy programs. The membership of the client rights and human rights committee for a multicounty program or local management entity shall include a representative from each of the participating counties. (1985-589, s. 2; 2001-437, s. 1.3; 2009-190, s. 1.)

§ 122C-65. Offenses relating to clients.

(a) For the protection of clients receiving treatment or habilitation in a 24-hour facility, it is unlawful for any individual who is not a developmentally disabled client in a facility:

(1) To assist, advise, or solicit, or to offer to assist, advise, or solicit a client of a facility to leave without authority;

(2) To transport or to offer to transport a client of a facility to or from any place without the facility's authority;

(3) To receive or to offer to receive a minor client of a facility into any place, structure, building, or conveyance for the purpose of engaging in any act that would constitute a sex offense, or to solicit a minor client of a facility to engage in any act that would constitute a sex offense;

(4) To hide an individual who has left a facility without authority; or

(5) To engage in, or offer to engage in an act with a client of a facility that would constitute a sex offense.

(b) Violation of this section is a Class 1 misdemeanor. (1899, c. 1, s. 53; Rev., s. 3694; C.S., s. 6171; 1963, c. 1184, ss. 1, 6; 1985, c. 589, s. 2; 1989, c. 625, s. 11; 1993, c. 539, s. 921; 1994, Ex. Sess., c. 24, s. 14(c).)

§ 122C-66. Protection from abuse and exploitation; reporting.

(a) An employee of or a volunteer at a facility who, other than as a part of generally accepted medical or therapeutic procedure, knowingly causes pain or injury to a client or borrows or takes personal property from a client is guilty of a Class 1 misdemeanor. Any employee or volunteer who uses reasonable force to carry out the provisions of G.S. 122C-60 or to protect himself or others from a violent client does not violate this subsection.

(b) An employee of a facility who witnesses or has knowledge of a violation of subsection (a) or of an accidental injury to a client shall report the violation or accidental injury to authorized personnel designated by the facility. No employee making a report may be threatened or harassed by any other employee or volunteer on account of the report. Violation of this subsection is a Class 3 misdemeanor punishable only by a fine, not to exceed five hundred dollars ($500.00).

(c) The identity of an individual who makes a report under this section or who cooperates in an ensuing investigation may not be disclosed without his consent, except to persons authorized by the facility or by State or federal law to investigate or prosecute these incidents, or in a grievance or personnel hearing or civil or criminal action in which a reporting individual is testifying, or when disclosure is legally compelled or authorized by judicial discovery. This subsection shall not be interpreted to require the disclosure of the identity of an individual where it is otherwise prohibited by law.

(d) An employee who makes a report in good faith under this section is immune from any civil liability that might otherwise occur for the report. In any case involving liability, making of a report under this section is prima facie evidence that the maker acted in good faith.

(e) The duty imposed by this section is in addition to any duty imposed by G.S. 7B-301 or G.S. 108A-102.

(f) The facility shall investigate or provide for the investigation of all reports made under the provisions of this section. (1985, c. 589, s. 2; 1993, c. 539, ss. 922, 923; 1994, Ex. Sess., c. 24, s. 14(c); 1998-202, s. 13(ee).)

§ 122C-67. Other rules regarding abuse, exploitation, neglect not prohibited.

G.S. 122C-66 does not prohibit the Commission from adopting rules for State and area facilities and does not prohibit other facilities from issuing policies regarding other forms of prohibited abuse, exploitation, or neglect. (1985, c. 589, s. 2.)

§ 122C-68. Reserved for future codification purposes.

§ 122C-69. Reserved for future codification purposes.

§ 122C-70. Reserved for future codification purposes.

Part 2. Advance Instruction for Mental Health Treatment.

§ 122C-71. Purpose.

(a)   The General Assembly recognizes as a matter of public policy the fundamental right of an individual to control the decisions relating to the individual's mental health care.

(b)   The purpose of this Part is to establish an additional, nonexclusive method for an individual to exercise the right to consent to or refuse mental health treatment when the individual lacks sufficient understanding or capacity to make or communicate mental health treatment decisions.

(c)   This Part is intended and shall be construed to be consistent with the provisions of Article 3 of Chapter 32A of the General Statutes, provided that in the event of a conflict between the provisions of this Part and Article 3 of Chapter 32A, the provisions of this Part control. (1997-442, s. 2; 1998-198, s. 2.)

§ 122C-72. Definitions.

As used in this Part, unless the context clearly requires otherwise, the following terms have the meanings specified:

(1)   "Advance instruction for mental health treatment" or "advance instruction" means a written instrument, signed in the presence of two qualified witnesses who believe the principal to be of sound mind at the time of the signing, and acknowledged before a notary public, pursuant to which the principal makes a declaration of instructions, information, and preferences regarding the principal's mental health treatment and states that the principal is aware that the advance instruction authorizes a mental health treatment provider to act according to the instruction. It may also state the principal's instructions regarding, but not limited to, consent to or refusal of mental health treatment when the principal is incapable.

(2)   "Attending physician" means the physician who has primary responsibility for the care and treatment of the principal.

(3)   Repealed by Session Laws 1998-198, s. 2.

(4) "Incapable" means that, in the opinion of a physician or eligible psychologist, the person currently lacks sufficient understanding or capacity to make and communicate mental health treatment decisions. As used in this Part, the term "eligible psychologist" has the meaning given in G.S. 122C-3(13d).

(5) "Mental health treatment" means the process of providing for the physical, emotional, psychological, and social needs of the principal for the principal's mental illness. "Mental health treatment" includes, but is not limited to, electroconvulsive treatment (ECT), commonly referred to as "shock treatment", treatment of mental illness with psychotropic medication, and admission to and retention in a facility for care or treatment of mental illness.

(6) "Principal" means the person making the advance instruction.

(7) "Qualified witness" means a witness who affirms that the principal is personally known to the witness, that the principal signed or acknowledged the principal's signature on the advance instruction in the presence of the witness, that the witness believes the principal to be of sound mind and not to be under duress, fraud, or undue influence, and that the witness is not:

a. The attending physician or mental health service provider or an employee of the physician or mental health treatment provider;

b. An owner, operator, or employee of an owner or operator of a health care facility in which the principal is a patient or resident; or

c. Related within the third degree to the principal or to the principal's spouse. (1997-442, s. 2; 1998-198, s. 2.)

§ 122C-73. Scope, use, and authority of advance instruction for mental health treatment.

(a) Any adult of sound mind may make an advance instruction regarding mental health treatment. The advance instruction may include consent to or refusal of mental health treatment.

(b) An advance instruction may include, but is not limited to, the names and telephone numbers of individuals to be contacted in case of a mental health crisis, situations that may cause the principal to experience a mental health crisis, responses that may assist the principal to remain in the principal's home during a mental health crisis, the types of assistance that may help stabilize the principal if it becomes necessary to enter a facility, and medications that the principal is taking or has taken in the past and the effects of those medications.

(c) An individual shall not be required to execute or to refrain from executing an advance instruction as a condition for insurance coverage, as a condition for receiving mental or physical health services, as a condition for receiving privileges while in a facility, or as a condition of discharge from a facility.

(c1) A principal, through an advance instruction, may grant or withhold authority for mental health treatment, including, but not limited to, the use of psychotropic medication, electroconvulsive treatment, and admission to and retention in a facility for the care or treatment of mental illness.

(d) A principal may nominate, by advance instruction for mental health treatment, the guardian of the person of the principal if a guardianship proceeding is thereafter commenced. The court shall make its appointment in accordance with the principal's most recent nomination in an unrevoked advance instruction for mental health treatment, except for good cause shown.

(e) If, following the execution of an advance instruction for mental health treatment, a court of competent jurisdiction appoints a guardian of the person of the principal, or a general guardian with powers over the person of the principal, the guardian shall follow the advance instruction consistent with G.S. 35A-1201(a)(5).

(f) An advance instruction for mental health treatment may be combined with a health care power of attorney or general power of attorney that is executed in accordance with the requirements of Chapter 32A of the General Statutes so long as each form shall be executed in accordance with its own statute. (1997-442, s. 2; 1998-198, s. 2.)

§ 122C-74. Effectiveness and duration; revocation.

(a) A validly executed advance instruction becomes effective upon its proper execution and remains valid unless revoked.

(b) The attending physician or other mental health treatment provider may consider valid and rely upon an advance instruction, or a copy of that advance instruction that is obtained from the Advance Health Care Directive Registry maintained by the Secretary of State pursuant to Article 21 of Chapter 130A of the General Statutes, in the absence of actual knowledge of its revocation or invalidity.

(c) An attending physician or other mental health treatment provider may presume that a person who executed an advance instruction in accordance with this Part was of sound mind and acted voluntarily when he or she executed the advance instruction.

(d) An attending physician or other mental health treatment provider shall act in accordance with an advance instruction when the principal has been determined to be incapable. If a patient is incapable, an advance instruction executed in accordance with this Article is presumed to be valid.

(e) The attending physician or mental health treatment provider shall continue to obtain the principal's informed consent to all mental health treatment decisions when the principal is capable of providing informed consent or refusal, as required by G.S. 122C-57. Unless the principal is deemed incapable by the attending physician or eligible psychologist, the instructions of the principal at the time of treatment shall supersede the declarations expressed in the principal's advance instruction.

(f) The fact of a principal's having executed an advance instruction shall not be considered an indication of a principal's capacity to make or communicate mental health treatment decisions at such times as those decisions are required.

(g) Upon being presented with an advance instruction, an attending physician or other mental health treatment provider shall make the advance instruction a part of the principal's medical record. When acting under authority of an advance instruction, an attending physician or other mental health treatment provider shall comply with the advance instruction unless:

(1) Compliance, in the opinion of the attending physician or other mental health treatment provider, is not consistent with generally accepted community practice standards of treatment to benefit the principal;

(2) Compliance is not consistent with the availability of treatments requested;

(3) Compliance is not consistent with applicable law;

(4) The principal is committed to a 24-hour facility pursuant to Article 5 of Chapter 122C of the General Statutes, and treatment is authorized in compliance with G.S. 122C-57 and rules adopted pursuant to it; or

(5) Compliance, in the opinion of the attending physician or other mental health treatment provider, is not consistent with appropriate treatment in case of an emergency endangering life or health.

In the event that one part of the advance instruction is unable to be followed because of one or more of the above, all other parts of the advance instruction shall nonetheless be followed.

(h) If the attending physician or other mental health treatment provider is unwilling at any time to comply with any part or parts of an advance instruction for one or more of the reasons set out in subdivisions (1) through (5) of subsection (g), the attending physician or other mental health care treatment provider shall promptly notify the principal and, if applicable, the health care agent and shall document the reason for not complying with the advance instruction and shall document the notification in the principal's medical record.

(i) An advance instruction does not limit any authority provided in Article 5 of G.S. 122C either to take a person into custody, or to admit, retain, or treat a person in a facility.

(j) An advance instruction may be revoked at any time by the principal so long as the principal is not incapable. The principal may exercise this right of revocation in any manner by which the principal is able to communicate an intent to revoke and by notifying the revocation to the treating physician or other mental health treatment provider. The attending physician or other mental health treatment provider shall note the revocation as part of the principal's medical record. (1997-442, s. 2; 1998-198, s. 2; 2001-455, s. 5; 2001-513, s. 30(b).)

§ 122C-75. Reliance on advance instruction for mental health treatment.

(a) An attending physician or eligible psychologist who in good faith determines that the principal is or is not incapable for the purpose of deciding whether to proceed or not to proceed according to an advance instruction, is not subject to criminal prosecution, civil liability, or professional disciplinary action for making and acting upon that determination.

(b) In the absence of actual knowledge of the revocation of an advance instruction, no attending physician or other mental health treatment provider shall be subject to criminal prosecution or civil liability or be deemed to have engaged in unprofessional conduct as a result of the provision of treatment to a principal in accordance with this Part unless the absence of actual knowledge resulted from the negligence of the attending physician or mental health treatment provider.

(c) An attending physician or mental health treatment provider who administers or does not administer mental health treatment according to and in good faith reliance upon the validity of an advance instruction is not subject to criminal prosecution, civil liability, or professional disciplinary action resulting from a subsequent finding of an advance instruction's invalidity.

(d) No attending physician or mental health treatment provider who administers or does not administer treatment under authorization obtained pursuant to this Part shall incur liability arising out of a claim to the extent that the claim is based on lack of informed consent or authorization for this action.

(e) This section shall not be construed as affecting or limiting any liability that arises out of a negligent act or omission in connection with the medical diagnosis, care, or treatment of a principal under an advance instruction or that arises out of any deviation from reasonable medical standards. (1997-442, s. 2; 1998-198, s. 2.)

§ 122C-76. Penalty.

It is a Class 2 misdemeanor for a person, without authorization of the principal, willfully to alter, forge, conceal, or destroy an instrument, the reinstatement or revocation of an instrument, or any other evidence or document reflecting the principal's desires and interests, with the intent or effect of affecting a mental health treatment decision. (1997-442, s. 2.)

§ 122C-77. Statutory form for advance instruction for mental health treatment.

(a) This Part shall not be construed to invalidate an advance instruction for mental health treatment that was executed prior to January 1, 1999, and was otherwise valid.

(b) The use of the following or similar form after the effective date of this Part in the creation of an advance instruction for mental health treatment is lawful, and, when used, it shall specifically meet the requirements and be construed in accordance with the provisions of this Part.

"ADVANCE INSTRUCTION FOR MENTAL HEALTH TREATMENT

I, _____, being an adult of sound mind, willfully and voluntarily make this advance instruction for mental health treatment to be followed if it is determined by a physician or eligible psychologist that my ability to receive and evaluate information effectively or communicate decisions is impaired to such an extent that I lack the capacity to refuse or consent to mental health treatment. "Mental health treatment" means the process of providing for the physical, emotional, psychological, and social needs of the principal. "Mental health treatment" includes electroconvulsive treatment (ECT), commonly referred to as "shock treatment", treatment of mental illness with psychotropic medication, and admission to and retention in a facility for care or treatment of mental illness.

I understand that under G.S. 122C-57, other than for specific exceptions stated there, mental health treatment may not be administered without my express and informed written consent or, if I am incapable of giving my informed consent, the express and informed consent of my legally responsible person, my health care agent named pursuant to a valid health care power of attorney, or my consent expressed in this advance instruction for mental health treatment. I understand that I may become incapable of giving or withholding informed consent for mental health treatment due to the symptoms of a diagnosed mental disorder. These symptoms may include:

PSYCHOACTIVE MEDICATIONS

If I become incapable of giving or withholding informed consent for mental health treatment, my instructions regarding psychoactive medications are as follows: (Place initials beside choice.)

_____ I consent to the administration of the following medications:

_____ I do not consent to the administration of the following medications:

_____
_____

_____
_____

Conditions or limitations:_____
—

_____
_____

_____
_____

ADMISSION TO AND RETENTION IN FACILITY

If I become incapable of giving or withholding informed consent for mental health treatment, my instructions regarding admission to and retention in a health care facility for mental health treatment are as follows: (Place initials beside choice.)

_____ I consent to being admitted to a health care facility for mental health treatment.

My facility preference is_____

_____ I do not consent to being admitted to a health care facility for mental health treatment.

This advance instruction cannot, by law, provide consent to retain me in a facility for more than 10 days.

Conditions or limitations_____
_____

ADDITIONAL INSTRUCTIONS

These instructions shall apply during the entire length of my incapacity.

In case of mental health crisis, please contact:

1.
Name:_____

Home Address:_____

Home Telephone Number:_____

Work Telephone Number:_____

Relationship to Me:_____

2. Name:_____

Home Address:_____

Home Telephone Number:_____

Work Telephone Number:_____

Relationship to Me:_____

3. My Physician:

Name:_____

Telephone Number:_____

4. My Therapist:

Name:_____

Telephone Number:_____

The following may cause me to experience a mental health crisis:
_____
_____

The following may help me avoid a hospitalization:_____

_____

_____

I generally react to being hospitalized as
follows:_____
_____
_____

Staff of the hospital or crisis unit can help me by doing the following:

_____
_____
_____

I give permission for the following person or people to visit me:

_____
_____
_____

Instructions concerning any other medical interventions, such as electroconvulsive (ECT) treatment (commonly referred to as "shock treatment"):

_____
_____
_____

Other
instructions:_____
_____
_____
_____
_____

_____ I have attached an additional sheet of instructions to be followed and considered part of this advance instruction.

SHARING OF INFORMATION BY PROVIDERS

I understand that the information in this document may be shared by my mental health treatment provider with any other mental health treatment provider who may serve me when necessary to provide treatment in accordance with this advance instruction.

Other instructions about sharing of information:

_____
_____
_____

SIGNATURE OF PRINCIPAL

By signing here, I indicate that I am mentally alert and competent, fully informed as to the contents of this document, and understand the full impact of having made this advance instruction for mental health treatment.

Signature of Principal   Date

NATURE OF WITNESSES

I hereby state that the principal is personally known to me, that the principal signed or acknowledged the principal's signature on this advance instruction for mental health treatment in my presence, that the principal appears to be of sound mind and not under duress, fraud, or undue influence, and that I am not:

a. The attending physician or mental health service provider or an employee of the physician or mental health treatment provider;

b. An owner, operator, or employee of an owner or operator of a health care facility in which the principal is a patient or resident; or

c. Related within the third degree to the principal or to the principal's spouse.

AFFIRMATION OF WITNESSES

We affirm that the principal is personally known to us, that the principal signed or acknowledged the principal's signature on this advance instruction for mental health treatment in our presence, that the principal appears to be of sound mind and not under duress, fraud, or undue influence, and that neither of us is:

A person appointed as an attorney-in-fact by this document;

The principal's attending physician or mental health service provider or a relative of the physician or provider;

The owner, operator, or relative of an owner or operator of a facility in which the principal is a patient or resident; or

A person related to the principal by blood, marriage, or adoption.

Witnessed by:

Witness:_____
Date:_____

Witness:_____
Date:_____

STATE OF NORTH CAROLINA

COUNTY OF_____

CERTIFICATION OF NOTARY PUBLIC

STATE OF NORTH CAROLINA

COUNTY OF

I, _____, a Notary Public for the County cited above in the State of North Carolina, hereby certify that _____ appeared before me and swore or affirmed to me and to the witnesses in my presence that this instrument is an advance instruction for mental health treatment, and that he/she willingly and voluntarily made and executed it as his/her free act and deed for the purposes expressed in it.

I further certify that _____ and _____, witnesses, appeared before me and swore or affirmed that they witnessed _____ sign the attached advance instruction for mental health treatment, believing him/her to be of sound mind; and also swore that at the time they witnessed the signing they were not (i) the attending physician or mental health treatment provider or an employee of the physician or mental health treatment provider and (ii) they were not an owner, operator, or employee of an owner or operator of a health care facility in which the principal is a patient or resident, and (iii) they were not related within the third degree to the principal or to the principal's spouse. I further certify that I am satisfied as to the genuineness and due execution of the instrument.

This is the _____ day of_____,_____

_____
Notary Public

My Commission expires:

NOTICE TO PERSON MAKING AN INSTRUCTION FOR MENTAL HEALTH TREATMENT

This is an important legal document. It creates an instruction for mental health treatment. Before signing this document you should know these important facts:

This document allows you to make decisions in advance about certain types of mental health treatment. The instructions you include in this declaration will be followed if a physician or eligible psychologist determines that you are incapable of making and communicating treatment decisions. Otherwise you will be considered capable to give or withhold consent for the treatments. Your instructions may be overridden if you are being held in accordance with civil commitment law. Under the Health Care Power of Attorney you may also appoint a person as your health care agent to make treatment decisions for you if you become incapable. You have the right to revoke this document at any time you have not been determined to be incapable. YOU MAY NOT REVOKE THIS ADVANCE INSTRUCTION WHEN YOU ARE FOUND INCAPABLE BY A PHYSICIAN OR OTHER AUTHORIZED MENTAL HEALTH TREATMENT PROVIDER. A revocation is effective when it is communicated to your attending physician or other provider. The physician or other provider shall note the revocation in your medical record. To be valid, this advance instruction must be signed by two qualified witnesses, personally known to you, who are present when you sign or acknowledge your signature. It must also be acknowledged before a notary public.

NOTICE TO PHYSICIAN OR OTHER MENTAL HEALTH TREATMENT PROVIDER

Under North Carolina law, a person may use this advance instruction to provide consent for future mental health treatment if the person later becomes incapable of making those decisions. Under the Health Care Power of Attorney the person may also appoint a health care agent to make mental health treatment decisions for the person when incapable. A person is "incapable" when in the opinion of a physician or eligible psychologist the person currently lacks sufficient understanding or capacity to make and communicate mental health treatment decisions. This document becomes effective upon its proper execution and remains valid unless revoked. Upon being presented with this advance instruction, the physician or other provider must make it a part of the person's medical record. The attending physician or other mental health treatment provider must act in accordance with the statements expressed in the advance instruction when the person is determined to be incapable, unless compliance is not consistent with G.S. 122C-74(g). The physician or other mental health treatment provider shall promptly notify the principal and, if applicable, the health care agent, and document noncompliance with any part of an advance instruction in the principal's medical record. The physician or other mental health treatment provider may rely upon the authority of a signed, witnessed, dated, and notarized advance instruction, as provided in G.S. 122C-75. (1997-442, s. 2; 1998-198, s. 2; 1998-217, s. 53(a)(5).)

§ 122C-78. Reserved for future codification purposes.

§ 122C-79. Reserved for future codification purposes.

Article 3A.

Miscellaneous Provisions.

§ 122C-80. Criminal history record check required for certain applicants for employment.

(a) Definition. - As used in this section, the term "provider" applies to an area authority/county program and any provider of mental health, developmental disability, and substance abuse services that is licensable under Article 2 of this Chapter.

(b) Requirement. - An offer of employment by a provider licensed under this Chapter to an applicant to fill a position that does not require the applicant to have an occupational license is conditioned on consent to a State and national criminal history record check of the applicant. If the applicant has been a resident of this State for less than five years, then the offer of employment is conditioned on consent to a State and national criminal history record check of the applicant. The national criminal history record check shall include a check of the applicant's fingerprints. If the applicant has been a resident of this State for five years or more, then the offer is conditioned on consent to a State criminal history record check of the applicant. A provider shall not employ an applicant who refuses to consent to a criminal history record check required by this section. Except as otherwise provided in this subsection, within five business days of making the conditional offer of employment, a provider shall submit a request to the Department of Justice under G.S. 114-19.10 to conduct a criminal history record check required by this section or shall submit a request to a private entity to conduct a State criminal history record check required by this section. Notwithstanding G.S. 114-19.10, the Department of Justice shall return the results of national criminal history record checks for employment positions not covered by Public Law 105-277 to the Department of Health and Human Services, Criminal Records Check Unit. Within five business days of receipt of the national criminal history of the person, the Department of Health and Human Services, Criminal Records Check Unit, shall notify the provider as to whether the information received may affect the employability of the applicant. In no case shall the results of the national criminal history record check be shared with the provider. Providers shall make available upon request verification that a criminal history check has been completed on any staff covered by this section. A county that has adopted an appropriate local ordinance and has access to the Division of Criminal Information data bank may conduct on behalf of a provider a State criminal history record check required by this section without the provider having to submit a request to the Department of Justice. In such a case, the county shall commence with the State criminal history record check required by this section within five business days of the conditional offer of employment by the provider. All criminal history information received by the provider is confidential and may not be disclosed, except to the applicant as provided in subsection (c) of this section. For purposes of this subsection, the term "private entity" means a business regularly engaged in conducting criminal history record checks utilizing public records obtained from a State agency.

(c) Action. - If an applicant's criminal history record check reveals one or more convictions of a relevant offense, the provider shall consider all of the following factors in determining whether to hire the applicant:

(1) The level and seriousness of the crime.

(2) The date of the crime.

(3) The age of the person at the time of the conviction.

(4) The circumstances surrounding the commission of the crime, if known.

(5) The nexus between the criminal conduct of the person and the job duties of the position to be filled.

(6) The prison, jail, probation, parole, rehabilitation, and employment records of the person since the date the crime was committed.

(7) The subsequent commission by the person of a relevant offense.

The fact of conviction of a relevant offense alone shall not be a bar to employment; however, the listed factors shall be considered by the provider. If the provider disqualifies an applicant after consideration of the relevant factors, then the provider may disclose information contained in the criminal history record check that is relevant to the disqualification, but may not provide a copy of the criminal history record check to the applicant.

(d) Limited Immunity. - A provider and an officer or employee of a provider that, in good faith, complies with this section shall be immune from civil liability for:

(1) The failure of the provider to employ an individual on the basis of information provided in the criminal history record check of the individual.

(2) Failure to check an employee's history of criminal offenses if the employee's criminal history record check is requested and received in compliance with this section.

(e) Relevant Offense. - As used in this section, "relevant offense" means a county, state, or federal criminal history of conviction or pending indictment of a crime, whether a misdemeanor or felony, that bears upon an individual's fitness to have responsibility for the safety and well-being of persons needing mental health, developmental disabilities, or substance abuse services. These crimes include the criminal offenses set forth in any of the following Articles of Chapter 14 of the General Statutes: Article 5, Counterfeiting and Issuing Monetary Substitutes; Article 5A, Endangering Executive and Legislative Officers; Article 6, Homicide; Article 7A, Rape and Other Sex Offenses; Article 8, Assaults; Article 10, Kidnapping and Abduction; Article 13, Malicious Injury or Damage by Use of Explosive or Incendiary Device or Material; Article 14, Burglary and Other Housebreakings; Article 15, Arson and Other Burnings; Article 16, Larceny; Article 17, Robbery; Article 18, Embezzlement; Article 19, False Pretenses and Cheats; Article 19A, Obtaining Property or Services by False or Fraudulent Use of Credit Device or Other Means; Article 19B, Financial Transaction Card Crime Act; Article 20, Frauds; Article 21, Forgery; Article 26, Offenses Against Public Morality and Decency; Article 26A, Adult Establishments; Article 27, Prostitution; Article 28, Perjury; Article 29, Bribery; Article 31, Misconduct in Public Office; Article 35, Offenses Against the Public Peace; Article 36A, Riots, Civil Disorders, and Emergencies; Article 39, Protection of Minors; Article 40, Protection of the Family; Article 59, Public Intoxication; and Article 60, Computer-Related Crime. These crimes also include possession or sale of drugs in violation of the North Carolina Controlled Substances Act, Article 5 of Chapter 90 of the General Statutes, and alcohol-related offenses such as sale to underage persons in violation of G.S. 18B-302 or driving while impaired in violation of G.S. 20-138.1 through G.S. 20-138.5.

(f) Penalty for Furnishing False Information. - Any applicant for employment who willfully furnishes, supplies, or otherwise gives false information on an employment application that is the basis for a criminal history record check under this section shall be guilty of a Class A1 misdemeanor.

(g) Conditional Employment. - A provider may employ an applicant conditionally prior to obtaining the results of a criminal history record check regarding the applicant if both of the following requirements are met:

(1) The provider shall not employ an applicant prior to obtaining the applicant's consent for criminal history record check as required in subsection (b) of this section or the completed fingerprint cards as required in G.S. 114-19.10.

(2) The provider shall submit the request for a criminal history record check not later than five business days after the individual begins conditional employment. (2000-154, s. 4; 2001-155, s. 1; 2004-124, ss. 10.19D(c), (h); 2005-4, ss. 1, 2, 3, 4, 5(a); 2007-444, s. 3; 2012-12, s. 2(tt).)

§ 122C-81. National accreditation benchmarks.

(a) As used in this section, the term:

(1) "National accreditation" applies to accreditation by an entity approved by the Secretary that accredits mental health, developmental disabilities, and substance abuse services.

(2) "Provider" applies to only those providers of services, including facilities, requiring national accreditation, which services are designated by the Secretary pursuant to subsection (b) of this section.

(b) The Secretary, through the Medicaid State Plan, Medicaid waiver, or rules adopted by the Secretary, shall designate the mental health, developmental disabilities, and substance abuse services that require national accreditation.

(c) Providers enrolled with the Medicaid program prior to July 1, 2008, and providing services that require national accreditation approved by the Secretary pursuant to subsection (b) of this section, shall successfully complete national accreditation requirements within three years of enrollment with the Medicaid program. Providers shall meet the following benchmarks to ensure continuity of care for consumers in the event the provider does not make sufficient progress in achieving national accreditation in a timely manner:

(1)   Nine months prior to the accreditation deadline - Formal selection of an accrediting agency as documented by a letter from the agency to the provider acknowledging the provider's selection of that accrediting agency. A provider failing to meet this benchmark shall be prohibited from admitting new clients to service. If a provider fails to meet this benchmark, then the LMEs shall work with the provider to transfer all the provider's entire case load to another provider within four months of the date of the provider's failure to meet the benchmark. The transfer of the case load shall be in increments such that not fewer than twenty-five percent (25%) of the provider's total caseload shall be transferred per month. The Department shall terminate the provider's enrollment in the Medicaid program within four months of the provider's failure to meet the benchmark.

(2)   Six months prior to the accreditation deadline - An on-site accreditation review scheduled by the accrediting agency as documented by a letter from the agency to the facility. A provider failing to meet this benchmark will be prohibited from admitting new clients to service. If a provider fails to meet this benchmark, then the LMEs shall work with the provider to transfer the provider's entire case load to another provider within three months of the date of the provider's failure to meet the benchmark. The transfer of the case load shall be in increments such that not fewer than thirty-three percent (33%) of the provider's total caseload shall be transferred per month. The Department shall terminate the provider's enrollment in the Medicaid program within three months of the provider's failure to meet the benchmark.

(3)   Three months prior to the accreditation deadline - Completion of an on-site accreditation review, receipt of initial feedback from accrediting agency, and submission of a Plan of Correction for any deficiencies noted by the accrediting agency. A provider failing to meet this benchmark shall be prohibited from admitting new clients to service. If a provider fails to meet this benchmark, then the LMEs shall work with the provider to transfer the provider's entire case load to another provider within two months of the date of the provider's failure to meet the benchmark. The transfer of the case load shall be in increments such that not fewer than fifty percent (50%) of the provider's total caseload shall be transferred per month. The Department shall terminate the provider's enrollment

in the Medicaid program within two months of the provider's failure to meet the benchmark.

(4) Accreditation deadline - Approval as fully accredited by the national accrediting agency. A provider failing to meet this requirement shall be prohibited from admitting new clients to service. The LMEs will work with a provider failing to meet this deadline to transition clients currently receiving service to other providers within 60 days. The Department shall terminate the provider's enrollment in the Medicaid program within 60 days of the provider's failure to meet the benchmark.

(5) A provider that has its enrollment terminated in the Medicaid program as a result of failure to meet benchmarks for national accreditation or failure to continue to be nationally accredited may not apply for re-enrollment in the Medicaid program for at least one year following its enrollment termination.

(d) Providers enrolled in the Medicaid program or contracting for State-funded services on or after July 1, 2008, and providing services which require national accreditation shall successfully complete all accreditation requirements and be awarded national accreditation within one year of enrollment in the Medicaid program or within two years following the provider's first contract to deliver a State-funded service requiring national accreditation. Providers providing services that require national accreditation shall be required to discontinue service delivery and shall have their Medicaid enrollment and any service contracts terminated if they do not meet the following benchmarks for demonstrating sufficient progress in achieving national accreditation following the date of enrollment in the Medicaid program or initial contract for State-funded services:

(1) Three months - On-site accreditation review scheduled by accrediting agency as documented by a letter from the agency to the provider and completion of self-study and self-evaluation protocols distributed by the selected accrediting agency.

(2) Six months - On-site accreditation review scheduled by accrediting agency as documented by a letter from the agency to the provider.

(3) Nine months - Completion of on-site accreditation review, receipt of initial feedback from accrediting agency, plan to address any deficiencies identified developed.

(4) If a provider's Medicaid enrollment or service delivery contracts are terminated as a result of failure to meet accreditation benchmarks or failure to continue to be nationally accredited, the provider will work with the LME to transition consumers served by the provider to other service providers in an orderly fashion within 60 days of notification by the LME of such failure.

(5) A provider that has its Medicaid enrollment or service delivery contracts terminated as a result of failure to meet accreditation benchmarks or failure to continue to be nationally accredited may not reapply for enrollment in the Medicaid program or enter into any new service delivery contracts for at least one year following enrollment or contract termination. (2008-107, s. 10.15A(c).)

Article 4.

Organization and System for Delivery of Mental Health, Developmental Disabilities, and Substance Abuse Services.

Part 1. Policy.

§ 122C-101. Policy.

Within the public system of mental health, developmental disabilities, and substance abuse services, there are area, county, and State facilities. An area authority or county program is the locus of coordination among public services for clients of its catchment area. (1985, c. 589, s. 2; 1989, c. 625, s. 13; 1993, c. 396, s. 3; 2001-437, s. 1.4.)

§ 122C-102. State Plan for Mental Health, Developmental Disabilities, and Substance Abuse Services; system performance measures.

(a) Purpose of State Plan. - The Department shall develop and implement a State Plan for Mental Health, Developmental Disabilities, and Substance Abuse Services. The purpose of the State Plan is to provide a strategic template regarding how State and local resources shall be organized and used to provide services. The State Plan shall be issued every three years beginning July 1,

2007. It shall identify specific goals to be achieved by the Department, area authorities, and county programs over a three-year period of time and benchmarks for determining whether progress is being made towards those goals. It shall also identify data that will be used to measure progress towards the specified goals. In order to increase the ability of the State, area authorities, county programs, private providers, and consumers to successfully implement the goals of the State Plan, the Department shall not adopt or implement policies that are inconsistent with the State Plan without first consulting with the Joint Legislative Oversight Committee on Mental Health, Developmental Disabilities, and Substance Abuse Services.

(b) Content of State Plan. - The State Plan shall include the following:

(1) Vision and mission of the State Mental Health, Developmental Disabilities, and Substance Abuse Services system.

(2) Repealed by Session Laws 2006-142, s. 2(a), effective July 19, 2006.

(3) Protection of client rights and consumer involvement in planning and management of system services.

(4) Provision of services to targeted populations, including criteria for identifying targeted populations.

(5) Compliance with federal mandates in establishing service priorities in mental health, developmental disabilities, and substance abuse.

(6) Description of the core services that are available to all individuals in order to improve consumer access to mental health, developmental disabilities, and substance abuse services at the local level.

(7) Service standards for the mental health, developmental disabilities, and substance abuse services system.

(8) Implementation of the uniform portal process.

(9) Strategies and schedules for implementing the service plan, including consultation on Medicaid policy with area and county programs, qualified providers, and others as designated by the Secretary, intersystem collaboration, promotion of best practices, technical assistance, outcome-based monitoring, and evaluation.

(10) A plan for coordination of the State Plan for Mental Health, Developmental Disabilities, and Substance Abuse Services with the Medicaid State Plan, and NC Health Choice.

(11) A business plan to demonstrate efficient and effective resource management of the mental health, developmental disabilities, and substance abuse services system, including strategies for accountability for non-Medicaid and Medicaid services.

(12) Strategies and schedules for implementing a phased in plan to eliminate disparities in the allocation of State funding across county programs and area authorities by January 1, 2007, including methods to identify service gaps and to ensure equitable use of State funds to fill those gaps among all counties.

(c) Repealed by Session Laws 2013-360, s. 12A.8(c), effective July 1, 2013. (2001-437, s. 1.5; 2006-142, s. 2(a); 2011-291, s. 2.42; 2013-360, s. 12A.8(c).)

§§ 122C-103 through 122C-110. Reserved for future codification purposes.

Part 2. State, County and Area Authority.

§ 122C-111. Administration.

The Secretary shall administer and enforce the provisions of this Chapter and the rules of the Commission and shall operate State facilities. An area director or program director shall (i) manage the public mental health, developmental disabilities, and substance abuse system for the area authority or county program according to the local business plan, and (ii) enforce applicable State laws, rules of the Commission, and rules of the Secretary. The Secretary in cooperation with area and county program directors and State facility directors shall provide for the coordination of public services between area authorities, county programs, and State facilities. The area authority or county program shall monitor the provision of mental health, developmental disabilities, and substance abuse services for compliance with the law, which monitoring and management shall not supersede or duplicate the regulatory authority or functions of agencies of the Department. (1963, c. 1166, s. 3; 1973, c. 476, s. 133; 1985, c. 589, s. 2; 2001-437, s. 1.6; 2002-164, s. 4.2; 2006-142, s. 4(b).)

§ 122C-112: Repealed by Session Laws 2001-437, s. 1.7(a), effective July 1, 2002.

§ 122C-112.1. Powers and duties of the Secretary.

(a)   The Secretary shall do all of the following:

(1)   Oversee development and implementation of the State Plan for Mental Health, Developmental Disabilities, and Substance Abuse Services.

(2)   Enforce the provisions of this Chapter and the rules of the Commission and the Secretary.

(3)   Establish a process and criteria for the submission, review, and approval or disapproval of LME business plans submitted by area authorities and county programs for the management of mental health, developmental disabilities, and substance abuse services.

(4)   Adopt rules specifying the content and format of LME business plans.

(5)   Review LME business plans and, upon approval of the plan, certify the submitting area authority or county program to manage the delivery of mental health, developmental disabilities, and substance abuse services in the applicable catchment area.

(6)   Establish comprehensive, cohesive oversight and monitoring procedures and processes to ensure continuous compliance by area authorities, county programs, and all providers of public services with State and federal policy, law, and standards. The procedures shall include the development and use of critical performance measures and report cards for each area authority and county program.

(7)   Conduct regularly scheduled monitoring and oversight of area authority, county programs, and all providers of public services. Monitoring and oversight shall be used to assess compliance with the LME business plan and implementation of core LME functions. Monitoring shall also include the examination of LME and provider performance on outcome measures including adherence to best practices, the assessment of consumer satisfaction, and the review of client rights complaints.

(8) Make findings and recommendations based on information and data collected pursuant to subdivision (7) of this subsection and submit these findings and recommendations to the applicable area authority board, county program director, board of county commissioners, providers of public services, and to the Local Consumer Advocacy Office.

(9) Provide ongoing and focused technical assistance to area authorities and county programs in the implementation of the LME functions and the establishment and operation of community-based programs. The technical assistance required under this subdivision includes, but is not limited to, the technical assistance required under G.S. 122C-115.4(d)(2). The Secretary shall include in the State Plan a mechanism for monitoring the Department's success in implementing this duty and the progress of area authorities and county programs in achieving these functions.

(10) Operate State facilities and adopt rules pertaining to their operation.

(11) Develop a unified system of services provided at the community level, by State facilities, and by providers enrolled or under a contract with the State and an area authority or county program.

(12) Adopt rules governing the expenditure of all funds for mental health, developmental disabilities, and substance abuse programs and services.

(13) Adopt rules to implement the appeal procedure authorized by G.S. 122C-151.2.

(14) Implement the uniform portal process developed under rules adopted by the Commission for Mental Health, Developmental Disabilities, and Substance Abuse Services in accordance with G.S. 122C-114.

(15) Except as provided in G.S. 122C-26(4), adopt rules establishing procedures for waiver of rules adopted by the Secretary under this Chapter.

(16) Notify the clerks of superior court of changes in the designation of State facility regions and of facilities designated under G.S. 122C-252.

(17) Promote public awareness and understanding of mental health, mental illness, developmental disabilities, and substance abuse.

(18) Administer and enforce rules that are conditions of participation for federal or State financial aid.

(19) Carry out G.S. 122C-361.

(20) Monitor the fiscal and administrative practices of area authorities and county programs to ensure that the programs are accountable to the State for the management and use of federal and State funds allocated for mental health, developmental disabilities, and substance abuse services. The Secretary shall ensure maximum accountability by area authorities and county programs for rate-setting methodologies, reimbursement procedures, billing procedures, provider contracting procedures, record keeping, documentation, and other matters pertaining to financial management and fiscal accountability. The Secretary shall further ensure that the practices are consistent with professionally accepted accounting and management principles.

(21) Provide technical assistance, including conflict resolution, to counties in the development and implementation of area authority and county program business plans and other matters, as requested by the county.

(22) Develop a methodology to be used for calculating county resources to reflect cash and in-kind contributions of the county.

(23) Adopt rules establishing program evaluation and management of mental health, developmental disabilities, and substance abuse services.

(24) Adopt rules regarding the requirements of the federal government for grants-in-aid for mental health, developmental disabilities, or substance abuse programs which may be made available to area authorities or county programs or the State. This section shall be liberally construed in order that the State and its citizens may benefit from the grants-in-aid.

(25) Adopt rules for determining minimally adequate services for purposes of G.S. 122C-124.1 and G.S. 122C-125.

(26) Establish a process for approving area authorities and county programs to provide services directly in accordance with G.S. 122C-141.

(27) Sponsor training opportunities in the fields of mental health, developmental disabilities, and substance abuse.

(28) Enforce the protection of the rights of clients served by State facilities, area authorities, county programs, and providers of public services.

(29) Adopt rules for the enforcement of the protection of the rights of clients being served by State facilities, area authorities, county programs, and providers of public services.

(30) Prior to requesting approval to close a State facility under G.S. 122C-181(b):

a. Notify the Joint Legislative Commission on Governmental Operations, the Joint Legislative Oversight Committee on Health and Human Services, and members of the General Assembly who represent catchment areas affected by the closure; and

b. Present a plan for the closure to the members of the Joint Legislative Oversight Committee on Health and Human Services, the House of Representatives Appropriations Subcommittee on Health and Human Services, and the Senate Appropriations Committee on Health and Human Services for their review, advice, and recommendations. The plan shall address specifically how patients will be cared for after closure, how support services to community-based agencies and outreach services will be continued, and the impact on remaining State facilities. In implementing the plan, the Secretary shall take into consideration the comments and recommendations of the committees to which the plan is presented under this subdivision.

(31) Ensure that the State Plan for Mental Health, Developmental Disabilities, and Substance Abuse Services is coordinated with the Medicaid State Plan and NC Health Choice.

(32) Implement standard forms, quality measures, contracts, processes, and procedures to be used by all area authorities and county programs with other public and private service providers. The Secretary shall consult with LMEs, CFACs, counties, and qualified providers regarding the development of any forms, processes, and procedures required under this subdivision. Any document, process, or procedure developed under this subdivision shall place an obligation upon providers to transmit to LMEs timely client information and outcome data. The Secretary shall also adopt rules regarding what constitutes a clean claim for purposes of billing.

When implementing this subdivision, the Secretary shall balance the need for LMEs to exercise discretion in the discharge of their LME functions with the need of qualified providers for a uniform system of doing business with public entities.

(33) Develop and implement critical performance indicators to be used to hold LMEs accountable for managing the mental health, developmental disabilities, and substance abuse services system. The performance system indicators shall be implemented no later than July 1, 2007.

(34) Adopt rules for the implementation of a co-payment graduated schedule to be used by LMEs and by contractual provider agencies under G.S. 122C-146. The co-payment graduated schedule shall be developed to require a co-payment for services identified by the Secretary. Families whose family income is three hundred percent (300%) or greater of the federal poverty level are eligible for services with the applicable co-payment.

(35) Develop and adopt rules governing a statewide data system containing waiting list information obtained annually from each LME as required under G.S. 122C-115.4(b)(8). The rules adopted shall establish standardized criteria to be used by LMEs to ensure that the waiting list data are consistent across LMEs. The Department shall use data collected from LMEs under G.S. 122C-115.4(b)(8) for statewide planning and needs projections. The creation of the statewide waiting list data system does not create an entitlement to services for individuals on the waiting list. The Department shall report annually to the Joint Legislative Oversight Committee on Health and Human Services its recommendations based on data obtained annually from each LME. The report shall indicate the services that are most needed throughout the State, plans to address unmet needs, and any cost projections for providing needed services.

(36) The Department shall ensure that developmental disability services funded from State appropriations to or allocations from the Division of Mental Health, Developmental Disabilities, and Substance Abuse Services, including CAP-MRDD are authorized on a quarterly, semiannual, or annual basis, in accordance with guidelines issued by the Department, unless a change in the individual's person-centered plan indicates a different authorization frequency.

(37) The Department shall develop new developmental disability service definitions for developmental disability services funded from State appropriations to or allocations from the Division of Mental Health,

Developmental Disabilities, and Substance Abuse Services, including CAP-MRDD that allow for person-centered and self-directed supports.

(38)   Adopt rules establishing a procedure for single-county disengagement from an area authority operating under a 1915(b)/(c) Medicaid Waiver.

(39)   Develop and use a standard contract for all local management entity/managed care organizations for operation of the 1915(b)/(c) Medicaid Waiver that requires compliance by each LME/MCO with all provisions of the contract to operate the 1915(b)/(c) Medicaid Waiver and with all applicable provisions of State and federal law.

(b)   The Secretary may do the following:

(1)   Acquire, by purchase or otherwise in the name of the Department, equipment, supplies, and other personal property necessary to carry out the mental health, developmental disabilities, and substance abuse programs.

(2)   Promote and conduct research in the fields of mental health, developmental disabilities, and substance abuse; promote best practices.

(3)   Receive donations of money, securities, equipment, supplies, or any other personal property of any kind or description that shall be used by the Secretary for the purpose of carrying out mental health, developmental disabilities, and substance abuse programs. Any donations shall be reported to the Office of State Budget and Management as determined by that office.

(4)   Accept, allocate, and spend any federal funds for mental health, developmental disabilities, and substance abuse activities that may be made available to the State by the federal government. This Chapter shall be liberally construed in order that the State and its citizens may benefit fully from these funds. Any federal funds received shall be deposited with the Department of State Treasurer and shall be appropriated by the General Assembly for the mental health, developmental disabilities, or substance abuse purposes specified.

(5)   Enter into agreements authorized by G.S. 122C-346.

(6)   Notwithstanding G.S. 126-18, authorize funds for contracting with a person, firm, or corporation for aid or assistance in locating, recruiting, or

arranging employment of health care professionals in any facility listed in G.S. 122C-181.

(7) Contract with one or more private providers or other public service agencies to serve clients of an area authority or county program and reallocate program funds to pay for services under the contract if the Secretary finds all of the following:

a. The area authority or county program refuses or has failed to provide the services to clients within its catchment area, or provide specialty services in another catchment area, in a manner that is at least adequate.

b. Clients within the area authority or county program catchment area will either not be served or will suffer an unreasonable hardship if required to obtain the services from another area authority or county program.

c. There is at least one private provider or public service agency within the area authority or county program catchment area, or within reasonable proximity to the catchment area, willing and able to provide services under contract.

Before contracting with a private provider as authorized under this subdivision, the Secretary shall provide written notification to the area authority or county program and to the applicable participating boards of county commissioners of the Secretary's intent to contract and shall provide the area authority or county program and the applicable participating boards of county commissioners an opportunity to be heard.

(8) Contract with one or more private providers or other public service agencies to serve clients from more than one area authority or county program and reallocate the funds of the applicable programs to pay for services under the contract if the Secretary finds either that there is no other area authority or county program available to act as the administrative entity under contract with the provider or that the area authority or county program refuses or has failed to properly manage and administer the contract with the contract provider, and clients will either not be served or will suffer unreasonable hardship if services are not provided under the contract. Before contracting with a private provider as authorized under this subdivision, the Secretary shall provide written notification to the area authority or county program and the applicable participating boards of county commissioners of the Secretary's intent to contract and shall provide the area authority or county program and the

applicable participating boards of county commissioners an opportunity to be heard.

(9) Require reports of client characteristics, staffing patterns, agency policies or activities, services, or specific financial data of the area authority, county program, and providers of public services. The reports shall not identify individual clients of the area authority or county program unless specifically required by State law or by federal law or regulation or unless valid consent for the release has been given by the client or legally responsible person. (2001-437, s. 1.7(b); 2006-142, s. 4(m); 2007-410, s. 2; 2007-504, s. 2.2; 2009-186, s. 2; 2011-291, ss. 2.43, 2.44; 2012-151, s. 7(b); 2013-85, s. 3.)

§ 122C-113. Cooperation between Secretary and other agencies.

(a) The Secretary shall cooperate with other State agencies to coordinate services for the treatment and habilitation of individuals who are mentally ill, developmentally disabled, or substance abusers. The Secretary shall also coordinate with these agencies to provide public education to promote a better understanding of mental illness, developmental disabilities, and substance abuse.

(b) The Secretary shall promote cooperation among area facilities, State facilities, and local agencies to facilitate the provision of services to individuals who are mentally ill, developmentally disabled, or substance abusers.

(b1) The Secretary shall cooperate with the State Board of Education and the Division of Juvenile Justice of the Department of Public Safety in coordinating the responsibilities of the Department of Health and Human Services, the State Board of Education, the Division of Juvenile Justice of the Department of Public Safety, and the Department of Public Instruction for adolescent substance abuse programs. The Department of Health and Human Services, through its Division of Mental Health, Developmental Disabilities, and Substance Abuse Services, in cooperation with the Division of Juvenile Justice of the Department of Public Safety, shall be responsible for intervention and treatment in non-school based programs. The State Board of Education and the Department of Public Instruction, in consultation with the Division of Juvenile Justice of the Department of Public Safety, shall have primary responsibility for in-school education, identification, and intervention services, including student assistance programs.

(c) The Secretary shall adopt rules to assure this coordination. (1963, c. 1166, s. 3; 1973, c. 476, s. 133; 1977, c. 679, s. 7; 1981, c. 51, s. 3; 1985, c. 589, s. 2; 1987, c. 863, s. 1; 1989, c. 625, s. 14; 1993, c. 522, s. 9; 1997-443, s. 11A.118(a); 1998-202, s. 4(s); 2000-137, s. 4(v); 2011-145, s. 19.1(l).)

§ 122C-114. Powers and duties of the Commission.

(a) The Commission shall have authority as provided by this Chapter, Chapters 90 and 148 of the General Statutes, and by G.S. 143B-147.

(b) The Commission shall adopt rules regarding all of the following:

(1) The development of a process for screening, triage, and referral, including a uniform portal process, for implementation by the Secretary as required under G.S. 122C-112.1(14).

(2) LME monitoring of providers of mental health, developmental disabilities, and substance abuse services.

(3) LME provision of technical assistance to providers of mental health, developmental disabilities, and substance abuse services.

(4) The requirements of a qualified public or private provider as that term is used in G.S. 122C-141. In adopting rules under this subsection, the Commission shall take into account the need to ensure fair competition among providers. (C.S., s. 6153; 1929, c. 265, s. 1; 1933, c. 342, s. 1; 1943, cc. 32, 164; 1945, c. 952, s. 9; 1947, c. 537, s. 5; 1957, c. 1232, s. 1; 1959, c. 348, s. 3; c. 1002, s. 3; c. 1028, ss. 1, 2, 3, 5; 1963, c. 451, s. 1; c. 1166, s. 10; 1973, c. 476, s. 133; 1977, c. 679, s. 7; 1981, c. 51, s. 3; 1985, c. 589, s. 2; 2007-504, s. 2.3; 2012-66, s. 1.)

§ 122C-115. Duties of counties; appropriation and allocation of funds by counties and cities.

(a) A county shall provide mental health, developmental disabilities, and substance abuse services in accordance with rules, policies, and guidelines adopted pursuant to statewide restructuring of the management responsibilities for the delivery of services for individuals with mental illness, intellectual or other developmental disabilities, and substance abuse disorders under a 1915(b)/(c) Medicaid Waiver through an area authority. Beginning July 1, 2012, the catchment area of an area authority shall contain a minimum population of at least 300,000. Beginning July 1, 2013, the catchment area of an area authority shall contain a minimum population of at least 500,000. To the extent this section conflicts with G.S. 153A-77 or G.S. 122C-115.1, the provisions of this section control.

(a1) Effective July 1, 2012, the Department shall reduce the administrative funding for LMEs that do not comply with the minimum population requirement of 300,000 to a rate consistent with the funding rate provided to LMEs with a population of 300,000.

(a2) Effective July 1, 2013, the Department shall reassign management responsibilities for Medicaid funds and State funds away from LMEs that are not in compliance with the minimum population requirement of 500,000 to LMEs that are fully compliant with all catchment area requirements, including the minimum population requirements specified in this section.

(a3) A county that wishes to disengage from a local management entity/managed care organization and realign with another multicounty area authority operating under the 1915(b)/(c) Medicaid Waiver may do so with the approval of the Secretary. The Secretary shall adopt rules to establish a process for county disengagement that shall ensure, at a minimum, the following:

(1) Provision of services is not disrupted by the disengagement.

(2) The disengaging county either is in compliance or plans to merge with an area authority that is in compliance with population requirements provided in G.S. 122C-115(a) of this section.

(3) The timing of the disengagement is accounted for and does not conflict with setting capitation rates.

(4) Adequate notice is provided to the affected counties, the Department of Health and Human Services, and the General Assembly.

(5) Provision for distribution of any real property no longer within the catchment area of the area authority.

(b) Counties shall and cities may appropriate funds for the support of programs that serve the catchment area, whether the programs are physically located within a single county or whether any facility housing a program is owned and operated by the city or county. Counties and cities may make appropriations for the purposes of this Chapter and may allocate for these purposes other revenues not restricted by law, and counties may fund them by levy of property taxes pursuant to G.S. 153A-149(c)(22).

(c) Except as authorized in G.S. 122C-115.1, within a catchment area designated in the business plan pursuant to G.S. 122C-115.2, a board of county commissioners or two or more boards of county commissioners jointly shall establish an area authority with the approval of the Secretary.

(c1) Area authorities may add one or more additional counties to their existing catchment area upon the adoption of a resolution to that effect by a majority of the members of the area board and the approval of the Secretary.

(d) Except as otherwise provided in this subsection, counties shall not reduce county appropriations and expenditures for current operations and ongoing programs and services of area authorities or county programs because of the availability of State-allocated funds, fees, capitation amounts, or fund balance to the area authority or county program. Counties may reduce county appropriations by the amount previously appropriated by the county for one-time, nonrecurring special needs of the area authority or county program. (1977, c. 568, s. 1; c. 679, s. 7; 1979, c. 358, ss. 5, 23; 1981, c. 51, s. 3; 1985, c. 589, s. 2; 1989, c. 625, s. 14; 1995 (Reg. Sess., 1996), c. 749, s. 1; 1999-202, s. 1; 2001-437, s. 1.8; 2004-124, s. 10.26(a); 2006-66, s. 10.32(c), (d); 2007-504, s. 1.3; 2011-264, s. 2; 2012-151, ss. 1, 6; 2013-85, s. 4(a)-(c); 2013-363, s. 4.12(a); 2013-378, s. 11; 2013-410, s. 23(a).)

§ 122C-115.1. County governance and operation of mental health, developmental disabilities, and substance abuse services program.

(a) A county may operate a county program for mental health, developmental disabilities, and substance abuse services as a single county or, pursuant to Article 20 of Chapter 160A of the General Statutes, may enter into an interlocal agreement with one or more other counties for the operation of a multicounty program. An interlocal agreement shall provide for the following:

(1) Adoption and administration of the program budget in accordance with Chapter 159 of the General Statutes.

(2) Appointment of a program director to carry out the provisions of G.S. 122C-111 and duties and responsibilities delegated by the county. Except when specifically waived by the Secretary, the program director shall meet all the following minimum qualifications:

a. Masters degree.

b. Related experience.

c. Management experience.

d. Any other qualifications required under G.S. 122C-120.1.

(3) Repealed by Session Laws 2006-66, s. 10.32(e), effective July 1, 2007.

(4) Compliance with the provisions of this Chapter and the rules of the Commission and the Secretary.

(5) Written notification to the Secretary prior to the termination of the interlocal agreement.

(6) Appointment of an advisory committee. The interlocal agreement shall designate a county manager to whom the advisory committee shall report. The interlocal agreement shall also designate the appointing authorities. The appointing authorities shall make appointments that take into account sufficient citizen participation, equitable representation of the disability groups, and equitable representation of participating counties. The membership shall conform to the requirements provided in G.S. 122C-118.1.

(b) Before establishing a county program pursuant to this section, a county board of commissioners shall hold a public hearing with notice published at least 10 days before the hearing.

(c) A county shall ensure that the county program and the services provided through the county program comply with the provisions of this Chapter and the rules adopted by the Commission and the Secretary.

(d) A county program shall submit on a quarterly basis to the Secretary and the board of county commissioners service delivery reports that assess the quality and availability of public services within the county program's catchment area. The service delivery reports shall include the types of services delivered, number of recipients served, and services requested but not delivered due to staffing, financial, or other constraints. In addition, at least annually, a progress report shall be submitted to the Secretary and the board of county commissioners. The progress report shall include an assessment of the progress in implementing local service plans, goals, and outcomes. All reports shall be in a format and shall contain any additional information required by the Secretary or board of county commissioners.

(e) Within 30 days of the end of each quarter of the fiscal year, the program director and finance officer of the county program shall present to each member of the board of county commissioners a budgetary statement and balance sheet that details the assets, liabilities, and fund balance of the county program. This information shall be read into the minutes of the meeting at which it is presented. The program director or finance officer of the county program shall provide to the board of county commissioners ad hoc reports as requested by the board of county commissioners.

(f) In a single-county program, the program director shall be appointed by the county manager. In a multicounty program, the program director shall be appointed in accordance with the terms of the interlocal agreement.

Except when specifically waived by the Secretary, the program director in a single county program shall meet all the following minimum qualifications:

(1) Masters degree.

(2) Related experience.

(3) Management experience.

(4) Any other qualifications required under G.S. 122C-120.1.

(g) In a single-county program, an advisory committee shall be appointed by the board of county commissioners and shall report to the county manager. The appointments shall take into account sufficient citizen participation, equitable representation of the disability groups, and equitable representation of participating counties. The membership shall conform to the requirements in

G.S. 122C-118.1. In a multicounty program, the advisory committee shall be appointed in accordance with the terms of the interlocal agreement.

(h)   The county program may contract to provide services to governmental or private entities, including Employee Assistance Programs.

(i)   Except as otherwise specifically provided, this Chapter applies to counties that provide mental health, developmental disabilities, and substance abuse services through a county program. As used in the applicable sections of this Article, the terms "area authority", "area program", and "area facility" shall be construed to include "county program". (2001-437, s. 1.9; 2006-66, s. 10.32(e); 2006-142, s. 4(f), (g), (i), (j); 2012-151, s. 2(b).)

§ 122C-115.2. LME business plan required; content, process, certification.

(a)   Every county, through an area authority or county program, shall provide for the development, review, and approval of an LME business plan for the management and delivery of mental health, developmental disabilities, and substance abuse services. An LME business plan shall provide detailed information regarding how the area authority or county program will meet State standards, laws, and rules for ensuring quality mental health, developmental disabilities, and substance abuse services, including outcome measures for evaluating program effectiveness. The business plan shall be in effect for at least three State fiscal years. The Secretary shall develop a model business plan that illustrates compliance with this section, including specific State standards and rules adopted by the Secretary. The Secretary shall provide each LME with the model business plan to assist the LME in developing its business plan.

(b)   Business plans shall include the following:

(1)   Description of how the following core administrative functions will be carried out:

a.   Planning. - Local services plans that identify service gaps and methods for filling the gaps, ensure the availability of an array of services based on consumer needs, provision of core services, equitable service delivery among member counties, and prescribing the efficient and effective use of all funds for targeted services. Local planning shall be an open process involving key stakeholders.

b. Provider network development. - Ensuring available, qualified providers to deliver services based on the business plan. Development of new providers and monitoring provider performance and service outcomes. Provider network development shall address consumer choice and fair competition. For the purposes of this section, a "qualified provider" means a provider who meets the provider qualifications as defined by rules adopted by the Secretary.

c. Service management. - Implementation of uniform portal process. Service management shall include appropriate level and intensity of services, management of State hospitals/facilities bed days, utilization management, case management, and quality management. If services are provided directly by the area authority or county program, then the plan shall indicate how consumer choice and fair competition in the marketplace is ensured.

d. Financial management and accountability. - Carrying out business functions in an efficient and effective manner, cost-sharing, and managing resources dedicated to the public system.

e. Service monitoring and oversight. - Ensuring that services provided to consumers and families meet State outcome standards and ensure quality performance by providers in the network.

f. Evaluation. - Self-evaluation based on statewide outcome standards and participation in independent evaluation studies.

g. Collaboration. - Collaborating with other local service systems in ensuring access and coordination of services at the local level. Collaborating with other area authorities and county programs and the State in planning and ensuring the delivery of services.

h. Access. - Ensuring access to core and targeted services.

(2) Description of how the following will be addressed:

a. Reasonable administrative costs based on uniform State criteria for calculating administrative costs and costs or savings anticipated from consolidation.

b. Proposed reinvestment of savings toward direct services.

c. Compliance with the catchment area consolidation plan adopted by the Secretary.

d. Based on rules adopted by the Secretary, method for calculating county resources to reflect cash and in-kind contributions of the county.

e. Financial and services accountability and oversight in accordance with State and federal law.

f. The composition, appointments, selection process, and the process for notifying each board of county commissioners of all appointments made to the area authority board.

g. The population base of the catchment area to be served.

h. Use of local funds for the alteration, improvement, and rehabilitation of real property as authorized by and in accordance with G.S. 122C-147.

i. The resources available and needed within the catchment area to prevent out-of-community placements and shall include input from the community public agencies.

(3) Other matters determined by the Secretary to be necessary to effectively and efficiently ensure the provision of mental health, developmental disabilities, and substance abuse services through an area authority or county program.

(c) The county program or area authority proposing the business plan shall submit the proposed plan as approved by the board of county commissioners to the Secretary for review and certification. The Secretary shall review the business plan within 30 days of receipt of the plan. If the business plan meets all of the requirements of State law and standards adopted by the Secretary, then the Secretary shall certify the area authority or county program as a single-county area authority, a single-county program, a multicounty area authority, or a multicounty program. A business plan that demonstrates substantial compliance with the model business plan developed by the Secretary shall be deemed as meeting the requirements of State law and standards adopted by the Secretary. Implementation of the certified plan shall begin within 30 days of certification. If the Secretary determines that changes to the plan are necessary, then the Secretary shall so notify the submitting county program or area authority and the applicable participating boards of county commissioners and shall indicate in the notification the changes that need to be made in order for the proposed program to be certified. If the Secretary determines that a business plan needs substantial changes in order to be certifiable, the Secretary shall provide the LME submitting the plan with detailed information on each area of the plan that is in need of change, the particular State law or standard adopted by the Secretary that has not been met, and instructions or assistance on what changes need to be made in order for the plan to be certifiable. The submitting county program or area authority shall have 30 days from receipt of the Secretary's notice to make the requested changes and resubmit the amended plan to the Secretary for review. The Secretary shall provide whatever assistance is necessary to resolve outstanding issues. Amendments to the business plan shall be subject to the approval of the participating boards of county commissioners.

(d) Annually, in accordance with procedures established by the Secretary, each area authority and county program submitting a business plan shall enter into a memorandum of agreement with the Secretary for the purpose of ensuring that State funds are used in accordance with priorities expressed in the business plan.

(e) The Secretary may waive any requirements of this section that are inconsistent with or incompatible with contracts entered into between the Department and the area authority for the management responsibilities for the delivery of services for individuals with mental illness, intellectual or other developmental disabilities, and substance abuse disorders under a 1915(b)/(c) Medicaid Waiver. (2001-437, s. 1.9; 2002-164, s. 4.3; 2006-142, s. 4(c); 2007-504, s. 2.1; 2012-151, s. 9(b).)

§ 122C-115.3. Dissolution of area authority.

(a) Repealed by Session Laws 2013-85, s. 5(a), effective June 12, 2013.

(b) No county shall withdraw from an area authority nor shall an area authority be dissolved without prior approval of the Secretary.

(c), (d) Repealed by Session Laws 2013-85, s. 5(a), effective June 12, 2013.

(e) Any fund balance available to an area authority at the time of its dissolution that is not utilized to pay liabilities shall be transferred to the area authority contracted to operate the 1915(b)/(c) Medicaid Waiver in the catchment area of the dissolved area authority. If the fund balance transferred from the dissolved area authority is insufficient to constitute fifteen percent (15%) of the anticipated operational expenses arising from assumption of responsibilities from the dissolved area authority, the Secretary shall guarantee the operational reserves for the area authority assuming the responsibilities under the 1915(b)/(c) Medicaid Waiver until the assuming area authority has reestablished fifteen percent (15%) operational reserves.

(f), (g) Repealed by Session Laws 2013-85, s. 5(a), effective June 12, 2013. (2001-437, s. 1.9; 2011-102, s. 5; 2011-264, s. 3; 2013-85, s. 5(a)-(c).)

§ 122C-115.4. Functions of local management entities.

(a) Local management entities are responsible for the management and oversight of the public system of mental health, developmental disabilities, and substance abuse services at the community level. An LME shall plan, develop, implement, and monitor services within a specified geographic area to ensure expected outcomes for consumers within available resources.

(b) The primary functions of an LME are designated in this subsection and shall not be conducted by any other entity unless an LME voluntarily enters into a contract with that entity under subsection (c) of this section. The primary functions include all of the following:

(1) Access for all citizens to the core services and administrative functions described in G.S. 122C-2. In particular, this shall include the implementation of a 24-hour a day, seven-day a week screening, triage, and referral process and a uniform portal of entry into care.

(2) Provider monitoring, technical assistance, capacity development, and quality control. If at anytime the LME has reasonable cause to believe a violation of licensure rules has occurred, the LME shall make a referral to the Division of Health Service Regulation. If at anytime the LME has reasonable cause to believe the abuse, neglect, or exploitation of a client has occurred, the LME shall make a referral to the local Department of Social Services, Child Protective Services Program, or Adult Protective Services Program.

(3) Utilization management, utilization review, and determination of the appropriate level and intensity of services. An LME may participate in the development of person centered plans for any consumer and shall monitor the implementation of person centered plans. An LME shall review and approve person centered plans for consumers who receive State-funded services and shall conduct concurrent reviews of person centered plans for consumers in the LME's catchment area who receive Medicaid funded services.

(4) Authorization of the utilization of State psychiatric hospitals and other State facilities. Authorization of eligibility determination requests for recipients under a CAP-MR/DD waiver.

(5) Care coordination and quality management. This function involves individual client care decisions at critical treatment junctures to assure clients' care is coordinated, received when needed, likely to produce good outcomes, and is neither too little nor too much service to achieve the desired results. Care coordination is sometimes referred to as "care management." Care coordination shall be provided by clinically trained professionals with the authority and skills necessary to determine appropriate diagnosis and treatment, approve treatment and service plans, when necessary to link clients to higher levels of care quickly and efficiently, to facilitate the resolution of disagreements between providers and clinicians, and to consult with providers, clinicians, case managers, and utilization reviewers. Care coordination activities for high-risk/high-cost consumers or consumers at a critical treatment juncture include the following:

a. Assisting with the development of a single care plan for individual clients, including participating in child and family teams around the development of plans for children and adolescents.

b. Addressing difficult situations for clients or providers.

c. Consulting with providers regarding difficult or unusual care situations.

d. Ensuring that consumers are linked to primary care providers to address the consumer's physical health needs.

e. Coordinating client transitions from one service to another.

f. Conducting customer service interventions.

g. Assuring clients are given additional, fewer, or different services as client needs increase, lessen, or change.

h. Interfacing with utilization reviewers and case managers.

i. Providing leadership on the development and use of communication protocols.

j. Participating in the development of discharge plans for consumers being discharged from a State facility or other inpatient setting who have not been previously served in the community.

(6) Community collaboration and consumer affairs including a process to protect consumer rights, an appeals process, and support of an effective consumer and family advisory committee.

(7) Financial management and accountability for the use of State and local funds and information management for the delivery of publicly funded services.

(8) Each LME shall develop a waiting list of persons with intellectual or developmental disabilities that are waiting for specific services. The LME shall develop the list in accordance with rules adopted by the Secretary to ensure that waiting list data are collected consistently across LMEs. Each LME shall report this data annually to the Department. The data collected should include numbers of persons who are:

a. Waiting for residential services.

b. Potentially eligible for CAP-MRDD.

c. In need of other services and supports funded from State appropriations to or allocations from the Division of Mental Health, Developmental Disabilities, and Substance Abuse Services, including CAP-MRDD.

Subject to all applicable State and federal laws and rules established by the Secretary and the Commission, nothing in this subsection shall be construed to preempt or supersede the regulatory or licensing authority of other State or local departments or divisions.

(c) Subject to subsection (b) of this section and all applicable State and federal laws and rules established by the Secretary, an LME may contract with a public or private entity for the implementation of LME functions designated under subsection (b) of this section.

(d)   Except as provided in G.S. 122C-124.1 and G.S. 122C-125, the Secretary may neither remove from an LME nor designate another entity as eligible to implement any function enumerated under subsection (b) of this section unless all of the following applies:

(1)   The LME fails during the previous consecutive three months to achieve a satisfactory outcome on any of the critical performance measures developed by the Secretary under G.S. 122C-112.1(33).

(2)   The Secretary provides focused technical assistance to the LME in the implementation of the function. The assistance shall continue for at least three months or until the LME achieves a satisfactory outcome on the performance measure, whichever occurs first.

(3)   If, after three months of receiving technical assistance from the Secretary, the LME still fails to achieve or maintain a satisfactory outcome on the critical performance measure, the Secretary shall enter into a contract with another LME or agency to implement the function on behalf of the LME from which the function has been removed.

(e)   Notwithstanding subsection (d) of this section, in the case of serious financial mismanagement or serious regulatory noncompliance, the Secretary may temporarily remove an LME function after consultation with the Joint Legislative Oversight Committee on Health and Human Services.

(f)   The Commission shall adopt rules regarding the following matters:

(1)   The definition of a high risk consumer. Until such time as the Commission adopts a rule under this subdivision, a high risk consumer means a person who has been assessed as needing emergent crisis services three or more times in the previous 12 months.

(2)   The definition of a high cost consumer. Until such time as the Commission adopts a rule under this subdivision, a high cost consumer means a person whose treatment plan is expected to incur costs in the top twenty percent (20%) of expenditures for all consumers in a disability group.

(3) The notice and procedural requirements for removing one or more LME functions under subsection (d) of this section.

(g) The Commission shall adopt rules to ensure that the needs of members of the active and reserve components of the Armed Forces of the United States, veterans, and their family members are met by requiring:

(1) Each LME to have at least one trained care coordination person on staff to serve as the point of contact for TRICARE, the North Carolina National Guard's Integrated Behavioral Health System, the Army Reserve Department of Psychological Health, the United States Department of Veterans Affairs, the Division of Adult Correction, and related organizations to ensure that members of the active and reserve components of the Armed Forces of the United States, veterans, and their family members have access to State-funded services when they are not eligible for federally funded mental health or substance abuse services.

(2) LME staff members who provide screening, triage, or referral services to receive training to enhance the services provided to members of the active or reserve components of the Armed Forces of the United States, veterans, and their families. The training required by this subdivision shall include training on at least all of the following:

a. The number of persons who serve or who have served in the active or reserve components of the Armed Forces of the United States in the LME's catchment area.

b. The types of mental health and substance abuse disorders that these service personnel and their families may have experienced, including traumatic brain injury, posttraumatic stress disorder, depression, substance use disorders, potential suicide risks, military sexual trauma, and domestic violence.

c. Appropriate resources to which these service personnel and their families may be referred as needed. (2006-142, s. 4(d); 2007-323, ss. 10.49(l), (hh); 2007-484, ss. 18, 43.7(a)-(c); 2007-504, s. 1.2; 2008-107, s. 10.15(cc); 2009-186, s. 1; 2009-189, s. 1; 2011-145, s. 19.1(h); 2011-185, s. 6; 2011-291, s. 2.45; 2012-66, s. 2; 2012-83, s. 43.)

§ 122C-116. Status of area authority; status of consolidated human services agency.

(a) An area authority is a local political subdivision of the State.

(b) A consolidated human services agency is a department of the county. (1977, c. 568, s. 1; c. 679, s. 7; 1979, c. 358, s. 2; 1981, c. 51, ss. 3, 4; c. 539, s. 1; 1983, c. 280; c. 383, s. 2; 1985, c. 589, s. 2; 1995 (Reg. Sess., 1996), c. 690, s. 10; 2012-151, s. 2(a).)

§ 122C-117. Powers and duties of the area authority.

(a) The area authority shall do all of the following:

(1) Engage in comprehensive planning, budgeting, implementing, and monitoring of community-based mental health, developmental disabilities, and substance abuse services.

(2) Ensure the provision of services to clients in the catchment area, including clients committed to the custody of the Division of Juvenile Justice of the Department of Public Safety.

(3) Determine the needs of the area authority's clients and coordinate with the Secretary and with the Division of Juvenile Justice of the Department of Public Safety the provision of services to clients through area and State facilities.

(4) Develop plans and budgets for the area authority subject to the approval of the Secretary. The area authority shall submit the approved budget to the board of county commissioners and the county manager and provide quarterly reports on the financial status of the program in accordance with subsection (c) of this section.

(5) Assure that the services provided by the county through the area authority meet the rules of the Commission and Secretary.

(6) Comply with federal requirements as a condition of receipt of federal grants.

(7) Appoint an area director in accordance with G.S. 122C-121(d).

(8) Develop and submit to the board of county commissioners for approval the business plan required under G.S. 122C-115.2. A multicounty area authority shall submit the business plan to each participating board of county commissioners for its approval. The boards of county commissioners of a multicounty area authority shall jointly submit one approved business plan to the Secretary for approval and certification.

(9) Perform public relations and community advocacy functions.

(10) Recommend to the board of county commissioners the creation of local program services.

(11) Submit to the Secretary and the board of county commissioners service delivery reports, on a quarterly basis, that assess the quality and availability of public services within the area authority's catchment area. The service delivery reports shall include the types of services delivered, number of recipients served, and services requested but not delivered due to staffing, financial, or other constraints. In addition, at least annually, a progress report shall be submitted to the Secretary and the board of county commissioners. The progress report shall include an assessment of the progress in implementing local service plans, goals, and outcomes. All reports shall be in a format and shall contain any additional information required by the Secretary or board of county commissioners.

(12) Comply with this Article and rules adopted by the Secretary for the development and submission of and compliance with the area authority business plan.

(13) Coordinate with Treatment Accountability for Safer Communities for the provision of services to criminal justice clients.

(14) Maintain a 24-hour a day, seven day a week crisis response service. Crisis response shall include telephone and face-to-face capabilities. Crisis phone response shall include triage and referral to appropriate face-to-face crisis providers and shall be initiated within one hour of notification. Crisis services do not require prior authorization but shall be delivered in compliance with appropriate policies and procedures. Crisis services shall be designed for prevention, intervention, and resolution, not merely triage and transfer, and shall

be provided in the least restrictive setting possible, consistent with individual and family need and community safety.

(15) An LME that utilizes single stream funding shall, on a biannual basis, report on the allocation of service dollars and allow for public comment at a regularly scheduled LME board of directors meeting.

(16) Before an LME proposes to reduce State funding to HUD group homes and HUD apartments below the original appropriation of State funds, the LME must:

a. Receive approval of the reduction in funding from the Department, and

b. Hold a public hearing at an open LME board meeting to receive comment on the reduction in funding.

(17) Have the authority to borrow money with the approval of the Local Government Commission.

(a1) The area authority may contract to provide services to governmental or private entities, including Employee Assistance Programs.

(b) The governing unit of the area authority is the area board. All powers, duties, functions, rights, privileges, or immunities conferred on the area authority may be exercised by the area board.

(c) Within 30 days of the end of each quarter of the fiscal year, the area director and finance officer of the area authority shall provide the quarterly report of the area authority to the county finance officer. The county finance officer shall provide the quarterly report to the board of county commissioners at the next regularly scheduled meeting of the board. The clerk of the board of commissioners shall notify the area director and the county finance officer if the quarterly report required by this subsection has not been submitted within the required period of time. This information shall be delivered to the county and, at the request of the board of county commissioners, may be presented in person by the area director or the director's designee.

(d) A multicounty area authority shall provide to each board of county commissioners of participating counties a copy of the area authority's annual audit. The audit findings shall be presented in a format prescribed by the county and shall be read into the minutes of the meeting at which the audit findings are presented. (1971, c. 470, s. 1; 1973, c. 476, s. 133; c. 661; 1977, c. 568, s. 1; c. 679, s. 7; 1979, c. 358, ss. 1, 3, 14, 23; 1981, c. 51, s. 3; 1983, c. 383, s. 1; 1985, c. 589, s. 2; 1987, c. 830, s. 47(d); 1989, c. 625, s. 14; 1991, c. 215, s. 1; 1995 (Reg. Sess., 1996), c. 749, s. 2; 1997-443, s. 11A.118(a); 1998-202, s. 4(t); 2000-137, s. 4(w).; 2001-437, s. 1.10; 2001-487, s. 79.5; 2005-371, s. 2; 2006-142, s. 3(a); 2009-191, s. 1; 2011-145, s. 19.1(l); 2012-151, s. 9(a).)

§ 122C-118: Repealed by Session Laws 2001-437, s. 1.11.

§ 122C-118.1. Structure of area board.

(a) An area board shall have no fewer than 11 and no more than 21 voting members. The board of county commissioners, or the boards of county commissioners within the area, shall appoint members consistent with the requirements provided in subsection (b) of this section. The process for appointing members shall ensure participation from each of the constituent counties of a multicounty area authority. If the board or boards fail to comply with the requirements of subsection (b) of this section, the Secretary shall appoint the unrepresented category. The boards of county commissioners within a multicounty area with a catchment population of at least 1,250,000 shall have the option to appoint members of the area board in a manner or with a composition other than as required by this section by each county adopting a resolution to that effect and receiving written approval from the Secretary. A member of the board may be removed with or without cause by the initial appointing authority. The area board may declare vacant the office of an appointed member who does not attend three consecutive scheduled meetings without justifiable excuse. The chair of the area board shall notify the appropriate appointing authority of any vacancy. Vacancies on the board shall be filled by the initial appointing authority before the end of the term of the vacated seat or within 90 days of the vacancy, whichever occurs first, and the appointments shall be for the remainder of the unexpired term.

(b) Within the maximum membership provided in subsection (a) of this section, the membership of the area board shall reside within the catchment area and be composed as follows:

(1) At least one member who is a current county commissioner.

(2) The chair of the local Consumer and Family Advisory Committee (CFAC) or the chair's designee.

(3) At least one family member of the local CFAC, as recommended by the local CFAC, representing the interests of the following:

a. Individuals with mental illness.

b. Individuals in recovery from addiction.

c. Individuals with intellectual or other developmental disabilities.

(4) At least one openly declared consumer member of the local CFAC, as recommended by the local CFAC, representing the interests of the following:

a. Individuals with mental illness.

b. Individuals with intellectual or other developmental disabilities.

c. Individuals in recovery from addiction.

(5) An individual with health care expertise and experience in the fields of mental health, intellectual or other developmental disabilities, or substance abuse services.

(6) An individual with health care administration expertise consistent with the scale and nature of the managed care organization.

(7) An individual with financial expertise consistent with the scale and nature of the managed care organization.

(8) An individual with insurance expertise consistent with the scale and nature of the managed care organization.

(9) An individual with social services expertise and experience in the fields of mental health, intellectual or other developmental disabilities, or substance abuse services.

(10) An attorney with health care expertise.

(11) A member who represents the general public and who is not employed by or affiliated with the Department of Health and Human Services, as appointed by the Secretary.

(12) The President of the LME/MCO Provider Council or the President's designee to serve as a nonvoting member who shall participate only in Board activities that are open to the public.

(13) An administrator of a hospital providing mental health, developmental disabilities, and substance abuse emergency services to serve as a nonvoting member who shall participate only in Board activities that are open to the public.

Except as provided in subdivisions (12) and (13) of this subsection, an individual that contracts with a local management entity (LME) for the delivery of mental health, developmental disabilities, and substance abuse services may not serve on the board of the LME for the period during which the contract for services is in effect. No person registered as a lobbyist under Chapter 120C of the General Statutes shall be appointed to or serve on an area authority board. Of the members described in subdivisions (2) through (4) of this subsection, the boards of county commissioners shall ensure there is at least one member representing the interest of each of the following: (i) individuals with mental illness, (ii) individuals with intellectual or other developmental disabilities, and (iii) individuals in recovery from addiction.

(c) The board of county commissioners may elect to appoint a member of the area authority board to fill concurrently no more than two categories of membership if the member has the qualifications or attributes of the two categories of membership.

(d) Any member of an area board who is a county commissioner serves on the board in an ex officio capacity at the pleasure of the initial appointing authority, for a term not to exceed the earlier of three years or the member's service as a county commissioner. Any member of an area board who is a county manager serves on the board at the pleasure of the initial appointing authority, for a term not to exceed the earlier of three years or the duration of the member's employment as a county manager. The terms of members on the area board shall be for three years, except that upon the initial formation of an area board in compliance with subsection (a) of this section, one-third shall be appointed for one year, one-third for two years, and all remaining members for three years. Members shall not be appointed for more than three consecutive terms.

(e) Upon request, the board shall provide information pertaining to the membership of the board that is a public record under Chapter 132 of the General Statutes.

(f) An area authority that adds one or more counties to its existing catchment area under G.S. 122C-115(c1) shall ensure that the expanded catchment area is represented through membership on the area board, with or without adding area board members under this section, as provided in G.S. 122C-118.1(a). (2001-437, s. 1.11(b); 2002-159, s. 40(a); 2006-142, s. 4(e); 2007-504, s. 1.4; 2010-31, s. 10.7; 2012-151, s. 3(a); 2013-85, ss. 6, 7.)

§ 122C-118.2. Establishment of county commissioner advisory board.

(a) There is established a county commissioner advisory board for each catchment area, consisting of one county commissioner from each county in the catchment area, designated by the board of commissioners of each county. The county commissioner advisory board shall meet on a regular basis, and its duties shall include serving as the chief advisory board to the area authority and to the director of the area authority on matters pertaining to the delivery of services for individuals with mental illness, intellectual or other developmental disabilities, and substance abuse disorders in the catchment area. The county commissioner advisory board serves in an advisory capacity only to the area authority, and its duties do not include authority over budgeting, personnel matters, governance, or policymaking of the area authority.

(b) Each board of commissioners within the catchment area shall designate from its members the commissioner to serve on the county commissioner advisory board. Each board of commissioners may determine the manner of designation, the term of service, and the conditions under which its designee will serve on the county commissioner advisory board. (2013-85, s. 8.)

§ 122C-119. Organization of area board.

(a) The area board shall meet at least six times per year.

(b) Meetings shall be called by the area board chairman or by three or more members of the board after notifying the area board chairman in writing.

(c) Members of the area board elect the board's chairman. The term of office of the area board chairman shall be one year. A county commissioner area board member may serve as the area board chairman.

(d) The area board shall establish a finance committee that shall meet at least six times per year to review the financial strength of the area program. The finance committee shall have a minimum of three members, two of whom have expertise in budgeting and fiscal control. The member of the area board who is the county finance officer or individual with financial expertise shall serve as an ex officio member. All other finance officers of participating counties in a multicounty area authority may serve as ex officio members. If the area board so chooses, the entire area board may function as the finance committee; however, its required meetings as a finance committee shall be distinct from its meetings as an area board. (1971, c. 470, s. 1; 1973, c. 455; c. 476, s. 133; c. 1355; 1975, c. 400, ss. 1-4; 1977, c. 568, s. 1; 1979, c. 358, ss. 6, 23; c. 455; 1981, c. 52; 1983, c. 6; 1985, c. 589, s. 2; 1995 (Reg. Sess., 1996), c. 749, s. 4; 2001-437, s. 1.11(c).)

§ 122C-119.1. Area Authority board members' training.

All members of the governing body for an area authority shall receive initial orientation on board members' responsibilities and annual training provided by the Department which shall include fiscal management, budget development, and fiscal accountability. A member's refusal to be trained shall be grounds for removal from the board. (1995, c. 507, s. 23.3; 1995 (Reg. Sess., 1996), c. 749, s. 5; 2012-151, s. 4(a).)

§ 122C-120. Compensation of area board members.

(a) Area board members may receive as compensation for their services per diem and a subsistence allowance for each day during which they are engaged in the official business of the area board. The amount of the per diem and subsistence allowances shall be established by the area board. The amount of per diem allowance shall not exceed fifty dollars ($50.00). Reimbursement of subsistence expenses shall be at the rates allowed to State officers and employees under G.S. 138-6(a)(3).

(b) Area board members may be reimbursed for all necessary travel expenses and registration fees in amounts fixed by the board. (1979, c. 358, s. 28; 1985, c. 589, s. 2; 2000-67, s. 11.18.)

§ 122C-120.1. Job classifications; director and finance officer.

(a) The Office of State Human Resources shall develop a job classification for director of an area authority or county program that reflects the skills required of an individual operating a local management entity. The Office of State Human Resources shall also review the job classifications for area authority and county program finance officers to determine whether they reflect the skills necessary to manage the finances of a local management entity. The Commission shall adopt a job classification for director and any new or revised job classifications for finance officers no later than December 31, 2006.

(b) The job classifications developed under subsection (a) of this section shall apply to persons newly hired on or after January 1, 2007. (2006-142, s. 4(h); 2013-382, s. 9.1(c).)

§ 122C-121. Area director.

(a) The area director is an employee of the area board, shall serve at the pleasure of the board, and shall be appointed in accordance with G.S. 122C-117(7). As used in this subsection, "employee" means an individual and does not include a corporation, a partnership, a limited liability corporation, or any other business association.

(a1) The area board shall establish the area director's salary under Article 3 of Chapter 126 of the General Statutes. Notwithstanding G.S. 126-9(b), an area director may be paid a salary that is in excess of the salary ranges established by the State Human Resources Commission. Any salary that is higher than the maximum of the applicable salary range shall be supported by documentation of comparable salaries in comparable operations within the region and shall also include the specific amount the board proposes to pay the director. The area board shall not authorize any salary adjustment that is above the normal allowable salary range without obtaining prior approval from the Director of the Office of State Human Resources.

(a2)   The area board shall not provide the director with any benefits that are not also provided by the area board to all permanent employees of the area program, except that the area board may, in its discretion, offer severance benefits, relocation expenses, or both, to an applicant for the position of director as an incentive for the applicant to accept an offer of employment. The director shall be reimbursed only for allowable employment-related expenses at the same rate and in the same manner as other employees of the area program.

(b)   The area board shall evaluate annually the area director for performance based on criteria established by the Secretary and the area board. In conducting the evaluation, the area board shall consider comments from the board of county commissioners.

(c)   The area director is the administrative head of the area program. In addition to the duties under G.S. 122C-111, the area director shall:

(1)   Appoint, supervise, and terminate area program staff.

(2)   Administer area authority services.

(3)   Develop the budget of the area authority for review by the area board.

(4)   Provide information and advice to the board of county commissioners through the county manager.

(5)   Act as liaison between the area authority and the Department.

(d)   Except when specifically waived by the Secretary, the area director shall meet all the following minimum qualifications:

(1)   Masters degree.

(2)   Related experience.

(3)   Management experience.

(4)   Any other qualifications required under G.S. 122C-120.1. (1971, c. 470, s. 1; 1973, c. 476, s. 133; 1977, c. 568, s. 1; c. 679, s. 7; 1979, c. 358, s. 14; 1981, c. 51, s. 3; 1985, c. 589, s. 2; 2001-437, s. 1.12; 2006-142, s. 4(k); 2007-323, s. 6.20(a); 2012-151, s. 11(c); 2013-339, s. 1; 2013-382, s. 9.1(c).)

§ 122C-122: Repealed by Session Laws 2012-151, s. 12(a), effective July 12, 2012.

§ 122C-123. Other agency responsibility.

Notwithstanding the provisions of G.S. 122C-112(a)(10), G.S. 122C-117(a)(1), G.S. 122C-127, and G.S. 122C-131, other agencies of the Department, other State agencies, and other local agencies shall continue responsibility for services they provide for persons with developmental disabilities. (1987, c. 830, s. 47(e); 1989, c. 625, s. 14; 1995 (Reg. Sess., 1996), c. 690, s. 11.)

§ 122C-123.1. Area authority reimbursement to State for disallowed expenditures.

Any funds or part thereof of an area authority that are transferred by the area authority to any entity including a firm, partnership, corporation, company, association, joint stock association, agency, or nonprofit private foundation shall be subject to reimbursement by the area authority to the State when expenditures of the area authority are disallowed pursuant to a State or federal audit. (1999-237, s. 11.41.)

§ 122C-124: Repealed by Session Laws 2001-437, s. 1.13(a).

§ 122C-124.1. Actions by the Secretary when area authority or county program is not providing minimally adequate services.

(a) Notice of Likelihood of Action. - When the Secretary determines that there is a likelihood of suspension of funding, assumption of service delivery or management functions, or appointment of a caretaker board under this section within the ensuing 60 days, the Secretary shall so notify in writing the area authority board or the county program and the board of county commissioners of the area authority or county program. The notice shall state the particular deficiencies in program services or administration that must be remedied to avoid action by the Secretary under this section. The area authority board or county program shall have 60 days from the date it receives notice under this subsection to take remedial action to correct the deficiencies. The Secretary shall provide technical assistance to the area authority or county program in remedying deficiencies.

(b) Suspension of Funding; Assumption of Service Delivery or Management Functions. - If the Secretary determines that a county, through an area authority or county program, is not providing minimally adequate services to persons in need in a timely manner, or fails to demonstrate reasonable efforts to do so, the Secretary, after providing written notification of the Secretary's intent to the area authority or county program and to the board of county commissioners of the area authority or county program, and after providing the area authority or county program and the boards of county commissioners of the area authority or county program an opportunity to be heard, may:

(1) Withhold funding for the particular service or services in question from the area authority or county program and ensure the provision of these services through contracts with public or private agencies or by direct operation by the Department.

Upon suspension of funding, the Department shall direct the development and oversee implementation of a corrective plan of action and provide notification to the area authority or county program and the board of county commissioners of the area authority or county program of any ongoing concerns or problems with the area authority's or county program's finances or delivery of services.

(2) Assume control of the particular service or management functions in question or of the area authority or county program and appoint an administrator to exercise the powers assumed. This assumption of control shall have the effect of divesting the area authority or county program of its powers in G.S. 122C-115.1 and G.S. 122C-117 and all other service delivery powers conferred on the area authority or county program by law as they pertain to this service or management function. County funding of the area authority or county program shall continue when the State has assumed control of the catchment area or of the area authority or county program. At no time after the State has assumed this control shall a county withdraw funds previously obligated or appropriated to the area authority or county program.

Upon assumption of control of service delivery or management functions, the Department shall, in conjunction with the area authority or county program, develop and implement a corrective plan of action and provide notification to the area authority or county program and the board of county commissioners of the area authority or county program of the plan. The Department shall also keep the area authority board and the board of county commissioners informed of any ongoing concerns or problems with the delivery of services.

(c) Appointment of Caretaker Administrator. - In the event that a county, through an area authority or county program, fails to comply with the corrective plan of action required when funding is suspended or when the State assumes control of service delivery or management functions, the Secretary, after providing written notification of the Secretary's intent to the area authority or county program and the applicable participating boards of county commissioners of the area authority or county program, shall appoint a caretaker administrator, a caretaker board of directors, or both.

The Secretary may assign any of the powers and duties of the area director or program director or of the area authority board or board of county commissioners of the area authority or county program pertaining to the operation of mental health, developmental disabilities, and substance abuse services to the caretaker board or to the caretaker administrator as it deems necessary and appropriate to continue to provide direct services to clients, including the powers as to the adoption of budgets, expenditures of money, and all other financial powers conferred on the area authority or county program by law pertaining to the operation of mental health, developmental disabilities, and substance abuse services. County funding of the area authority or county program shall continue when the State has assumed control of the financial affairs of the program. At no time after the State has assumed this control shall a county withdraw funds previously obligated or appropriated to the area authority or county program. The caretaker administrator and the caretaker board shall perform all of these powers and duties. The Secretary may terminate the area director or program director when it appoints a caretaker administrator. Chapter 150B of the General Statutes shall apply to the decision to terminate the area director or program director. Neither party to any such contract shall be entitled to damages. After a caretaker board has been appointed, the General Assembly shall consider, at its next regular session, the future governance of the identified area authority or county program. (2001-437, s. 1.13(b); 2008-107, s. 10.15(ee).)

§ 122C-124.2. Actions by the Secretary to ensure effective management of behavioral health services under the 1915(b)/(c) Medicaid Waiver.

(a) For all local management entity/managed care organizations, the Secretary shall certify whether the LME/MCO is in compliance or is not in compliance with all requirements of subdivisions (1) through (3) of subsection (b) of this section. The Secretary's certification shall be made every six months beginning August 1, 2013. In order to ensure accurate evaluation of administrative, operational, actuarial and financial components, and overall performance of the LME/MCO, the Secretary's certification shall be based upon an internal and external assessment made by an independent external review agency in accordance with applicable federal and State laws and regulations. Beginning on February 1, 2014, and for all subsequent assessments for certification, the independent review will be made by an External Quality Review Organization approved by the Centers for Medicare and Medicaid Services and in accordance with applicable federal and State laws and regulations.

(b) The Secretary's certification under subsection (a) of this section shall be in writing and signed by the Secretary and shall contain a clear and unequivocal statement that the Secretary has determined the local management entity/managed care organization to be in compliance with all of the following requirements:

(1) The LME/MCO has made adequate provision against the risk of insolvency with respect to capitation payments for Medicaid enrollees. "Adequate provision" includes all of the following:

a. The LME/MCO has submitted to the Department all the financial records and reports required to be submitted to the Department under the Contract, including monthly balance sheets.

b. There are no consecutive three-month periods during which the LME/MCO's ratio of current assets to current liabilities is less than 1.0, based on a monthly review of the LME/MCO's balance sheets for each month of the three-month period, as determined by the Secretary.

c. An intradepartmental monitoring team, as designated by the Secretary and consisting of the Secretary or a designee, representatives of the Division of Medical Assistance, and representatives of the Division of Mental Health, Developmental Disabilities, and Substance Abuse Services, utilizing the monitoring team's solvency measures, determines that the LME/MCO has made adequate provisions against the risk of insolvency based on a quarterly review of the financial reports submitted to the Department by the LME/MCO.

(2)   The LME/MCO is making timely provider payments. The Secretary shall certify that an LME/MCO is making timely provider payments if there are no consecutive three-month periods during which the LME/MCO paid less than ninety percent (90%) of clean claims for covered services within the 30-day period following the LME/MCO's receipt of these claims during that three-month period. As used in this subdivision, a "clean claim" is a claim that can be processed without obtaining additional information from the provider of the service or from a third party. The term includes a claim with errors originating in the LME/MCO's claims system. The term does not include a claim from a provider who is under investigation by a governmental agency for fraud or abuse or a claim under review for medical necessity.

(3)   The LME/MCO is exchanging billing, payment, and transaction information with the Department and providers in a manner that complies with all applicable federal standards, including all of the following:

a.   Standards for information transactions and data elements specified in 42 U.S.C. § 1302d-2 of the Healthcare Insurance Portability and Accountability Act (HIPAA), as from time to time amended.

b.   Standards for health care claims or equivalent encounter information transactions specified in HIPAA regulations in 45 C.F.R. § 162.1102, as from time to time amended.

c.   Implementation specifications for Electronic Data Interchange standards published and maintained by the Accredited Standards Committee (ASC X12) and referenced in HIPAA regulations in 45 C.F.R. § 162.920, as from time to time amended.

(c)   If the Secretary does not provide a local management entity/managed care organization with the certification of compliance required by this section based upon the LME/MCO's failure to comply with any of the requirements specified in subdivisions (1) through (3) of subsection (b) of this section, the Secretary shall do the following:

(1)   Prepare a written notice informing the LME/MCO of the provisions of subdivision (1), (2), or (3) of subsection (c) of this section with which the

LME/MCO is deemed not to be in compliance and the reasons for the determination of noncompliance.

(2)   Cause the notice of the noncompliance to be delivered to the LME/MCO.

(3)   Not later than 10 days after the Secretary's notice of noncompliance is provided to the LME/MCO, assign the Contract of the noncompliant LME/MCO to a compliant LME/MCO.

(4)   Oversee the transfer of the operations and contracts from the noncompliant LME/MCO to the compliant LME/MCO in accordance with the provisions in subsection (e) of this section.

(d)   If, at any time, in the Secretary's determination, a local management entity/managed care organization is not in compliance with a requirement of the Contract other than those specified in subdivisions (1) through (3) of subsection (b) of this section, then the Secretary shall do all of the following:

(1)   Prepare a written notice informing the LME/MCO of the provisions of the Contract with which the LME/MCO is deemed not to be in compliance and the reasons therefor.

(2)   Cause the notice of the noncompliance to be delivered to the LME/MCO.

(3)   Allow the noncompliant LME/MCO 30 calendar days from the date of receipt of the notice to respond to the notice of noncompliance and to demonstrate compliance to the satisfaction of the Secretary.

(4)   Upon the expiration of the period allowed under subdivision (3) of this subsection, make a final determination on the issue of compliance and promptly notify the LME/MCO of the determination.

(5)   Upon a final determination that an LME/MCO is noncompliant, allow no more than 30 days following the date of notification of the final determination of noncompliance for the noncompliant LME/MCO to complete negotiations for a merger or realignment with a compliant LME/MCO that is satisfactory to the Secretary.

(6) If the noncompliant LME/MCO does not successfully complete negotiations with a compliant LME/MCO as described in subdivision (5) of this subsection, assign the Contract of the noncompliant LME/MCO to a compliant LME/MCO.

(7) Oversee the transfer of the operations and contracts from the noncompliant LME/MCO to the compliant LME/MCO in accordance with the provisions in subsection (e) of this section.

(e) If the Secretary assigns the Contract of a noncompliant local management entity/managed care organization to a compliant LME/MCO under subdivision (3) of subsection (c) of this section, or under subdivision (6) of subsection (d) of this section, the Secretary shall oversee the orderly transfer of all management responsibilities, operations, and contracts of the noncompliant LME/MCO to the compliant LME/MCO. The noncompliant LME/MCO shall cooperate with the Secretary in order to ensure the uninterrupted provision of services to Medicaid recipients. In making this transfer, the Secretary shall do all of the following:

(1) Arrange for the providers of services to be reimbursed from the remaining fund balance or risk reserve of the noncompliant LME/MCO, or from other funds of the Department if necessary, for proper, authorized, and valid claims for services rendered that were not previously paid by the noncompliant LME/MCO.

(2) Effectuate an orderly transfer of management responsibilities from the noncompliant LME/MCO to the compliant LME/MCO, including the responsibility of paying providers for covered services that are subsequently rendered.

(3) Oversee the dissolution of the noncompliant LME/MCO, including transferring to the compliant LME/MCO all assets of the noncompliant LME/MCO, including any balance remaining in its risk reserve after payments have been made under subdivision (1) of this subsection. Risk reserve funds of the noncompliant LME/MCO may be used only to pay authorized and approved provider claims. Any funds remaining in the risk reserve transferred under this subdivision shall become part of the compliant LME/MCO's risk reserve and subject to the same restrictions on the use of the risk reserve applicable to the compliant LME/MCO. If the risk reserves transferred from the noncompliant LME/MCO are insufficient, the Secretary shall guarantee any needed risk reserves for the compliant LME/MCO arising from the additional risks being assumed by the compliant LME/MCO until the compliant LME/MCO has

established fifteen percent (15%) risk reserves. All other assets shall be used to satisfy the liabilities of the noncompliant LME/MCO. In the event there are insufficient assets to satisfy the liabilities of the noncompliant LME/MCO, it shall be the responsibility of the Secretary to satisfy the liabilities of the noncompliant LME/MCO.

(4) Following completion of the actions specified in subdivisions (1) through (3) of this subsection, direct the dissolution of the noncompliant LME/MCO and deliver a notice of dissolution to the board of county commissioners of each of the counties in the dissolved LME/MCO. An LME/MCO that is dissolved by the Secretary in accordance with the provisions of this section may be dissolved at any time during the fiscal year.

(f) The Secretary shall provide a copy of each written, signed certification of compliance or noncompliance completed in accordance with this section to the Senate Appropriations Committee on Health and Human Services, the House Appropriations Subcommittee on Health and Human Services, the Legislative Oversight Committee on Health and Human Services, and the Fiscal Research Division.

(g) As used in this section, the following terms mean:

(1) Compliant local management entity/managed care organization. - An LME/MCO that has undergone an independent external assessment and been determined by the Secretary to be operating successfully and to have the capability of expanding.

(2) Contract. - The contract between the Department of Health and Human Services and a local management entity for the operation of the 1915(b)/(c) Medicaid Waiver. (2013-85, s. 2.)

§ 122C-125. Area Authority financial failure; State assumption of financial control.

At any time that the Secretary of the Department of Health and Human Services determines that an area authority is in imminent danger of failing financially and of failing to provide direct services to clients, the Secretary, after providing written notification of the Secretary's intent to the area board and after providing the area authority an opportunity to be heard, may assume control of the financial affairs of the area authority and appoint an administrator to exercise the powers assumed. This assumption of control shall have the effect of divesting the area authority of its powers as to the adoption of budgets, expenditures of money, and all other financial powers conferred in the area authority by law. County funding of the area authority shall continue when the State has assumed control of the financial affairs of the area authority. At no time after the State has assumed this control shall a county withdraw funds previously obligated or appropriated to the area authority. The Secretary shall adopt rules to define imminent danger of failing financially and of failing to provide direct services to clients.

Upon assumption of financial control, the Department shall, in conjunction with the area authority, develop and implement a corrective plan of action and provide notification to the area authority's board of directors of the plan. The Department shall also keep the county board of commissioners and the area authority's board of directors informed of any ongoing concerns or problems with the area authority's finances. (1995, c. 507, s. 23.2; 1995 (Reg. Sess., 1996), c. 749, s. 7; 1997-443, s. 11A.118(a).)

§ 122C-125.1: Repealed by Session Laws 2001-437, s. 1.13.

§ 122C-126: Repealed by Session Laws 2001-437, s. 1.13.

§ 122C-126.1. Confidentiality of competitive health care information.

(a) For the purposes of this section, competitive health care information means information relating to competitive health care activities by or on behalf of the area authority. Competitive health care information shall be confidential and not a public record under Chapter 132 of the General Statutes; provided that any contract entered into by or on behalf of an area authority shall be a public record, unless otherwise exempted by law, or the contract contains competitive health care information, the determination of which shall be as provided in subsection (b) of this section.

(b) If an area authority is requested to disclose any contract that the area authority believes in good faith contains or constitutes competitive health care information, the area authority may either redact the portions of the contract believed to constitute competitive health care information prior to disclosure or, if the entire contract constitutes competitive health care information, refuse disclosure of the contract. The person requesting disclosure of the contract may institute an action pursuant to G.S. 132-9 to compel disclosure of the contract or any redacted portion thereof. In any action brought under this subsection, the issue for decision by the court shall be whether the contract, or portions of the contract withheld, constitutes competitive health care information, and in making its determination, the court shall be guided by the procedures and standards applicable to protective orders requested under Rule 26(c)(7) of the Rules of Civil Procedure. Before rendering a decision, the court shall review the contract in camera and hear arguments from the parties. If the court finds that the contract constitutes or contains competitive health care information, the court may either deny disclosure or may make such other appropriate orders as are permitted under Rule 26(c) of the Rules of Civil Procedure.

(c)   Nothing in this section shall be deemed to prevent the Attorney General, the State Auditor, or an elected public body, in closed session, which has responsibility for the area authority, from having access to this confidential information. The disclosure to any public entity does not affect the confidentiality of the information. Members of the public entity shall have a duty not to further disclose the confidential information. (2012-151, s. 10.)

Part 2A. Consolidated Human Services.

§ 122C-127. Consolidated human services board; human services director.

(a)   Except as otherwise provided by this section and subject to any limitations that may be imposed by the board of county commissioners under G.S. 153A-77, a consolidated human services agency shall have the responsibility and authority set forth in G.S. 122C-117(a) to carry out the programs established in this Chapter in conformity with the rules and regulations of the Department and under the supervision of the Secretary in the same manner as an area authority. In addition to the powers conferred by G.S. 153A-77(d), a consolidated human services board shall have all the powers and duties of the governing unit of an area authority as provided by G.S. 122C-117(b), except that the consolidated human services board may not:

(1)   Appoint the human services director.

(2)   Transmit or present the budget for social services programs.

(3) Enter into contracts, including contracts to provide services to governmental or private entities, unless specifically authorized to do so by the board of county commissioners in accordance with county contracting policies and procedures.

(b) In addition to the powers conferred by G.S. 153A-77(e), a human services director shall have all the powers and duties of an area director as provided by G.S. 122C-121, except that the human services director may:

(1) Serve as the executive officer of the consolidated human services board only to the extent and in the manner authorized by the county manager.

(2) Appoint staff of the consolidated human services agency only upon the approval of the county manager.

The human services director is not an employee of the area board, but serves as an employee of the county under the direct supervision of the county manager. (1995 (Reg. Sess., 1996), c. 690, s. 12.)

§ 122C-128. Reserved for future codification purposes.

§ 122C-129. Reserved for future codification purposes.

§ 122C-130. Reserved for future codification purposes.

Part 3. Service Delivery System.

§ 122C-131. Composition of system.

Mental health, developmental disabilities, and substance abuse services of the public system in this State shall be delivered through area authorities and State facilities. (1985, c. 589, s. 2; 1989, c. 625, s. 15.)

§ 122C-132: Repealed by Session Laws 2001-437, s. 1.14.

§ 122C-132.1: Repealed by Session Laws 2001-437, s. 1.14.

§§ 122C-133 through 122C-140. Reserved for future codification purposes.

Part 4. Area Facilities.

§ 122C-141. Provision of services.

(a) The area authority or county program shall contract with other qualified public or private providers, agencies, institutions, or resources for the provision of services, and, subject to the approval of the Secretary, is authorized to provide services directly. The area authority or county program shall indicate in its local business plan how services will be provided and how the provision of services will address issues of access, availability of qualified public or private providers, consumer choice, and fair competition. The Secretary shall take into account these issues when reviewing the local business plan and considering approval of the direct provision of services. Unless an area authority or county program requests a shorter time, any approval granted by the Secretary shall be for not less than one year. The Secretary shall develop criteria for the approval of direct service provision by area authorities and county programs in accordance with this section and as evidenced by compliance with the local business plan. For the purposes of this section, a qualified public or private provider is a provider that meets the provider qualifications as defined by rules adopted by the Secretary.

(b) All area authority or county program services provided directly or under contract shall meet the requirements of applicable State statutes and the rules of the Commission and the Secretary. The Secretary may delay payments and, with written notification of cause, may reduce or deny payment of funds if an area authority or county program fails to meet these requirements.

(c) The area authority or board of county commissioners of a county program may contract with a health maintenance organization, certified and operating in accordance with the provisions of Article 67 of Chapter 58 of the General Statutes for the area authority or county program, to provide mental health, developmental disabilities, or substance abuse services to enrollees in a health care plan provided by the health maintenance organization. The terms of the contract must meet the requirements of all applicable State statutes and rules of the Commission and Secretary governing both the provision of services by an area authority or county program and the general and fiscal operation of an area authority or county program and the reimbursement rate for services rendered shall be based on the usual and customary charges paid by the health maintenance organization to similar providers. Any provision in conflict with a State statute or rule of the Commission or the Secretary shall be void; however, the presence of any void provision in that contract does not render void any other provision in that contract which is not in conflict with a State statute or rule of the Commission or the Secretary. Subject to approval by the Secretary and pending the timely reimbursement of the contractual charges, the area authority or county program may expend funds for costs which may be incurred by the area authority or county program as a result of providing the additional services under a contractual agreement with a health maintenance organization.

(d) If two or more counties enter into an interlocal agreement under Article 20 of Chapter 160A of the General Statutes to be a public provider of mental health, developmental disabilities, or substance abuse services ("public provider"), before an LME may enter into a contract with the public provider, all of the following must apply:

(1) The public provider must meet all the provider qualifications as defined by rules adopted by the Commission. A county that satisfies its duties under G.S. 122C-115(a) through a consolidated human services agency may not be considered a qualified provider for purposes of this subdivision.

(2) The LME must adopt a conflict of interest policy that applies to all provider contracts.

(3) The interlocal agreement must provide that any liabilities of the public provider shall be paid from its unobligated surplus funds and that if those funds are not sufficient to satisfy the indebtedness, the remaining indebtedness shall be apportioned to the participating counties.

(e) When enforcing rules adopted by the Commission, the Secretary shall ensure that there is fair competition among providers. (1977, c. 568, s. 1; c. 679, s. 7; 1979, c. 358, ss. 7, 18; 1981, c. 51, s. 3; c. 539, ss. 3, 4; c. 614, s. 7; 1985, c. 589, s. 2; 1987, c. 839; 1989, c. 625, s. 16; 2001-437, s. 1.15; 2006-142, s. 4(l); 2007-504, s. 2.4(a).)

§ 122C-142. Contract for services.

(a) When the area authority contracts with persons for the provision of services, it shall use the standard contract adopted by the Secretary and shall assure that these contracted services meet the requirements of applicable State statutes and the rules of the Commission and the Secretary. However, an area authority may amend the contract to comply with any court-imposed duty or responsibility. An area authority that is operating under a Medicaid waiver may amend the contract subject to the approval of the Secretary. Terms of the standard contract shall require the area authority to monitor the contract to assure that rules and State statutes are met. It shall also place an obligation upon the entity providing services to provide to the area authority timely data regarding the clients being served, the services provided, and the client outcomes. The Secretary may also monitor contracted services to assure that rules and State statutes are met.

(b) When the area authority contracts for services, it may provide funds to purchase liability insurance, to provide legal representation, and to pay any claim with respect to liability for acts, omissions, or decisions by members of the boards or employees of the persons with whom the area authority contracts. These acts, omissions, and decisions shall be ones that arise out of the performance of the contract and may not result from actual fraud, corruption, or actual malice on the part of the board members or employees. (1977, c. 568, s. 1; c. 679, s. 7; 1979, c. 358, s. 18; 1981, c. 51, s. 3; c. 539, ss. 3, 4; 1985, c. 589, s. 2; 2006-142, s. 1; 2006-259, s. 23; 2013-85, s. 9.)

§ 122C-142.1. Substance abuse services for those convicted of driving while impaired or driving while less than 21 years old after consuming alcohol or drugs.

(a) Services. - An area authority shall provide, directly or by contract, the substance abuse services needed by a person to obtain a certificate of completion required under G.S. 20-17.6 as a condition for the restoration of a drivers license. A person may obtain the required services from an area facility, from a private facility authorized by the Department to provide this service, or, with the approval of the Department, from an agency that is located in another state.

(a1) Authorization of a Private Facility Provider. - The Department shall authorize a private facility located in this State to provide substance abuse services needed by a person to obtain a certificate of completion if the private facility complies with all of the requirements of this subsection:

(1) Notifies both the designated area facility for the catchment area in which it is located and the Department of its intent to provide the services.

(2) Agrees to comply with the laws and rules concerning these services that apply to area facilities.

(3) Pays the Department the applicable fee for authorizing and monitoring the services of the facility. The initial fee is payable at the time the facility notifies the Department of its intent to provide the services and by July 1 of each year thereafter. Collected fees shall be used by the Division for program monitoring and quality assurance. The applicable fee is based upon the number of assessments completed during the prior fiscal year as set forth below:

Number of Assessments	Fee Amount
0-24	$250.00
25-99	$500.00
100 or more	$750.00.

(b) Assessments. - To conduct a substance abuse assessment, a facility shall give a client a standardized test approved by the Department to determine chemical dependency and shall conduct a clinical interview with the client. Based on the assessment, the facility shall recommend that the client either attend an alcohol and drug education traffic (ADET) school or obtain treatment. A recommendation shall be reviewed and signed by a certified alcoholism, drug abuse, or substance abuse counselor, as defined by the Commission, a Certified Substance Abuse Counselor, or by a physician certified by the American Society of Addiction Medicine (ASAM). The signature on the recommendation shall be the personal signature of the individual authorized to review the recommendation and not the signature of his or her agent. The signature shall reflect that the authorized individual has personally reviewed the recommendation and, with full knowledge of the contents of the recommendation, approved of the recommended treatment.

(b1) Persons Authorized to Conduct Assessments. - The following individuals are authorized to conduct a substance abuse assessment under subsection (b) of this section:

(1)   A Certified Substance Abuse Counselor (CSAC), as defined by the Commission.

(2)   A Licensed Clinical Addiction Specialist (LCAS), as defined by the Commission.

(3)   Repealed by Session Laws 2004-197, s. 2, effective October 1, 2008, and applicable to substance abuse assessments conducted on or after that date.

(4)   A person licensed by the North Carolina Medical Board or the North Carolina Psychology Board.

(5)   A physician certified by the American Society of Addiction Medicine (ASAM).

(c)   School or Treatment. - Attendance at an ADET school is required if none of the following applies and completion of a treatment program is required if any of the following applies:

(1)   The person took a chemical test at the time of the offense that caused the person's license to be revoked and the test revealed that the person had an alcohol concentration at any relevant time after driving of at least 0.15.

(2)   The person has a prior conviction of an offense involving impaired driving.

(3)   The substance abuse assessment identifies a substance abuse disability.

(d)   Standards. - An ADET school shall offer the curriculum established by the Commission and shall comply with the rules adopted by the Commission. A substance abuse treatment program offered to a person who needs the program to obtain a certificate of completion shall comply with the rules adopted by the Commission.

(d1)   Persons Authorized to Provide Instruction. - Beginning January 1, 2009, individuals who provide ADET school instruction as a Department-authorized ADETS instructor must have at least one of the following qualifications:

(1) A Certified Substance Abuse Counselor (CSAC), as defined by the Commission.

(2) A Licensed Clinical Addictions Specialist (LCAS), as defined by the Commission.

(3) A Certified Substance Abuse Prevention Consultant (CSAPC), as defined by the Commission.

(e) Certificate of Completion. - Any facility that issues a certificate of completion shall forward the original certificate of completion to the Department. The Department shall review the certificate of completion for accuracy and completeness. If the Department finds the certificate of completion to be accurate and complete, the Department shall forward it to the Division of Motor Vehicles of the Department of Transportation. If the Department finds the certificate of completion is not accurate or complete, the Department shall return the certificate of completion to the area facility for appropriate action.

(f) Fees. - A person who has a substance abuse assessment conducted for the purpose of obtaining a certificate of completion shall pay to the assessing agency a fee of one hundred dollars ($100). A person shall pay to a school a fee of one hundred sixty dollars ($160.00). A person shall pay to a treatment facility a fee of seventy-five dollars ($75.00). If the defendant is treated by an area mental health facility, G.S. 122C-146 applies after receipt of the seventy-five dollar ($75.00) fee.

A facility that provides to a person who is required to obtain a certificate of completion a substance abuse assessment, an ADET school, or a substance abuse treatment program may require the person to pay a fee required by this subsection before it issues a certificate of completion. As stated in G.S. 122C-146, however, an area facility may not deny a service to a person because the person is unable to pay.

A facility shall remit to the Department ten percent (10%) of each fee paid to the facility under this subsection by a person who attends an ADET school conducted by the facility. The Department may use amounts remitted to it under this subsection only to support, evaluate, and administer ADET schools.

(f1) Multiple Assessments. - If a person has more than one offense for which a certificate of completion is required under G.S. 20-17.6, the person shall pay the assessment fee required under subsection (f) of this section for each certificate of completion required. However, the facility shall conduct only one substance abuse assessment and recommend only one ADET school or treatment program for all certificates of completion required at that time, and the person shall pay the fee required under subsection (f) of this section for only one school or treatment program.

If any of the criteria in subdivisions (c)(1), (c)(2), or (c)(3) of this section are present in any of the offenses for which the person needs a certificate of completion, completion of a treatment program shall be required pursuant to subsection (c) of this section.

The provisions of this subsection do not apply to subsequent assessments performed after a certificate of completion has already been issued for a previous assessment.

(g) Out-of-State Services. - A person may obtain a substance abuse service needed to obtain a certificate of completion from a provider located in another state if the service offered by that provider is substantially similar to the service offered by a provider located in this State. A person who obtains a service from a provider located in another state is responsible for paying any fees imposed by the provider.

(h) Rules. - The Commission may adopt rules to implement this section. In developing rules for determining when a person needs to be placed in a substance abuse treatment program, the Commission shall consider diagnostic criteria such as those contained in the most recent revision of the Diagnostic and Statistical Manual or used by the American Society of Addiction Medicine (ASAM).

(i) Report. - The Department shall submit an annual report on substance abuse assessments to the Joint Legislative Commission on Governmental Operations. The report is due by February 1. Each facility that provides services needed by a person to obtain a certificate of completion shall file an annual report with the Department by October 1 that contains the information the Department needs to compile the report the Department is required to submit under this section.

The report submitted to the Joint Legislative Commission on Governmental Operations shall include all of the following information and any other information requested by that Commission:

(1) The number of persons required to obtain a certificate of completion during the previous fiscal year as a condition of restoring the person's drivers license under G.S. 20-17.6.

(2) The number of substance abuse assessments conducted during the previous fiscal year for the purpose of obtaining a certificate of completion.

(3) Of the number of assessments reported under subdivision (2) of this subsection, the number recommending attendance at an ADET school, the number recommending treatment, and, for those recommending treatment, the level of treatment recommended.

(4) Of the number of persons recommended for an ADET school or treatment under subdivision (3) of this subsection, the number who completed the school or treatment.

(5) The number of substance abuse assessments conducted by each facility and, of these assessments, the number that recommended attendance at an ADET school and the number that recommended treatment.

(6) The fees paid to a facility for providing services for persons to obtain a certificate of completion and the facility's costs in providing those services.

(j) Repealed by Session Laws 2013-360, s. 12A.8(a), effective July 1, 2013. (1995, c. 496, ss. 10, 13; 2001-370, s. 9; 2003-396, ss. 1, 3, 4; 2004-197, ss. 1, 2, 3; 2005-312, ss. 1, 2, 4; 2008-130, ss. 7, 8; 2013-360, s. 12A.8(a).)

§ 122C-143: Repealed by Session Laws 1993, c. 321, s. 220(d).

§ 122C-143.1. Policy guidance.

(a) The General Assembly shall, as it considers necessary, endorse as policy guidance long-range plans for the broad age/disability categories of persons to be served and the services to be provided by area authorities.

(b) The Secretary shall develop a payment policy that designates, within broad age/disability categories, the priority populations, based on their disability level and the types of service to be supported by State resources. The Secretary shall review the Department's payment policy annually to assure that payments are made consistent with the State's long-range plans.

(c) The Secretary shall ensure that the payment policy provides incentives designated to target resources consistent with legislative policy and with the State's long-range plans and to promote equal accessibility to services for individuals regardless of their catchment area.

(d) Upon request of the Secretary, each area authority shall develop, revise, or amend its local long-range plans to be consistent with the policy guidance set forth in the State's long-range plans. Local service implementation plans shall be subject to the approval of the Secretary.

(e) The Secretary shall ensure that the Department's requests for expansion funds for area authorities are consistent with the State's long-range plans and include consideration of needs identified by the area authorities and their local plans. (1993, c. 321, s. 220(e).)

§ 122C-143.2: Repealed by Session Laws 2001-437, s. 1.16, effective July 1, 2002.

§ 122C-144: Repealed by Session Laws 1993, c. 321, s. 220(f).

§ 122C-144.1. Budget format and reports.

(a) The area authority shall maintain its budget in accordance with the requirements of Article 3 of Subchapter III of Chapter 159 of the General Statutes, the Local Government Budget and Fiscal Control Act.

(b) The Secretary may require periodic reports of receipts and expenditures for all area authority services provided directly or under contract according to a format prescribed by the Secretary.

(c) In accordance with G.S. 159-34, the area authority shall have an audit completed and submit it to the Local Government Commission.

(d) The Secretary may require reports of client characteristics, staffing patterns, agency policies or activities, services, or specific financial data of the area authority, but the reports shall not identify individual clients of the area authority unless specifically required by State statute or federal statute or regulation, or unless valid consent for the release has been given by the client or legally responsible person. (1993, c. 321, s. 220(g).)

§ 122C-145: Renumbered as G.S. 122C-151.2 by Session Laws 1993, c. 321, s. 220.

§ 122C-146. Uniform co-payment schedule.

(a) The LME and its contractual provider agencies shall implement the co-payment schedule based on family income adopted by the Secretary under G.S. 122C-112.1(a)(34). The LME is responsible for determining the applicability of the co-payment to individuals authorized by the LME to receive services. An LME that provides services and its contractual provider agencies shall also make every reasonable effort to collect appropriate reimbursement for costs in providing these services from individuals or entities able to pay, including insurance and third-party payments. However, no individual may be refused services because of an inability to pay.

(b) Individuals may not be charged for free services, as required in "The Amendments to the Education of the Handicapped Act", P.L. 99-457, provided to eligible infants and toddlers and their families. This exemption from charges does not exempt insurers or other third-party payors from being charged for payment for these services, if the person who is legally responsible for any eligible infant or toddler is first advised that the person may or may not grant permission for the insurer or other payor to be billed for the free services.

(c) All funds collected from co-payments for LME operated services shall be used to provide services to individuals in targeted populations.

The collection of co-payments by an LME that provides services may not be used as justification for reduction or replacement of the budgeted commitment of local tax revenue. All funds collected from co-payments by contractual provider agencies shall be used to provide services to individuals in targeted populations. (1977, c. 568, s. 1; 1979, c. 358, s. 16; 1985, c. 589, s. 2; 1989 (Reg. Sess., 1990), c. 1003, s. 4; 1991, c. 215, s. 2; 1993, c. 487, s. 3; c. 553, s. 36; 2007-410, s. 1.)

§ 122C-147. Financing and title of area authority property.

(a) Repealed by Session Laws 1993, c. 321, s. 220(i).

(b) Unless otherwise specified by the Secretary, State appropriations to area authorities shall be used exclusively for the operating costs of the area authority; provided however:

(1) The Secretary may specify that designated State funds may be used by area authorities (i) for the purchase, alteration, improvement, or rehabilitation of real estate to be used as a facility or (ii) in contracting with a private, nonprofit corporation or with another governmental entity that operates facilities for the mentally ill, developmentally disabled, or substance abusers and according to the terms of the contract between the area authority and the private, nonprofit corporation or with the governmental entity, for the purchase, alteration, improvement, rehabilitation of real estate or, to make a lump sum down payment or periodic payments on a real property mortgage in the name of the private, nonprofit corporation or governmental entity.

(2) Upon cessation of the use of the facility by the area authority, if operated by the area authority, or upon termination, default, or nonrenewal of the contract if operated by a contractual agency, the Department shall be reimbursed in accordance with rules adopted by the Secretary for the Department's participation in the purchase of the facility.

(c) All real property purchased for use by the area authority shall be provided by local or federal funds unless otherwise allowed under subsection (b) of this section or by specific capital funds appropriated by the General Assembly. The title to this real property and the authority to acquire it is held by the area authority. Real property may not be acquired by means of an installment contract under G.S. 160A-20 unless the Local Government Commission has approved the acquisition. No deficiency judgment may be rendered against any unit of local government in any action for breach of a contractual obligation authorized by this subsection, and the taxing power of a unit of local government is not and may not be pledged directly or indirectly to secure any moneys due under a contract authorized by this subsection.

(d) The area authority may lease real property.

(e) Equipment necessary for the operation of the area authority may be obtained with local, State, federal, or donated funds, or a combination of these.

(f) The area authority may acquire or lease personal property. An acquisition may be accomplished by an installment contract under G.S. 160A-20 or by a lease-purchase agreement. An area authority may not acquire personal property by means of an installment contract under G.S. 160A-20 without the approval of the board or boards of commissioners of all the counties that comprise the area authority. The approval of a board of county commissioners shall be by resolution of the board and may have any necessary or proper conditions, including provisions for distribution of the proceeds in the event of disposition of the property by the area authority. The area authority may not acquire personal property by means of an installment contract under G.S. 160A-20 without the approval of the Local Government Commission, when required by that statute. No deficiency judgment may be rendered against any unit of local government in any action for breach of a contractual obligation authorized by this subsection, and the taxing power of a unit of local government is not and shall not be pledged directly or indirectly to secure any moneys due under a contract authorized by this subsection. Title to personal property may be held by the area authority.

(g) All area authority funds shall be spent in accordance with the rules of the Secretary. Failure to comply with the rules is grounds for the Secretary to stop participation in the funding of the particular program. The Secretary may withdraw funds from a specific program of services not being administered in accordance with an approved plan and budget after written notice and subject to an appeal as provided by G.S. 122C-145 and Chapter 150B of the General Statutes.

(h) Notwithstanding subsection (b) of this section and in addition to the purposes listed in that subsection, the funds allocated by the Secretary for services for members of the class identified in Willie M., et al. vs. Hunt, et al. (C-C-79-294, Western District) may be used for the purchase, alteration, improvement, or rehabilitation of real property owned or to be owned by a nonprofit corporation or by another governmental entity and used or to be used as a facility.

(i) Notwithstanding subsection (c) of this section and in addition to the purposes listed in that subsection, funds allocated by the Secretary for services for members of the class identified in Willie M., et al. vs. Hunt, et al. (C-C-79-294, Western District) may be used for the purchase, alteration, improvement, or rehabilitation of real property used by an area authority as long as the title to the real property is vested in the county where the property is located or is vested in another governmental entity. If the property ceases to be used in accordance with the annual plan, the unamortized part of funds spent under this subsection for the purchase, alteration, improvement, or rehabilitation of real property shall be returned to the Department, in accordance with the rules of the Secretary.

(j) Notwithstanding subsection (c) of this section the area authority, with the approval of the Secretary, may use local funds for the alteration, improvement, and rehabilitation of real property owned by a nonprofit corporation or by another governmental entity under contract with the area authority and used or to be used as a facility. Prior to the use of county appropriated funds for this purpose, the area authority shall obtain consent of the board or boards of commissioners of all the counties that comprise the area authority. The consent shall be by resolution of the affected board or boards of county commissioners and may have any necessary or proper conditions, including provisions for distribution of the proceeds in the event of disposition of the property. (1973, c. 476, s. 133; c. 613; 1977, c. 568, s. 1; c. 679, s. 7; 1979, c. 358, s. 29; 1981, c. 51, s. 3; 1983, c. 5; c. 25; c. 402; 1985, c. 589, s. 2; 1987, c. 720, s. 3; c. 784; 1989, c. 625, s. 17; 1993, c. 321, s. 220(h), (i); 1993 (Reg. Sess., 1994), c. 592, s. 1; 1995, c. 305, s. 1; 2012-151, s. 8.)

§ 122C-147.1. Appropriations and allocations.

(a) Except as provided in subsection (b) of this section, funds shall be appropriated by the General Assembly in broad age/disability categories. The Secretary shall allocate and account for funds in broad age/disability categories so that the area authority may, with flexibility, earn funds in response to local needs that are identified within the payment policy developed in accordance with G.S. 122C-143.1(b).

(b) When the General Assembly determines that it is necessary to appropriate funds for a more specific purpose than the broad age/disability category, the Secretary shall determine whether expenditure accounting, special reporting within earning from a broad fund, the Memorandum of Agreement, or some other mechanism allows the best accounting for the funds.

(b1) Notwithstanding subsection (b) of this section, funds appropriated by the General Assembly for crisis services shall not be allocated in broad disability or age/disability categories. Subsection (c) of this section shall not apply to funds appropriated by the General Assembly for crisis services.

(c) Funds that have been appropriated by the General Assembly for a more specific purpose than specified in subsection (a) of this section shall be converted to a broad age/disability category at the beginning of the second biennium following the appropriation, unless otherwise acted upon by the General Assembly.

(d) The Secretary shall allocate funds to area programs:

(1) To be earned in a purchase of service basis, at negotiated reimbursement rates, for services that are included in the payment policy and delivered to mentally ill, developmentally disabled, and substance abuse clients and for services that are included in the payment policy to other recipients; or

(2) To be paid under a grant on the basis of agreed-upon expenditures, when the Secretary determines that it would be impractical to pay on a purchase of service basis.

(d1) Notwithstanding subsections (b) and (d) of this section, each area program shall determine whether to earn the funds for crisis services and funds for services to substance abuse clients in a purchase-for-service basis, under a grant, or some combination of the two. Area programs shall account for funds expended on a grant basis according to procedures required by the Secretary and in a manner that is similar to funds expended in a purchase-for-service basis.

(e) After the close of a fiscal year, final payments of funds shall be made:

(1) Under the purchase of service basis, on the earnings of the area authority for the delivery to individuals within each age/disability group, of any services that are consistent with the payment policy established in G.S. 122C-143.1(b), up to the final allocation amount; or

(2) When awarded on an expenditure basis, on allowable actual expenditures, up to the final allocation amount.

Under rules adopted by the Secretary, final payments shall be adjusted on the basis of the audit required in G.S. 122C-144.1(d). (1993, c. 321, s. 220(j); 2007-323, ss. 10.49(b), (q).)

§ 122C-147.2. Purchase of services and reimbursement rates.

(a) When funds are used to purchase services, the following provisions apply:

(1) Reimbursement rates for specific types of service shall be negotiated between the Secretary and the area authority. The negotiation shall begin with the rate determined by a standardized cost-finding and rate-setting procedure approved by the Secretary.

(2) The reimbursement rate used for the payment of services shall incorporate operating and administrative costs, including costs for property in accordance with G.S. 122C-147.

(b) To ensure uniformity in rates charged to area programs and funded with State-allocated resources, the Division of Mental Health, Developmental Disabilities, and Substance Abuse Services of the Department of Health and Human Services may require a private agency that provides services under contract with an area program or county program, except for hospital services that have an established Medicaid rate, to complete an agency-wide uniform cost finding in accordance with subsection (a) of this section. The resulting cost shall be the maximum included for the private agency in the contracting area program's unit cost finding. If a private agency fails to timely and accurately complete the required agency-wide uniform cost finding in a manner acceptable to the Department's controller's office, the Department may suspend all Department funding and payment to the private agency until such time as an acceptable cost finding has been completed by the private agency and approved by the Department's controller's office. (1993, c. 321, s. 220(j); 2005-276, s. 10.30.)

§§ 122C-148 through 122C-150: Repealed by Session Laws 1993, c. 321, s. 220(k).

§ 122C-151. Responsibilities of those receiving appropriations.

(a) All resources allocated to and received by any area authority and used for programs of mental health, developmental disabilities, substance abuse or other related services are subject to the conditions specified in this Article and to the rules of the Commission and the Secretary and to the conditions of the Memorandum of Agreement specified in G.S. 122C-143.2.

(b) If an area authority fails to complete actions necessary for the development of a Memorandum of Agreement, fails to file required reports within the time limit set by the Secretary, or fails to comply with any other requirements specified in this Article, the Secretary may:

(1) Delay payments; and

(2) With written notification of cause and subject to an appeal as provided by G.S. 122C-151.2, reduce or deny payment of funds. Restoration of funds upon compliance is within the discretion of the Secretary. (1977, c. 568, s. 1; c. 679, s. 7; 1979, c. 358, s. 25; 1981, c. 51, s. 3; 1985, c. 589, s. 2; 1989, c. 625, s. 19; 1993, c. 321, s. 220(l).)

§ 122C-151.1: Repealed by Session Laws 1993, c. 321, s. 220(n), as amended by Session Laws 1993 (Regular Session, 1994), c. 591, s. 7.)

§ 122C-151.2. Appeal by area authorities and county programs.

(a) The area authority or county program may appeal to the Commission any action regarding rules under the jurisdiction of the Commission or rules under the joint jurisdiction of the Commission and the Secretary.

(b) The area authority or county program may appeal to the Secretary any action regarding rules under the jurisdiction of the Secretary.

(c) Appeals shall be conducted according to rules adopted by the Commission and Secretary and in accordance with Chapter 150B of the General Statutes. (1977, c. 568, s. 1; c. 679, s. 7; 1979, c. 358, ss. 7, 19; 1981, c. 51, s. 3; c. 614, s. 7; 1985, c. 589, s. 2; 1987, c. 720, s. 3; 1993, c. 321, s. 220(m); 2001-437, s. 1.17(a).)

§ 122C-151.3. Dispute with area authorities or county programs.

(a) An area authority or county program shall establish written procedures for resolving disputes over decisions of an area authority or county program that may be appealed to the State MH/DD/SA Appeals Panel under G.S. 122C-151.4. The procedures shall be informal and shall provide an opportunity for those who dispute the decision to present their position.

(b) This section does not apply to LME/MCOs, enrollees, applicants, providers of emergency services, or network providers subject to Chapter 108D of the General Statutes. (1993, c. 321, s. 220(o); 2001-437, s. 1.17(b); 2013-397, s. 2.)

§ 122C-151.4. Appeal to State MH/DD/SA Appeals Panel.

(a) Definitions. - The following definitions apply in this section:

(1) "Appeals Panel" means the State MH/DD/SA Appeals Panel established under this section.

(1a) "Client" means an individual who is admitted to or receiving public services from an area facility. "Client" includes the client's personal representative or designee.

(1b) "Contract" means a contract with an area authority or county program to provide services, other than personal services, to clients and other recipients of services.

(2) "Contractor" means a person who has a contract or who had a contract during the current fiscal year.

(3) "Former contractor" means a person who had a contract during the previous fiscal year.

(b) Appeals Panel. - The State MH/DD/SA Appeals Panel is established. The Panel shall consist of three members appointed by the Secretary. The Secretary shall determine the qualifications of the Panel members. Panel members serve at the pleasure of the Secretary.

(c) Who Can Appeal. - The following persons may appeal to the State MH/DD/SA Appeals Panel after having exhausted the appeals process at the appropriate area authority or county program:

(1) A contractor or a former contractor who claims that an area authority or county program is not acting or has not acted within applicable State law or rules in denying the contractor's application for endorsement or in imposing a particular requirement on the contractor on fulfillment of the contract;

(2) A contractor or a former contractor who claims that a requirement of the contract substantially compromises the ability of the contractor to fulfill the contract;

(3) A contractor or former contractor who claims that an area authority or county program has acted arbitrarily and capriciously in reducing funding for the type of services provided or formerly provided by the contractor or former contractor;

(4) A client or a person who was a client in the previous fiscal year, who claims that an area authority or county program has acted arbitrarily and capriciously in reducing funding for the type of services provided or formerly provided to the client directly by the area authority or county program; and

(5) A person who claims that an area authority or county program did not comply with a State law or a rule adopted by the Secretary or the Commission in developing the plans and budgets of the area authority or county program and that the failure to comply has adversely affected the ability of the person to participate in the development of the plans and budgets.

(d) Hearing. - All members of the State MH/DD/SA Appeals Panel shall hear an appeal to the Panel. An appeal shall be filed with the Panel within the time required by the Secretary and shall be heard by the Panel within the time required by the Secretary. A hearing shall be conducted at the place determined in accordance with the rules adopted by the Secretary. A hearing before the Panel shall be informal; no sworn testimony shall be taken and the rules of evidence do not apply. The person who appeals to the Panel has the burden of proof. The Panel shall not stay a decision of an area authority during an appeal to the Panel.

(e) Decision. - The State MH/DD/SA Appeals Panel shall make a written decision on each appeal to the Panel within the time set by the Secretary. A decision may direct a contractor, an area authority, or a county program to take an action or to refrain from taking an action, but it shall not require a party to the appeal to pay any amount except payment due under the contract. In making a decision, the Panel shall determine the course of action that best protects or benefits the clients of the area authority or county program. If a party to an appeal fails to comply with a decision of the Panel and the Secretary determines that the failure deprives clients of the area authority or county program of a type of needed service, the Secretary may use funds previously allocated to the area authority or county program to provide the service.

(f) Chapter 150B Appeal. - A person who is dissatisfied with a decision of the Panel may commence a contested case under Article 3 of Chapter 150B of the General Statutes. Notwithstanding G.S. 150B-2(1a), an area authority or county program is considered an agency for purposes of the limited appeal authorized by this section. If the need to first appeal to the State MH/DD/SA Appeals Panel is waived by the Secretary, a contractor may appeal directly to the Office of Administrative Hearings after having exhausted the appeals process at the appropriate area authority or county program.

(g) This section does not apply to LME/MCOs, enrollees, applicants, providers of emergency services, or network providers subject to Chapter 108D of the General Statutes. (1993, c. 321, s. 220(o); 2001-437, s. 1.17(c); 2008-107, s. 10.15A(h); 2011-398, s. 40; 2012-66, s. 3; 2013-397, s. 3.)

§ 122C-152. Liability insurance and waiver of immunity as to torts of agents, employees, and board members.

(a) An area authority, by securing liability insurance as provided in this section, may waive its governmental immunity from liability for damage by reason of death or injury to person or property caused by the negligence or tort of any agent, employee, or board member of the area authority when acting within the scope of his authority or within the course of his duties or employment. Governmental immunity is waived by the act of obtaining this insurance, but it is waived by only to the extent that the area authority is indemnified by insurance for the negligence or tort.

(b) Any contract of insurance purchased pursuant to this section shall be issued by a company or corporation licensed and authorized to execute insurance contracts in this State and shall by its terms adequately insure the area authority against any and all liability for any damages by reason of death or injury to a person or property proximately caused by the negligent acts or torts of the agents, employees, and board members of the area authority when acting within the course of their duties or employment. The area board shall determine the extent of the liability and what agents, employees by class, and board members are covered by any insurance purchased pursuant to this subsection. Any company or corporation that enters into a contract of insurance as described in this section with the authority, by this act waives any defense based upon the governmental immunity of the area authority.

(c) Any persons sustaining damages, or, in the case of death, his personal representative, may sue an area authority insured under this section for the recovery of damages in any court of competent jurisdiction in this State, but only in a county located within the geographic limits of the authority. It is no defense to any action that the negligence or tort complained of was in pursuance of a governmental or discretionary function of the area authority if, and to the extent that, the authority has insurance coverage as provided by this section.

(d) Except as expressly provided by subsection (c) of this section, nothing in this section deprives any area authority of any defense whatsoever to any action for damages or to restrict, limit, or otherwise affect any defense which the area authority may have at common law or by virtue of any statute. Nothing in this section relieves any person sustaining damages nor any personal representative of any decedent from any duty to give notice of a claim to the area authority or to commence any civil action for the recovery of damages within the applicable period of time prescribed or limited by statute.

(e) The area authority may incur liability pursuant to this section only with respect to a claim arising after the authority has procured liability insurance pursuant to this section and during the time when the insurance is in force.

(f) No part of the pleadings that relate to or allege facts as to a defendant's insurance against liability may be read or mentioned in the presence of the trial jury in any action brought pursuant to this section. This liability does not attach unless the plaintiff waives the right to have all issues of law or fact relating to insurance in the action determined by a jury. These issues shall be heard and determined by the judge, and the jury shall be absent during any motions, arguments, testimony, or announcement of findings of fact or conclusions of law with respect to insurance. (1981, c. 539, s. 2; 1985, c. 589, s. 2.)

§ 122C-153. Defense of agents, employees, and board members.

(a) Upon request made by or in behalf of any agent, employee, or board member or former agent, employee, or board member of the area authority, any area authority may provide for the defense of any civil or criminal action or proceeding brought against him either in his official or in his individual capacity, or both, on account of any act done or omission made, or any act allegedly done or omission allegedly made, in the scope and course of his duty as an agent, employee, or board member. The defense may be provided by the local board by employing counsel or by purchasing insurance that requires that the insurer provide the defense. Nothing in this section requires any area authority to provide for the defense of any action or proceeding of any nature.

(b) An area authority may budget funds for the purpose of paying all or part of the claim made or any civil judgment entered against any of its agents, employees, or board members or former agents, employees, or board members when a claim is made or judgment is rendered as damages on account of any act done or omission made, or any act allegedly done or omission allegedly made, in the scope and course of his duty as an agent, employee, or board member of the area authority. Nothing in this section shall authorize any area authority to budget funds for the purpose of paying any claim made or civil judgment against any of its agents, employees, or board members, or former agents, employees, or board members, if the authority finds that the agent, employee, or board member acted or failed to act because of actual fraud, corruption, or actual malice on his part. Any authority may budget for and purchase insurance coverage for payment of claims or judgments pursuant to this section. Nothing in this section requires any authority to pay any claim or judgment referred to, and the purchase of insurance coverage for payment of the claim or judgment may not be considered an assumption of any liability not covered by the insurance contract and may not be deemed an assumption of liability or payment of any claim or judgment in excess of the limits of coverage in the insurance contract.

(c) Subsection (b) of this section does not authorize an authority to pay all or part of a claim made or civil judgment entered or to provide a defense to a criminal charge unless (i) notice of the claim or litigation is given to the area authority before the time that the claim is settled or civil judgment is entered; and (ii) the area authority has adopted, and made available for public inspection, uniform standards under which claims made, civil judgments entered, or criminal charges against agents, employees, or board members or former agents, employees, or board members shall be defended or paid.

(d) The board or boards of county commissioners that establish the area authority and the Secretary may allocate funds not otherwise restricted by law, in addition to the funds allocated for the operation of the program, for the purpose of paying legal defense, judgments, and settlements under this section. (1981, c. 539, s. 2; 1985, c. 589, s. 2.)

§ 122C-154. Personnel.

Employees under the direct supervision of the area director are employees of the area authority. For the purpose of personnel administration, Chapter 126 of the General Statutes applies unless otherwise provided in this Article. Employees appointed by the county program director are employees of the county. In a multicounty program, employment of county program staff shall be as agreed upon in the interlocal agreement adopted pursuant to G.S. 122C-115.1. Notwithstanding G.S. 126-9(b), an employee of an area authority may be paid a salary that is in excess of the salary ranges established by the State Human Resources Commission. Any salary that is higher than the maximum of the applicable salary range shall be supported by documentation of comparable salaries in comparable operations within the region and shall also include the specific amount the board proposes to pay the employee. The area board shall not authorize any salary adjustment that is above the normal allowable salary range without obtaining prior approval from the Director of the Office of State Human Resources. (1971, c. 470, s. 1; 1973, c. 476, s. 133; 1977, c. 568, s. 1; c. 679, s. 7; 1979, c. 358, s. 14; 1981, c. 51, s. 3; 1985, c. 589, s. 2; 2001-437, s. 1.18; 2012-151, s. 11(b); 2013-382, s. 9.1(c).)

§ 122C-155. Supervision of services.

Unless otherwise specified, client services are the responsibility of a qualified professional. Direct medical and psychiatric services shall be provided by a qualified psychiatrist or a physician with adequate training and experience acceptable to the Secretary. (1971, c. 470, s. 1; 1973, c. 476, s. 133; 1977, c. 568, s. 1; c. 679, s. 7; 1979, c. 358, s. 14; 1981, c. 51, s. 3; 1985, c. 589, s. 2.)

§ 122C-156. Salary plan for employees of the area authority.

(a) The area authority shall establish a salary plan which shall set the salaries for employees of the area authority. The salary plan shall be in compliance with Chapter 126 of the General Statutes. In a multi-county area, the salary plan shall not exceed the highest paying salary plan of any county in that area. In a single-county area, the salary plan shall not exceed the county's salary plan. The salary plan limitations set forth in this section may be exceeded only if the area authority and the board or boards of county commissioners, as the case may be, jointly agree to exceed these limitations.

(b) An area authority may purchase life insurance or health insurance or both for the benefit of all or any class of authority officers or employees as a part of its compensation. An area authority may provide other fringe benefits for authority officers and employees.

(c) An area authority that is providing health insurance under subsection (b) of this section may provide health insurance for all or any class of former officers and employees of the area authority who are receiving benefits under Article 3 of Chapter 128 of the General Statutes. Health insurance may be paid entirely by the area authority, partly by the area authority and former officer or employee, or entirely by the former officer or employee, at the option of the area board. (1977, c. 568, s. 1; 1979, c. 358, ss. 15, 23; 1985, c. 589, s. 2.)

§ 122C-157. Establishment of a professional reimbursement policy.

The area authority shall adopt and enforce a professional reimbursement policy. This policy shall (i) require that fees for the provision of services received directly under the supervision of the area authority shall be paid to the area authority, (ii) prohibit employees of the area authority from providing services on a private basis which require the use of the resources and facilities of the area authority, and (iii) provide that employees may not accept dual compensation and dual employment unless they have the written permission of the area authority. (1977, c. 568, s. 1; 1979, c. 358, s. 17; 1985, c. 589, s. 2.)

§ 122C-158. Privacy of personnel records.

(a) Notwithstanding the provisions of G.S. 132-6 or any other State statute concerning access to public records, personnel files of employees or applicants for employment maintained by an area authority are subject to inspection and may be disclosed only as provided by this section. For purposes of this section, an employee's personnel file consists of any information in any form gathered by the area authority with respect to that employee, including his application, selection or nonselection, performance, promotions, demotions, transfers, suspensions and other disciplinary actions, evaluation forms, leave, salary, and termination of employment. As used in this section, "employee" includes former employees of the area authority.

(b) The following information with respect to each employee is a matter of public record:

(1) Name.

(2) Age.

(3) Date of original employment or appointment to the area authority.

(4) The terms of any contract by which the employee is employed whether written or oral, past and current, to the extent that the agency has the written contract or a record of the oral contract in its possession.

(5) Current position.

(6) Title.

(7) Current salary.

(8) Date and amount of each increase or decrease in salary with that area authority.

(9) Date and type each promotion, demotion, transfer, suspension, separation, or other change in position classification with that area authority.

(10) Date and general description of the reasons for each promotion with that area authority.

(11) Date and type of each dismissal, suspension, or demotion for disciplinary reasons taken by the area authority. If the disciplinary action was a dismissal, a copy of the written notice of the final decision of the area authority setting forth the specific acts or omissions that are the basis of the dismissal.

(12) The office to which the employee is currently assigned.

(b1) For the purposes of this subsection, the term "salary" includes pay, benefits, incentives, bonuses, and deferred and all other forms of compensation paid by the employing entity.

(b2) The area authority shall determine in what form and by whom this information will be maintained. Any person may have access to this information for the purpose of inspection, examination, and copying during regular business hours, subject only to rules for the safekeeping of public records as the area authority may have adopted. Any person denied access to this information may apply to the appropriate division of the General Court of Justice for an order compelling disclosure, and the court shall have jurisdiction to issue these orders.

(c) All information contained in an employee's personnel file, other than the information made public by subsection (b) of this section, is confidential and is open to inspection only in the following instances:

(1) The employee or an authorized agent may examine portions of his personnel file except (i) letters of reference solicited before employment, and (ii) information concerning a medical disability, mental or physical, that a prudent physician would not divulge to a patient.

(2) A licensed physician designated in writing by the employee may examine the employee's medical record.

(3) An area authority employee having supervisory authority over the employee may examine all material in the employee's personnel file.

(4) By order of a court of competent jurisdiction, any person may examine the part of an employee's personnel file that is ordered by the court.

(5) An official of an agency of the State or federal government, or any political subdivision of the State, may inspect any part of a personnel file pursuant to G.S. 122C-25(b) or G.S. 122C-192(a) or when the inspection is considered by the official having custody of the records to be inspected to be necessary and essential to the pursuance of a proper function of the inspecting agency. No information may be divulged for the purpose of assisting in a criminal prosecution of the employee or for the purpose of assisting in an investigation of the employee's tax liability. However, the official having custody

of the records may release the name, address, and telephone number from a personnel file for the purpose of assisting in a criminal investigation.

(6) An employee may sign a written release, to be placed with the employee's personnel file, that permits the person with custody of the file to provide, either in person, by telephone or by mail, information specified in the release to prospective employers, educational institutions, or other persons specified in the release.

(7) The area authority may tell any person of the employment or nonemployment, promotion, demotion, suspension, or other disciplinary action, reinstatement, transfer, or termination of an employee and the reasons for that personnel action. Before releasing the information, the area authority shall determine in writing that the release is essential to maintaining public confidence in the administration of services or to maintaining the level and quality of services. This written determination shall be retained as a record for public inspection and shall become part of the employee's personnel file.

(d) Even if considered part of an employee's personnel file, the following information need not be disclosed to an employee nor to any other person:

(1) Testing or examination material used solely to determine individual qualifications for appointment, employment, or promotion in the area authority service, when disclosure would compromise the objectivity or the fairness of the testing or examination process.

(2) Investigative reports or memoranda and other information concerning the investigation of possible criminal action of an employee, until the investigation is completed and no criminal action taken, or until the criminal action is concluded.

(3) Information that might identify an undercover law-enforcement officer or a law-enforcement informer.

(4) Notes, preliminary drafts, and internal communications concerning an employee. In the event these materials are used for any official personnel decision, then the employee or an authorized agent has a right to inspect these materials.

(e) The area authority may permit access, subject to limitations it may impose, to selected personnel files by a professional representative of a training, research, or academic institution if that representative certifies that he will not release information identifying the employees whose files are opened and that the information will be used solely for statistical, research, or teaching purposes. This certification shall be retained by the area authority as long as each personnel file so examined is retained.

(f) The area authority that maintains personnel files containing information other than the information mentioned in subsection (b) of this section shall establish procedures whereby an employee who objects to material in the employee's file on grounds that it is inaccurate or misleading may seek to have the material removed from the file or may place in the file a statement relating to the material.

(g) Permitting access, other than that authorized by this section, to a personnel file of an employee of an area authority is a Class 3 misdemeanor and is punishable only by a fine, not to exceed five hundred dollars ($500.00).

(h) Anyone who, knowing that he is not authorized to do so, examines, removes, or copies information in a personnel file of an employee of an area authority is guilty of a Class 3 misdemeanor and is punishable only by a fine, not to exceed five hundred dollars ($500.00). (1983, c. 281; 1985, c. 589, s. 2; 1993, c. 539, ss. 924, 925; 1994, Ex. Sess., c. 24, s. 14(c); 2007-508, s. 3; 2010-169, s. 18(d).)

§§ 122C-159 through 122C-169. Reserved for future codification purposes.

Part 4A. Consumer and Family Advisory Committees.

§ 122C-170. Local Consumer and Family Advisory Committees.

(a) Area authorities and county programs shall establish committees made up of consumers and family members to be known as Consumer and Family Advisory Committees (CFACS). A local CFAC shall be a self-governing and a self-directed organization that advises the area authority or county program in its catchment area on the planning and management of the local public mental health, developmental disabilities, and substance abuse services system.

Each CFAC shall adopt bylaws to govern the selection and appointment of its members, their terms of service, the number of members, and other procedural matters. At the request of either the CFAC or the governing board of the area authority or county program, the CFAC and the governing board shall execute an agreement that identifies the roles and responsibilities of each party, channels of communication between the parties, and a process for resolving disputes between the parties.

(b) Each of the disability groups shall be equally represented on the CFAC, and the CFAC shall reflect as closely as possible the racial and ethnic composition of the catchment area. The terms of members shall be three years, and no member may serve more than three consecutive terms. The CFAC shall be composed exclusively of:

(1) Adult consumers of mental health, developmental disabilities, and substance abuse services.

(2) Family members of consumers of mental health, developmental disabilities, and substance abuse services.

(c) The CFAC shall undertake all of the following:

(1) Review, comment on, and monitor the implementation of the local business plan.

(2) Identify service gaps and underserved populations.

(3) Make recommendations regarding the service array and monitor the development of additional services.

(4) Review and comment on the area authority or county program budget.

(5) Participate in all quality improvement measures and performance indicators.

(6) Submit to the State Consumer and Family Advisory Committee findings and recommendations regarding ways to improve the delivery of mental health, developmental disabilities, and substance abuse services.

(d) The director of the area authority or county program shall provide sufficient staff to assist the CFAC in implementing its duties under subsection

(c) of this section. The assistance shall include data for the identification of service gaps and underserved populations, training to review and comment on business plans and budgets, procedures to allow participation in quality monitoring, and technical advice on rules of procedure and applicable laws. (2006-142, s. 5; 2012-151, s. 5.)

§ 122C-171. State Consumer and Family Advisory Committee.

(a) There is established the State Consumer and Family Advisory Committee (State CFAC). The State CFAC shall be shall be a self-governing and self-directed organization that advises the Department and the General Assembly on the planning and management of the State's public mental health, developmental disabilities, and substance abuse services system.

(b) The State CFAC shall be composed of 21 members. The members shall be composed exclusively of adult consumers of mental health, developmental disabilities, and substance abuse services; and family members of consumers of mental health, developmental disabilities, and substance abuse services. The terms of members shall be three years, and no member may serve more than two consecutive terms. Vacancies shall be filled by the appointing authority. The members shall be appointed as follows:

(1) Nine by the Secretary. The Secretary's appointments shall reflect each of the disability groups. The terms shall be staggered so that terms of three of the appointees expire each year.

(2) Three by the President Pro Tempore of the Senate, one each of whom shall come from the three State regions for institutional services (Eastern Region, Central Region, and Western Region). The terms of the appointees shall be staggered so that the term of one appointee expires every year.

(3) Three by the Speaker of the House of Representatives, one each of whom shall come from the three State regions for institutional services (Eastern Region, Central Region, and Western Region). The terms of the appointees shall be staggered so that the term of one appointee expires every year.

(4) Three by the Council of Community Programs, one each of whom shall come from the three State regions for institutional services (Eastern Region,

Central Region, and Western Region). The terms of the appointees shall be staggered so that the term of one appointee expires every year.

(5) Three by the North Carolina Association of County Commissioners, one each of whom shall come from the three State regions for institutional services (Eastern Region, Central Region, and Western Region). The terms of the appointees shall be staggered so that the term of one appointee expires every year.

(c) The State CFAC shall undertake all of the following:

(1) Review, comment on, and monitor the implementation of the State Plan for Mental Health, Developmental Disabilities, and Substance Abuse Services.

(2) Identify service gaps and underserved populations.

(3) Make recommendations regarding the service array and monitor the development of additional services.

(4) Review and comment on the State budget for mental health, developmental disabilities, and substance abuse services.

(5) Participate in all quality improvement measures and performance indicators.

(6) Receive the findings and recommendations by local CFACs regarding ways to improve the delivery of mental health, developmental disabilities, and substance abuse services.

(7) Provide technical assistance to local CFACs in implementing their duties.

(d) The Secretary shall provide sufficient staff to assist the State CFAC in implementing its duties under subsection (c) of this section. The assistance shall include data for the identification of service gaps and underserved populations, training to review and comment on the State Plan and departmental budget, procedures to allow participation in quality monitoring, and technical advice on rules of procedure and applicable laws.

(e) State CFAC members shall receive the per diem and allowances prescribed by G.S. 138-5 for State boards and commissions. (2006-142, s. 5; 2009-50, s. 1.)

§§ 122C-172 through 122C-180. Reserved for future codification purposes.

Part 5. State Facilities.

§ 122C-181. Secretary's jurisdiction over State facilities.

(a) Except as provided in subsection (b) of this section, the Secretary shall operate the following facilities:

(1) Psychiatric Hospitals:

a. Cherry Hospital.

a1. (Contingent effective date, see Editor's note) Central Regional Hospital.

b. (Contingent repeal date, see Editor's note) Dorothea Dix Hospital.

c. (Contingent repeal date, see Editor's note) John Umstead Hospital.

d. Broughton Hospital.

(2) Developmental Centers:

a. Caswell Developmental Center.

b. Repealed by Session Laws 2007-177, s. 1, effective July 5, 2007.

b1. J. Iverson Riddle Developmental Center.

c. Murdoch Developmental Center.

d. through e. Repealed by Session Laws 2007-177, s. 1, effective July 5, 2007.

(3) Alcohol and Drug Treatment Centers:

a. Walter B. Jones Alcohol and Drug Abuse Treatment Center.

b. Repealed by Session Laws 2007-177, s. 1, effective July 5, 2007.

c. Julian F. Keith Alcohol and Drug Abuse Treatment Center.

d. R.J. Blackley Alcohol and Drug Treatment Center.

(4) Neuro-Medical Treatment Centers:

a. through c. Repealed by Session Laws 2007-177, s. 1, effective July 5, 2007.

d. Black Mountain Neuro-Medical Treatment Center.

e. O'Berry Neuro-Medical Treatment Center.

f. Longleaf Neuro-Medical Treatment Center.

(5) Residential Programs for Children:

a. Whitaker School.

b. Wright School.

(b) Subject to the requirements of subsection (c) of this section, the Secretary may, with the approval of the Governor and Council of State, close any State facility.

(c) Closure of a State facility under subsection (b) of this section becomes effective on the earlier of the 31st legislative day or the day of adjournment of the next regular session of the General Assembly that begins at least 10 days after the date the closure is approved, unless a different effective date applies under this subsection. If a bill that specifically disapproves the State facility closure is introduced in either house of the General Assembly before the thirty-first legislative day of that session, the closure becomes effective on the earlier of either the day an unfavorable final action is taken on the bill or the day that session of the General Assembly adjourns without ratifying a bill that specifically disapproves the State facility closure. If the Secretary specifies a later effective date for closure than the date that would otherwise apply under this subsection, the later date applies. Closure of a State facility does not become effective if the closure is specifically disapproved by a bill enacted into law before it becomes effective. Notwithstanding any rule of either house of the General Assembly, any member of the General Assembly may introduce a bill during the first 30 legislative days of any regular session to disapprove closure of a facility that has been approved by the Governor and Council of State as provided in subsection (b) of this section. Nothing in this subsection shall be construed to impair the Secretary's power or duty otherwise imposed by law to close a State facility temporarily for the protection of health and safety. (Code, ss. 2227, 2240; 1899, c. 1, s. 1; Rev., s. 4542; C.S., s. 6151; 1945, c. 952, s. 8; 1947, c. 537, s. 2; 1949, c. 1206, s. 1; 1955, c. 887, s. 1; 1959, c. 348, s. 1; c. 1002, s. 1; c. 1008; c. 1028, ss. 1-4; 1961, c. 513; c. 1173, ss. 1, 2, 4; 1963, c. 1166, ss. 2, 10, 12; c. 1184, s. 6; 1967, c. 151; 1969, c. 982; 1973, c. 476, ss. 128, 133, 138; 1975, c. 19, s. 41; 1977, c. 679, s. 7; 1981, c. 51, s. 3; c. 77; c. 412, s. 4; 1983, c. 383, s. 9; 1985, c. 589, s. 2; 1989, c. 145, s. 1; 1991, c. 689, s. 136; 2001-437, s. 1.19; 2001-487, s. 80(a); 2007-177, ss. 1, 2.)

§ 122C-182. Authority to contract with area authorities.

To establish a coordinated system of services for its clients, a State facility shall contract with an area authority. Contracted services shall meet the rules of the Commission and the Secretary. (1985, c. 589, s. 2.)

§ 122C-183. Appointment of employees as police officers who may arrest without warrant.

The director of each State facility may appoint as special police officers the number of employees of their respective facilities they consider necessary. Within the grounds of the State facility the employees appointed as special police officers have all the powers of police officers of cities. They have the right to arrest without warrant individuals committing violations of the State law or the ordinances or rules of that facility in their presence and to bring the offenders before a magistrate who shall proceed as in other criminal cases. (1899, c. 1, s. 55; 1901, c. 627; Rev., s. 4569; C.S., s. 6181; 1921, c. 207; 1957, c. 1232, s. 12; 1959, c. 1002, s. 12; 1973, c. 108, s. 73; c. 673, s. 12.1; 1981, c. 635, s. 5; 1985, c. 589, s. 2.)

§ 122C-184. Oath of special police officers.

Before exercising the duties of a special police officer, the employees appointed under G.S. 122C-183 shall take an oath or affirmation of office before an officer empowered to administer oaths. The oath or affirmation shall be filed with the records of the Department. The oath or affirmation of office is:

State of North Carolina: _____County.

I, _____, do solemnly swear (or affirm) that I will well and truly execute the duties of office of special police officer in and for the State facility called_____, according to the best of my skill and ability and according to law; and that I will use my best endeavors to enforce all the ordinances of said facility, and to suppress nuisances, and to suppress and prevent disorderly conduct within these grounds. So help me, God.

Sworn and subscribed before me, this _____ day of_____, A.D. _____.

(1899, c. 1, s. 56; 1901, c. 627; Rev., s. 4570; C.S., s. 6182; 1963, c. 1166, s. 11; 1973, c. 108, s. 74; c. 476, s. 133; 1985, c. 589, s. 2.)

§ 122C-185. Application of funds belonging to State facilities.

(a) All moneys and proceeds of property donated to any State facility shall be deposited into the State treasury and accounted for in the appropriate fund as determined by the Secretary and approved by the Office of State Budget and Management. All moneys and proceeds of property donated in which there are special directions for their application and the interest earned on these funds shall be spent as the donor has directed and except as required for deposit with the State treasury, shall not be subject to the provisions of the State Budget Act except for capital improvements projects which shall be authorized and executed in accordance with G.S. 143C-8-8 and G.S. 143C-8-9.

(b) Proceeds from the transfer or sale of surplus, obsolete, or unused equipment of State facilities shall be deposited and accounted for in accordance with G.S. 143-49(4).

(c) The net proceeds from the sale, lease, rental, or other disposition of real estate owned by a State facility shall be deposited and accounted for in accordance with G.S. 146-30.

(d) All proceeds from the operation of vending facilities as defined in G.S. 111-42(d) and operated by State facilities shall be deposited and accounted for in accordance with the State Budget Act, Chapter 143C of the General Statutes.

(e) All other revenues and other receipts collected by a State facility shall be deposited to the credit of the State treasury in accordance with G.S. 147-77. (1899, c. 1, s. 34; Rev., s. 4552; C.S., s. 6167; 1963, c. 1166, s. 13; 1973, c. 476, s. 133; 1985, c. 589, s. 2; 2000-140, s. 93.1(a); 2001-424, s. 12.2(b); 2006-203, s. 68.)

§ 122C-186. General Assembly visitors of State facilities.

The members of the General Assembly are ex officio visitors of all State facilities, provided that the common law right of visitation of a State facility is abrogated to the extent that it does not include the right to access to confidential information. This right of access is only as granted by statute. (1963, c. 1184, s. 1; 1973, c. 476, s. 133; 1985, c. 589, s. 2.)

§§ 122C-187 through 122C-190. Reserved for future codification purposes.

Part 6. Quality Assurance.

§ 122C-191. Quality of services.

(a) The assurance that services provided are of the highest possible quality within available resources is an obligation of the area authority and the Secretary.

(b) Each area authority and State facility shall comply with the rules of the Commission regarding quality assurance activities, including: program evaluation; utilization and peer review; and staff qualifications, privileging, supervision, education, and training. These rules may not nullify compliance otherwise required by Chapter 126 of the General Statutes.

(c)   Each area authority and State facility shall develop internal processes to monitor and evaluate the level of quality obtained by all its programs and services including the activities prescribed in the rules of the Commission.

(d)   The Secretary shall develop rules for a review process to monitor area facilities and State facilities for compliance with the required quality assurance activities as well as other rules of the Commission and the Secretary. The rules may provide that the Secretary has the authority to determine whether applicable standards of practice have been met.

(e)   For purposes of peer review functions only:

(1)   A member of a duly appointed quality assurance committee who acts without malice or fraud shall not be subject to liability for damages in any civil action on account of any act, statement, or proceeding undertaken, made, or performed within the scope of the functions of the committee.

(2)   The proceedings of a quality assurance committee, the records and materials it produces, and the material it considers shall be confidential and not considered public records within the meaning of G.S. 132-1,
" 'Public records' defined," and shall not be subject to discovery or introduction into evidence in any civil action against a facility or a provider of professional health services that results from matters which are the subject of evaluation and review by the committee. No person who was in attendance at a meeting of the committee shall be required to testify in any civil action as to any evidence or other matters produced or presented during the proceedings of the committee or as to any findings, recommendations, evaluations, opinions, or other actions of the committee or its members. However, information, documents or records otherwise available are not immune from discovery or use in a civil action merely because they were presented during proceedings of the committee, and nothing herein shall prevent a provider of professional health services from using such otherwise available information, documents or records in connection with an administrative hearing or civil suit relating to the medical staff membership, clinical privileges or employment of the provider. Documents otherwise available as public records within the meaning of G.S. 132-1 do not lose their status as public records merely because they were presented or considered during proceedings of the committee. A member of the committee or a person who testifies before the committee may be subpoenaed and be

required to testify in a civil action as to events of which the person has knowledge independent of the peer review process, but cannot be asked about the person's testimony before the committee for impeachment or other purposes or about any opinions formed as a result of the committee hearings.

(3) Peer review information that is confidential and is not subject to discovery or use in civil actions under this section may be released to a professional standards review organization that contracts with an agency of this State or the federal government to perform any accreditation or certification function, including the Joint Commission on Accreditation of Healthcare Organizations. Information released under this subdivision shall be limited to that which is reasonably necessary and relevant to the standards review organization's determination to grant or continue accreditation or certification. Information released under this subdivision retains its confidentiality and is not subject to discovery or use in any civil actions as provided under this subsection, and the standards review organization shall keep the information confidential subject to this section. (1977, c. 568, s. 1; 1979, c. 358, s. 1; 1983, c. 383, s. 1; 1985, c. 589, s. 2; 1989 (Reg. Sess., 1990), c. 1053, s. 1; 1998-212, s. 12.35C(d); 1999-222, s. 1; 2004-149, s. 2.7.)

§ 122C-192. Review and protection of information.

(a) Notwithstanding G.S. 8-53, G.S. 8-53.3, or any other law relating to confidentiality of communications involving a patient or client, as needed to ensure quality assurance activities, the Secretary may review any writing or other record concerning the admission, discharge, medication, treatment, medical condition, or history of a client of an area authority or State facility. The Secretary may also review the personnel records of employees of an area authority or State facility.

(b) An area authority, State facility, its employees, and any other individual interviewed in the course of an inspection are immune from liability for damages resulting from disclosure of any information to the Secretary.

Except as required by law, it is unlawful for the Secretary or his representative to disclose:

(1) Any confidential or privileged information obtained under this section unless the client or his legally responsible person authorizes disclosure in writing; or

(2) The name of anyone who has furnished information concerning an area authority or State facility without that individual's consent.

Violation of this subsection is a Class 3 misdemeanor punishable only by a fine, not to exceed five hundred dollars ($500.00).

(c) The Secretary shall adopt rules to ensure that unauthorized disclosure does not occur.

(d) All confidential or privileged information obtained under this section and the names of individuals providing such information are not public records under Chapter 132 of the General Statutes. (1985, c. 589, s. 2; 1993, c. 539, s. 926; 1994, Ex. Sess., c. 24, s. 14(c).)

§ 122C-193. Reserved for future codification purposes.

Part 7. Contested Case Hearings for Eligible Assaultive and Violent Children.

§§ 122C-194 through 122C-200: Repealed by Session Laws 2000-67, s. 11.21(e).

Article 5.

Procedure for Admission and Discharge of Clients.

Part I. General Provisions.

§ 122C-201. Declaration of policy.

It is State policy to encourage voluntary admissions to facilities. It is further State policy that no individual shall be involuntarily committed to a 24-hour facility unless that individual is mentally ill or a substance abuser and dangerous to self or others. All admissions and commitments shall be accomplished under conditions that protect the dignity and constitutional rights of the individual.

It is further State policy that, except as provided in G.S. 122C-212(b), individuals who have been voluntarily admitted shall be discharged upon application and that involuntarily committed individuals shall be discharged as soon as a less restrictive mode of treatment is appropriate. (1973, c. 723, s. 1; c. 726, s. 1; c. 1084; c. 1408, s. 1; 1977, c. 400, s. 1; 1979, c. 915, ss. 2, 11; 1983, c. 638, s. 1; c. 864, s. 4; 1985, c. 589, s. 2; 1995 (Reg. Sess., 1996), c. 739, s. 2.)

§ 122C-202. Applicability of Article.

This Article applies to all facilities unless expressly provided otherwise. Specific provisions that are delineated by the disability of the client, whether mentally ill, mentally retarded, developmentally disabled, or substance abuser, also apply to all facilities for that client's disability. Provisions that refer to a specific facility or type of facility apply only to the designated facility or facilities. (1985, c. 589, s. 2; 1989, c. 625, s. 20.)

§ 122C-202.1. Hospital privileges.

Nothing in this Article related to admission, commitment, or treatment shall be deemed to mandate hospitals to grant or deny to any individuals privileges to practice in hospitals. (1985, c. 589, s. 2.)

§ 122C-203. Admission or commitment and incompetency proceedings to have no effect on one another.

The admission or commitment to a facility of an alleged mentally ill individual, an alleged substance abuser, or an alleged mentally retarded or developmentally disabled individual under the provisions of this Article shall in no way affect incompetency proceedings as set forth in Chapter 35A or former Chapters 33 or 35 of the General Statutes and incompetency proceedings under those Chapters shall have no effect upon admission or commitment proceedings under this Article. (1963, c. 1184, s. 1; 1985, c. 589, s. 2; 1989, c. 625, s. 21; 1989 (Reg. Sess., 1990), c. 1024, s. 26(b).)

§ 122C-204. Civil liability for corruptly attempting admission or commitment.

Nothing in this Article relieves from liability in any suit instituted in the courts of this State any individual who unlawfully, maliciously, and corruptly attempts to admit or commit any individual to any facility under this Article. (1963, c. 1184, s. 1; 1985, c. 589, s. 2.)

§ 122C-205. Return of clients to 24-hour facilities.

(a)   When a client of a 24-hour facility who:

(1)   Has been involuntarily committed;

(2)   Is being detained pending a judicial hearing;

(3)   Has been voluntarily admitted but is a minor or incompetent adult;

(4)   Has been placed on conditional release from the facility; or

(5)   Has been involuntarily committed or voluntarily admitted and is the subject of a detainer placed with the 24-hour facility by an appropriate official

escapes or breaches a condition of his release, if applicable, the responsible professional shall notify or cause to be notified immediately the appropriate law enforcement agency in the county of residence of the client, the appropriate law enforcement agency in the county where the facility is located, and the appropriate law enforcement agency in any county where there are reasonable grounds to believe that the client may be found. The responsible professional shall determine the amount of personal identifying and background information reasonably necessary to divulge to the law enforcement agency or agencies under the particular circumstances involved in order to assure the expeditious return of the client to the 24-hour facility involved and protect the general public.

(b)   When a competent adult who has been voluntarily admitted to a 24-hour facility escapes or breaches a condition of his release, the responsible professional, in the exercise of accepted professional judgment, practice, and standards, will determine if it is reasonably foreseeable that:

(1)   The client may cause physical harm to others or himself;

(2) The client may cause damage to property;

(3) The client may commit a felony or a violent misdemeanor; or

(4) That the health or safety of the client may be endangered

unless he is immediately returned to the facility. If the responsible professional finds that any or all of these occurrences are reasonably foreseeable, he will follow the same procedures as those set forth in subsection (a) of this section.

(c) Upon receipt of notice of an escape or breach of a condition of release as described in subsections (a) and (b) of this section, an appropriate law enforcement officer shall take the client into custody and have the client returned to the 24-hour facility from which the client has escaped or has been conditionally released. Transportation of the client back to the 24-hour facility shall be provided in the same manner as described in G.S. 122C-251 and G.S. 122C-408(b). Law enforcement agencies who are notified of a client's escape or breach of conditional release shall be notified of the client's return by the responsible 24-hour facility. Under the circumstances described in this section, the initial notification by the 24-hour facility of the client's escape or breach of conditional release shall be given by telephone communication to the appropriate law enforcement agency or agencies and, if available and appropriate, by Division of Criminal Information (DCI) message to any law enforcement agency in or out of state and by entry into the National Crime Information Center (NCIC) telecommunications system. As soon as reasonably possible following notification, written authorization to take the client into custody shall also be issued by the 24-hour facility. Under this section, law enforcement officers shall have the authority to take a client into custody upon receipt of the telephone notification or Division of Criminal Information message prior to receiving written authorization. The notification of a law enforcement agency does not, in and of itself, render this information public information within the purview of Chapter 132 of the General Statutes. However, the responsible law enforcement agency shall determine the extent of disclosure of personal identifying and background information reasonably necessary, under the circumstances, in order to assure the expeditious return of a client to the 24-hour facility involved and to protect the general public and is authorized to make such disclosure. The responsible law enforcement agency may also place any appropriate message or entry into either the Division of Criminal Information System or National Crime Information System, or both, as appropriate.

(d) In the situations described in subsections (a) and (b) of this section, the responsible professional shall also notify or cause to be notified as soon as practicable:

(1) The next of kin of the client or legally responsible person for the client;

(2) The clerk of superior court of the county of commitment of the client;

(3) The area authority of the county of residence of the client, if appropriate;

(4) The physician or eligible psychologist who performed the first examination for a commitment of the client, if appropriate; and

(5) Any official who has placed a detainer on a client as described in subdivision (a)(5) of this section

of the escape or breach of condition of the client's release upon occurrence of either action and of his subsequent return to the facility. (1899, c. 1, s. 27; Rev., s. 4563; C.S., s. 6175; 1927, c. 114; 1945, c. 952, s. 12; 1953, c. 256, s. 1; 1955, c. 887, s. 3; 1973, c. 673, s. 11; 1983, c. 548; 1985, c. 589, s. 2; c. 695, s. 2; 1985 (Reg. Sess., 1986), c. 863, ss. 12-14; 1987, c. 749, s. 1.)

§ 122C-205.1. Discharge of clients who escape or breach the condition of release.

(a) As described in G.S. 122C-205(a), when a client of a 24-hour facility escapes or breaches the condition of his release and does not return to the facility, the facility shall:

(1) If the client was admitted under Part 2 of this Article or under Parts 3 or 4 of this Article to a nonrestrictive facility, discharge the client based on the professional judgment of the responsible professional;

(2) If the client was admitted under Part 3 or Part 4 of this Article to a restrictive facility, discharge the client when the period for continued treatment, as specified by the court, expires;

(3) If the client was admitted pending a district court hearing under Part 7 of this Article, request that the court consider dismissal or continuance of the case at the initial district court hearing; or

(4) If the client was committed under Part 7 of this Article, discharge the client when the commitment expires.

(b) As described in G.S. 122C-205(a), when a client of a 24-hour facility who was admitted under Part 8 of this Article escapes or breaches the conditions of his release and does not return to the facility, the facility may discharge the client from the facility based on the professional judgment of the responsible professional and following consultation with the appropriate area authority or physician.

(c) Upon discharge of the client, the 24-hour facility shall notify all the persons directed to be notified of the client's escape or breach of conditional release under 122C-205(a), (b) and (d) that the client has been discharged.

(d) If the client is returned to the 24-hour facility subsequent to discharge from the facility, applicable admission or commitment procedures shall be followed, when appropriate. (1987, c. 674, s. 1.)

§ 122C-206. Transfers of clients between 24-hour facilities.

(a) Before transferring a voluntary adult client from one 24-hour facility to another, the responsible professional at the original facility shall: (i) get authorization from the receiving facility that the facility will admit the client; (ii) get consent from the client; and (iii) if consent to share information is granted by the client, notify the next of kin of the time and location of the transfer. The preceding requirements of this paragraph may be waived if the client has been admitted under emergency procedures to a State facility not serving the client's region of the State. Following an emergency admission, the client may be transferred to the appropriate State facility without consent according to the rules of the Commission.

(b) Before transferring a respondent held for a district court hearing or a committed respondent from one 24-hour facility to another, the responsible professional at the original facility shall:

(1) Obtain authorization from the receiving facility that the facility will admit the respondent; and

(2) Provide reasonable notice to the respondent, or legally responsible person, of the reason for the transfer and document the notice in the client's record.

No later that 24 hours after the transfer, the responsible professional at the original facility shall notify the petitioner, the clerk of court, and, if consent is granted by the respondent, the next of kin, that the transfer is completed. If the transfer is completed before the judicial commitment hearing, these proceedings shall be initiated by the receiving facility.

(c) Minors and incompetent adults, admitted pursuant to Parts 3 and 4 of this Article, may be transferred from one 24-hour facility to another following the same procedures specified in subsection (b) of this section. In addition, the legally responsible person shall be consulted before the proposed transfer. If the transfer is completed before the judicial determination required in G.S. 122C-223 or G.S. 122C-232, these proceedings shall be initiated by the receiving facility.

(c1) If a client described in subsections (b) or (c) of this section is to be transferred from one 24-hour facility to another and transportation is needed, the responsible professional at the original facility shall notify the clerk of court or magistrate, and the clerk of court or magistrate shall issue a custody order for transportation of the client as provided by G.S. 122C-251.

(d) Minors and incompetent adults, admitted pursuant to Part 5 of this Article, may be transferred from one 24-hour facility to another provided that prior to transfer the responsible professional at the original facility shall:

(1) Obtain authorization from the receiving facility that the facility will admit the client; and

(2) Provide reasonable notice to the client regarding the reason for transfer and document the notice in the client's record; and

(3) Provide reasonable notice to and consult with the legally responsible person regarding the reason for the transfer and document the notice and consultation in the client's record.

No later than 24 hours after the transfer, the responsible professional at the original facility shall notify the legally responsible person that the transfer is completed.

(e) The responsible professional may transfer a client from one facility to another for emergency medical treatment, emergency medical evaluation, or emergency surgery without notice to or consent from the client. Within a reasonable period of time the responsible professional shall notify the next of kin or the legally responsible person of the client of the transfer.

(f) When a client is transferred to another facility solely for medical reasons, the client shall be returned to the original facility when the medical care is completed unless the responsible professionals at both facilities concur that discharge of the client who is not subject to G.S. 122C-266(b) is appropriate.

(g) The Commission may adopt rules to implement this section. (1919, c. 330; C.S., S. 6163; 1925, c. 51, s. 1; 1945, c. 925, s. 5; 1947, c. 537, s. 9; c. 623, s. 1; 1953, c. 675, s. 15; 1955, c. 1274, s. 1; 1959, c. 1002, s. 11; 1963, c. 1166, ss. 10, 12; 1973, c. 475, s. 1; c. 476, s. 133; c. 673, ss. 7, 8; c. 1436, ss. 6, 7; 1977, c. 679, s. 7; 1981, c. 51, s. 3; c. 328, ss. 1, 2; 1985, c. 589, s. 2; 1985 (Reg. Sess., 1986), c. 863, s. 15; 1991, c. 704, s. 1.)

§ 122C-207. Confidentiality.

Court records made in all proceedings pursuant to this Article are confidential, and are not open to the general public except as provided for by G. S. 122C-54(d). (1977, c. 696, s. 1; 1979, c. 164, s. 2; c. 915, s. 20; 1985, c. 589, s. 2.)

§ 122C-208. Voluntary admission not admissible in involuntary proceeding.

Except when considering treatment history as it pertains to an involuntary outpatient commitment, the fact that an individual has been voluntarily admitted for treatment shall not be competent evidence in an involuntary commitment proceeding. (1985, c. 589, s. 2.)

§ 122C-209. Voluntary admissions acceptance.

Nothing contained in Parts 2 through 5 of this Article requires a private physician or private facility to accept an individual as a client for examination or treatment. Examination or treatment at a private facility or by a private physician is at the expense of the individual to the extent that charges are not disposed of by contract between the area authority and private facility. (1985, c. 589, s. 2.)

§ 122C-210. Guardian to pay expenses out of estate.

It is the duty of the guardian who has legal custody of the estate of an incompetent individual held pursuant to the provisions of this Article in a facility to supply funds for his support in the facility during the stay as long as there are sufficient funds for that purpose over and beyond maintaining and supporting those individuals who may be legally dependent on the estate. (1985, c. 589, s. 2.)

§ 122C-210.1. Immunity from liability.

No facility or any of its officials, staff, or employees, or any physician or other individual who is responsible for the custody, examination, management, supervision, treatment, or release of a client and who follows accepted professional judgment, practice, and standards is civilly liable, personally or otherwise, for actions arising from these responsibilities or for actions of the client. This immunity is in addition to any other legal immunity from liability to which these facilities or individuals may be entitled and applies to actions performed in connection with, or arising out of, the admission or commitment of any individual pursuant to this Article. (1899, c. 1, s. 31; Rev., s. 4560; C.S., s. 6172; 1961, c. 511, s. 1; 1973, c. 673, s. 10; 1983, c. 638, s. 15; c. 864, s. 4; 1985, c. 589, s. 2; 1995 (Reg. Sess., 1996), c. 739, s. 3.)

§ 122C-210.2. Research at State facilities for the mentally ill.

(a) For research purposes, State facilities for the mentally ill may be designated by the Secretary as facilities for the voluntary admission of adults who are not admissible as clients otherwise. Designation of these facilities shall be made in accordance with rules of the Secretary that assure the protection of those admitted for research purposes.

(b) Individuals may be admitted to such designated facilities on either an outpatient or inpatient basis.

(c) The Human Rights Committee of the designated facility shall monitor the care of individuals admitted for research during their participation in any research program.

(d) For these individuals admitted to such designated facilities for research purposes only, the following provisions shall apply:

(1) A written application for admission pursuant to G.S. 122C-211(a) and an examination by a physician within 24 hours of admission shall be provided to each of these individuals;

(2) They shall be exempt from the provisions of G.S. 122C-57(a) governing the rights to treatment and to a treatment plan; the requirements of G.S. 122C-61(2) and G.S. 122C-212(b); and the requirements of any single portal of entry and exit plan; however, nothing in this section shall take away the individual's right to be informed of the potential risks and alleged benefits of their participation in any research program;

(3) The Secretary shall exempt these individuals from the provisions of Article 7 of Chapter 143 of the General Statutes requiring payment for treatment in a State institution. The Secretary may also authorize reasonable compensation to be paid to individuals participating in research projects for their services; provided, that the compensation is paid from research grant funds; and

(4) The Commission shall adopt rules regarding the admission, care and discharge of those individuals admitted for research purposes only. (1987, c. 358, s. 1.)

Part 2. Voluntary Admissions and Discharges, Competent Adults, Facilities for the Mentally Ill and Substance Abusers.

§ 122C-211. Admissions.

(a) Except as provided in subsections (b) through (f1) of this section, any individual, including a parent in a family unit, in need of treatment for mental illness or substance abuse may seek voluntary admission at any facility by presenting himself for evaluation to the facility. No physician's statement is necessary, but a written application for evaluation or admission, signed by the individual seeking admission, is required. The application form shall be available at all times at all facilities. However, no one shall be denied admission because application forms are not available. An evaluation shall determine whether the individual is in need of care, treatment, habilitation or rehabilitation for mental illness or substance abuse or further evaluation by the facility. Information provided by family members regarding the individual's need for treatment shall be reviewed in the evaluation. An individual may not be accepted as a client if the facility determines that the individual does not need or cannot benefit from the care, treatment, habilitation, or rehabilitation available and that the individual is not in need of further evaluation by the facility. The facility shall give to an individual who is denied admission a referral to another facility or facilities that may be able to provide the treatment needed by the client.

(b) In 24-hour facilities the application shall acknowledge that the applicant may be held by the facility for a period of 72 hours after any written request for release that the applicant may make, and shall acknowledge that the 24-hour facility may have the legal right to petition for involuntary commitment of the applicant during that period. At the time of application, the facility shall tell the applicant about procedures for discharge.

(c) Any individual who voluntarily seeks admission to a 24-hour facility in which medical care is an integral component of the treatment shall be examined and evaluated by a physician of the facility within 24 hours of admission. The evaluation shall determine whether the individual is in need of treatment for mental illness or substance abuse or further evaluation by the facility. If the evaluating physician determines that the individual will not benefit from the treatment available, the individual shall not be accepted as a client.

(d) Any individual who voluntarily seeks admission to any 24-hour facility, other than one in which medical care is an integral component of the treatment, shall have a medical examination within 30 days before or after admission if it is reasonably expected that the individual will receive treatment for more than 30 days or shall produce a current, valid physical examination report, signed by a physician, completed within 12 months prior to the current admission. When applicable, this examination may be included in an examination conducted to meet the requirements of G.S. 122C-223 or G.S. 122C-232.

(e) When an individual from a single portal area seeks admission to an area or State 24-hour facility, the admission shall follow the procedures as prescribed in the area plan. When an individual from a single portal area presents himself for admission to the facility directly and is in need of an emergency admission, the individual may be accepted for admission. The facility shall notify the area authority within 24 hours of the admission. Further planning of treatment for the client is the joint responsibility of the area authority and the facility as prescribed in the area plan.

(f) A family unit may voluntarily seek admission to a 24-hour substance abuse facility that is able to provide, directly or by contract, treatment, habilitation, or rehabilitation services that will specifically address the family unit's needs. These services shall include gender-specific substance abuse treatment, habilitation, or rehabilitation for the parent as well as assessment, well-child care, and, as needed, early intervention services for the child. A family unit that voluntarily seeks admission to a 24-hour substance abuse facility shall be evaluated by the facility to determine whether the family unit would benefit from the services of the facility. A facility shall not accept a family unit as a client if the facility determines that the family unit does not need or cannot benefit from the care, habilitation, or rehabilitation available at the facility. The facility shall give to a family unit that is denied admission a referral to another facility or facilities that may be able to provide treatment needed by the family unit. Except as otherwise provided, this section applies to a parent in a family unit seeking admission under this section.

(f1) An individual in need of treatment for mental illness may be admitted to a facility pursuant to an advance instruction for mental health treatment or pursuant to the authority of a health care agent named in a valid health care power of attorney, provided that the individual is incapable, as defined in G.S. 122C-72(4) at the time of the need for admission. An individual admitted to a facility pursuant to an advance instruction for mental health treatment may not be retained for more than 10 days, except as provided for in subsection (b) of this section. When a health care power of attorney authorizes a health care agent to seek the admission of an incapable individual, the health care agent shall act for the individual in applying for admission to a facility and in consenting to medical treatment at the facility when consent is required, provided that the individual is incapable.

(g) As used in this Part, the term "family unit" means a parent and the parent's dependent children under the age of three years. (1945, c. 952, s. 471½; 1963, c. 1184, s. 22; 1973, c. 723, s. 1; c. 1084; 1983, c. 383, s. 4; 1985, c. 589, s. 2; 1985 (Reg. Sess., 1986), c. 863, s. 16; 1989, c. 287; 1998-47, s. 1(a); 1998-198, s. 6; 1998-217, s. 53(a)(1), (2); 1999-456, s. 5.)

§ 122C-212. Discharges.

(a) Except as provided in subsections (b) and (c) of this section, an individual who has been voluntarily admitted to a facility shall be discharged upon his own request. A request for discharge from a 24-hour facility shall be in writing.

(b) An individual who has been voluntarily admitted to a 24-hour facility may be held for 72 hours after his written application for discharge is submitted.

(c) When an individual from a single portal area who has been voluntarily admitted to an area or State 24-hour facility is discharged, the discharge shall follow the procedures as prescribed in the area plan. (1973, c. 723, s. 1; c. 1084; 1983, c. 383, s. 4; 1985, c. 589, s. 2.)

§§ 122C-213 through 122C-220. Reserved for future codification purposes.

Part 3. Voluntary Admissions and Discharges, Minors, Facilities for the Mentally Ill and Substance Abusers.

§ 122C-221. Admissions.

(a) Except as otherwise provided in this Part, a minor may be admitted to a facility if the minor is mentally ill or a substance abuser and in need of treatment. Except as otherwise provided in this Part, the provisions of G.S. 122C-211 shall apply to admissions of minors under this Part. Except as provided in G.S. 90-21.5, in applying for admission to a facility, in consenting to medical treatment when consent is required, and in any other legal procedure under this Article, the legally responsible person shall act for the minor. If a minor reaches the age of 18 while in treatment under this Part, further treatment is authorized only on the written authorization of the client or under the provisions of Part 7 or Part 8 of Article 5 of this Chapter.

(b)   The Commission shall adopt rules governing procedures for admission to 24-hour facilities not falling within the category of facilities where freedom of movement is restricted. These rules shall be designed to ensure that no minor is improperly admitted to or improperly remains in a 24-hour facility. (1973, c. 1084; 1983, c. 302, s. 1; 1985, c. 589, s. 2; 1987, c. 370, s. l.)

§ 122C-222. Admissions to State facilities.

Admission of a minor who is a resident of a county that is not in a single portal area shall be made to a State facility following screening and upon referral by an area authority, a physician, or an eligible psychologist. Further planning of treatment and discharge for the minor is the joint responsibility of the State facility and the person making the referral. (1987, c. 370, s. 1.)

§ 122C-223. Emergency admission to a 24-hour facility.

(a)   In an emergency situation, when the legally responsible person does not appear with the minor to apply for admission, a minor who is mentally ill or a substance abuser and in need of treatment may be admitted to a 24-hour facility upon his own written application. The application shall serve as the initiating document for the hearing required by G.S. 122C-224.

(b)   Within 24 hours of admission, the facility shall notify the legally responsible person of the admission unless notification is impossible due to an inability to identify, to locate, or to contact him after all reasonable means to establish contact have been attempted.

(c)   If the legally responsible person cannot be located within 72 hours of admission, the responsible professional shall initiate proceedings for juvenile protective services as described in Article 3 of Chapter 7B of the General Statutes in either the minor's county of residence or in the county in which the facility is located.

(d) Within 24 hours of an emergency admission to a State facility, the State facility shall notify the area authority and, as appropriate, the minor's physician or eligible psychologist. Further planning of treatment and discharge for the minor is the joint responsibility of the State facility and the appropriate person in the community. (1973, c. 1084; 1983, c. 302, s. 1; 1985, c. 589, s. 2; 1987, c. 370, s. 1; 1998-202, s. 13(ff).)

§ 122C-224. Judicial review of voluntary admission.

(a) When a minor is admitted to a 24-hour facility where the minor will be subjected to the same restrictions on his freedom of movement present in the State facilities for the mentally ill, or to similar restrictions, a hearing shall be held by the district court in the county in which the 24-hour facility is located within 15 days of the day that the minor is admitted to the facility. A continuance of not more than five days may be granted.

(b) Before the admission, the facility shall provide the minor and his legally responsible person with written information describing the procedures for court review of the admission and informing them about the discharge procedures. They shall also be informed that, after a written request for discharge, the facility may hold the minor for 72 hours during which time the facility may apply for a petition for involuntary commitment.

(c) Within 24 hours after admission, the facility shall notify the clerk of court in the county where the facility is located that the minor has been admitted and that a hearing for concurrence in the admission must be scheduled. At the time notice is given to schedule a hearing, the facility shall notify the clerk of the names and addresses of the legally responsible person and the responsible professional. (1975, c. 839; 1977, c. 756; 1979, c. 171, s. 1; 1983, c. 889, ss. 1, 2; 1985, c. 589, s. 2; 1987, c. 370, s. 1.)

§ 122C-224.1. Duties of clerk of court.

(a) Within 48 hours of receipt of notice that a minor has been admitted to a 24-hour facility wherein his freedom of movement will be restricted, an attorney shall be appointed for the minor in accordance with rules adopted by the Office of Indigent Defense Services. When a minor has been admitted to a State facility for the mentally ill, the attorney appointed shall be the attorney employed in accordance with G.S. 122C-270(a) through (c). All minors shall be conclusively presumed to be indigent, and it shall not be necessary for the court to receive from any minor an affidavit of indigency. The attorney shall be paid a reasonable fee in accordance with rules adopted by the Office of Indigent Defense Services. The judge may require payment of the attorney's fee from a person other than the minor as provided in G.S. 7A-450.1 through G.S. 7A-450.4.

(b) Upon receipt of notice that a minor has been admitted to a 24-hour facility wherein his freedom of movement will be restricted, the clerk shall calendar a hearing to be held within 15 days of admission for the purpose of review of the minor's admission. Notice of the time and place of the hearing shall be given as provided in G.S. 1A-1, Rule 4(j) to the attorney in lieu of the minor, as soon as possible but not later than 72 hours before the scheduled hearing. Notice of the hearing shall be sent to the legally responsible person and the responsible professional as soon as possible but not later than 72 hours before the hearing by first-class mail postage prepaid to the individual's last known address.

(c) The clerk shall schedule all hearings and rehearings and send all notices as required by this Part. (1987, c. 370, s. 1; 2000-144, s. 37.)

§ 122C-224.2. Duties of the attorney for the minor.

(a) The attorney shall meet with the minor within 10 days of his appointment but not later than 48 hours before the hearing. In addition, the attorney shall inform the minor of the scheduled hearing and shall give the minor a copy of the notice of the time and place of the hearing no later than 48 hours before the hearing.

(b) The attorney shall counsel the minor concerning the hearing procedure and the potential effects of the hearing proceeding on the minor. If the minor does not wish to appear, the attorney shall file a motion with the court before the scheduled hearing to waive the minor's right to be present at the hearing procedure except during the minor's own testimony. If the attorney determines that the minor does not wish to appear before the judge to provide his own testimony, the attorney shall file a separate motion with the court before the hearing to waive the minor's right to testify.

(c) In all actions on behalf of the minor, the attorney shall represent the minor until formally relieved of the responsibility by the judge. (1987, c. 370, s. 1.)

§ 122C-224.3. Hearing for review of admission.

(a) Hearings shall be held at the 24-hour facility in which the minor is being treated, if it is located within the judge's district court district as defined in G.S. 7A-133, unless the judge determines that the court calendar will be disrupted by such scheduling. In cases where the hearing cannot be held in the 24-hour facility, the judge may schedule the hearing in another location, including the judge's chambers. The hearing may not be held in a regular courtroom, over objection of the minor's attorney, if in the discretion of the judge a more suitable place is available.

(b) The minor shall have the right to be present at the hearing unless the judge rules favorably on the motion of the attorney to waive the minor's appearance. However, the minor shall retain the right to appear before the judge to provide his own testimony and to respond to the judge's questions unless the judge makes a separate finding that the minor does not wish to appear upon motion of the attorney.

(c) Certified copies of reports and findings of physicians, psychologists and other responsible professionals as well as previous and current medical records are admissible in evidence, but the minor's right, through his attorney, to confront and cross-examine witnesses may not be denied.

(d) Hearings shall be closed to the public unless the attorney requests otherwise.

(e) A copy of all documents admitted into evidence and a transcript of the proceedings shall be furnished to the attorney, on request, by the clerk upon the direction of a district court judge. The copies shall be provided at State expense.

(f) For an admission to be authorized beyond the hearing, the minor must be (1) mentally ill or a substance abuser and (2) in need of further treatment at the 24-hour facility to which he has been admitted. Further treatment at the admitting facility should be undertaken only when lesser measures will be insufficient. It is not necessary that the judge make a finding of dangerousness in order to support a concurrence in the admission.

(g) The court shall make one of the following dispositions:

(1) If the court finds by clear, cogent, and convincing evidence that the requirements of subsection (f) have been met, the court shall concur with the voluntary admission and set the length of the authorized admission of the minor for a period not to exceed 90 days; or

(2) If the court determines that there exist reasonable grounds to believe that the requirements of subsection (f) have been met but that additional diagnosis and evaluation is needed before the court can concur in the admission, the court may make a one time authorization of up to an additional 15 days of stay, during which time further diagnosis and evaluation shall be conducted; or

(3) If the court determines that the conditions for concurrence or continued diagnosis and evaluation have not been met, the judge shall order that the minor be released.

(h) The decision of the District Court in all hearings and rehearings is final. Appeal may be had to the Court of Appeals by the State or by any party on the record as in civil cases. The minor may be retained and treated in accordance with this Part, pending the outcome of the appeal, unless otherwise ordered by the District Court or the Court of Appeals. (1987, c. 370; 1987 (Reg. Sess., 1988), c. 1037, s. 113.)

§ 122C-224.4. Rehearings.

(a) A minor admitted to a 24-hour facility upon order of the court for further diagnosis and evaluation shall have the right to a rehearing if the responsible professional determines that the minor is in need of further treatment beyond the time authorized by the court for diagnosis and evaluation.

(b) A minor admitted to a 24-hour facility upon the concurrence of the court shall have the right to a rehearing for further concurrence in continued treatment before the end of the period authorized by the court. The court shall review the continued admission in accordance with the hearing procedures in this Part. The court may order discharge of the minor if the minor no longer meets the criteria for admission. If the minor continues to meet the criteria for admission the court shall concur with the continued admission of the minor and set the length of the authorized admission for a period not to exceed 180 days. Subsequent rehearings shall be scheduled at the end of each subsequent authorized treatment period, but no longer than every 180 days.

(c) The responsible professional shall notify the clerk, no later than 15 days before the end of the authorized admission, that continued stay beyond the authorized admission is recommended for the minor. The clerk shall calendar the rehearing to be held before the end of the current authorized admission. (1987, c. 370, s. 1.)

§ 122C-224.5. Transportation.

When it is necessary for a minor to be transported to a location other than the treating facility for the purpose of a hearing, transportation shall be provided under the provisions of G.S. 122C-251. However, the 24-hour facility may obtain permission from the court to routinely provide transportation of minors to and from hearings. (1987, c. 370, s. 1.)

§ 122C-224.6. Treatment pending hearing and after authorization for or concurrence in admission.

(a) Pending the initial hearing and after authorization for further diagnosis and evaluation, or concurrence in admission, the responsible professional may administer to the minor reasonable and appropriate medication and treatment that is consistent with accepted medical standards and consistent with Article 3 of this Chapter.

(b) The responsible professional may release the minor conditionally for periods not in excess of 30 days on specified appropriate conditions. Violation of the conditions is grounds for return of the minor to the 24-hour facility. A law enforcement officer, on request of the responsible professional, shall take the minor into custody and return him to the facility in accordance with G.S. 122C-205. (1987, c. 370, s. 1.)

§ 122C-224.7. Discharge.

(a) The responsible professional shall unconditionally discharge a minor from treatment at any time that it is determined that the minor is no longer mentally ill or a substance abuser, or no longer in need of treatment at the facility.

(b) The legally responsible person may file a written request for discharge from the facility at any time. The facility may hold the minor in the facility for 72 hours after receipt of the request for discharge. If the responsible professional believes that the minor is mentally ill and dangerous to himself or others, he may file a petition for involuntary commitment under the provisions of Part 7 of this Article. If the responsible professional believes that the minor is a substance abuser and dangerous to himself or others, he may file a petition for involuntary commitment under the provisions of Part 8 of this Article. If an order authorizing the holding of the minor under involuntary commitment procedures is issued, further treatment and holding shall follow the provisions of Part 7 or Part 8 whichever is applicable. If an order authorizing the holding of the minor under involuntary commitment procedures is not issued, the minor shall be discharged.

(c) If a client reaches age 18 while in treatment, and the client refuses to sign an authorization for continued treatment within 72 hours of reaching 18, he shall be discharged unless the responsible professional obtains an order to hold the client under the provisions of Part 7 or Part 8 of this Article pursuant to an involuntary commitment. (1975, c. 839; 1977, c. 756; 1979, c. 171, s. 1; 1983, c. 889, ss. 1, 2; 1985, c. 589, s. 2; 1987, c. 370, s. 1.)

§§ 122C-225 through 122C-230. Reserved for future codification purposes.

Part 4. Voluntary Admissions and Discharges, Incompetent Adults, Facilities for the Mentally Ill and Substance Abusers.

§ 122C-231. Admissions.

Except as otherwise provided in this Part an incompetent adult may be admitted to a facility when the individual is mentally ill or a substance abuser and in need of treatment. The provisions of G.S. 122C-211 shall apply to admissions of an incompetent adult under this Part except that the legally responsible person shall act for the individual, in applying for admission to a facility, in consenting to medical treatment when consent is required, in giving or receiving any legal notice, and in any other legal procedure under this Article. (1973, c. 1084; 1983, c. 302, s. 1; 1985, c. 589, s. 2.)

§ 122C-232. Judicial determination.

(a) When an incompetent adult is admitted to a 24-hour facility where the incompetent adult will be subjected to the same restrictions on his freedom of movement present in the State facilities for the mentally ill, or to similar restrictions, a hearing shall be held in the district court in the county in which the 24-hour facility is located within 10 days of the day that the incompetent adult is admitted to the facility. A continuance of not more than five days may be granted upon motion of:

(1) The court;

(2) Respondent's counsel; or

(3) The responsible professional.

The Commission shall adopt rules governing procedures for admission to other 24-hour facilities not falling within the category of facilities where freedom of movement is restricted; these rules shall be designed to ensure that no incompetent adult is improperly admitted to or remains in a facility.

(b) In any case requiring the hearing described in subsection (a) of this section, no petition is necessary; the written application for voluntary admission shall serve as the initiating document for the hearing. The court shall determine whether the incompetent adult is mentally ill or a substance abuser and is in need of further treatment at the facility. Further treatment at the facility should be undertaken only when lesser measures will be insufficient. If the court finds by clear, cogent, and convincing evidence that these requirements have been met, the court shall concur with the voluntary admission of the incompetent adult. If the court finds that these requirements have not been met, it shall order that the incompetent adult be released. A finding of dangerousness to self or others is not necessary to support the determination that further treatment should be undertaken.

(c)   Unless otherwise provided in this Part, the hearing specified in subsection (a) of this section, including the provisions for representation of indigent incompetent adults, all subsequent proceedings, and conditional release are governed by the involuntary commitment procedures of Part 7 of this Article.

(d)   In addition to the notice of hearings and rehearings to the incompetent adult and his counsel required under Part 7 of this Article, notice shall be given by the clerk to the legally responsible person, or his successor. The legally responsible person, or his successor may also file with the clerk of court a written waiver of his right to receive notice. (1975, c. 839; 1977, c. 756; 1979, c. 171, s. 1; 1983, c. 889, ss. 1, 2; 1985, c. 589, s. 2.)

§ 122C-233. Discharges.

(a)   Except as provided in subsection (b) of this section, an incompetent adult shall be discharged upon the request of the legally responsible person as provided in G.S. 122C-212.

(b)   After the court has concurred in the admission of an incompetent adult to a 24-hour facility as provided in G.S. 122C-232, only the facility or the court may release the incompetent adult at any time when either determines that the incompetent adult does not need further treatment at the facility. If the legally responsible person believes that release is in the best interest of the incompetent adult, and the facility refuses release, the legally responsible person may apply to the court for a hearing for discharge. (1975, c. 839; 1977, c. 756; 1979, c. 171, s. 1; 1983, c. 889, ss. 1, 2; 1985, c. 589, s. 2.)

§§ 122C-234 through 122C-240: Reserved for future codification purposes.

Part 5. Voluntary Admissions and Discharges, Minors and Adults, Facilities for Individuals with Developmental Disabilities.

§ 122C-241. Admissions.

(a) Except as provided in subsection (c) of this section an individual with developmental disabilities may be admitted to a facility for the developmentally disabled in order that he receive care, habilitation, rehabilitation, training, or treatment. Application for admission is made as follows:

(1) A minor with developmental disabilities may be admitted upon application by both the father and the mother if they are living together and, if not, by the parent or parents having custody or by the legally responsible person.

(2) An adult with developmental disabilities who has been adjudicated incompetent under Chapter 35A or former Chapters 33 or 35 of the General Statutes may be admitted upon application by his guardian.

(3) An adult with developmental disabilities who has not been adjudicated incompetent under Chapter 35A or former Chapters 33 or 35 of the General Statutes may be admitted upon his own application.

(b) Prior to admission to a 24-hour facility, the individual shall be examined and evaluated by a physician or psychologist to determine whether the individual is developmentally disabled. In addition, the individual shall be examined and evaluated by a qualified developmental disabilities professional no sooner than 31 days prior to admission or within 72 hours after admission to determine whether the individual is in need of care, habilitation, rehabilitation, training or treatment by the facility. If the evaluating professional determines that the individual will not benefit from an admission, the individual shall not be admitted as a client.

(c) An admission to an area or State 24-hour facility of an individual from a single portal area shall follow the procedures as prescribed in the area plan. When an individual from a single portal area presents himself or is presented for admission to a State facility for the mentally retarded directly and is in need of an emergency admission, he may be accepted for admission. The State facility shall notify the area authority within 24 hours of the admission and further planning of treatment for the individual is the joint responsibility of the area authority and the State facility as prescribed in the area plan. (1963, c. 1184, s. 6; 1965, c. 800, s. 12; 1973, c. 476, s. 133; 1977, c. 679, s. 7; 1981, c. 51, s. 3; 1983, c. 383, s. 7; 1985, c. 589, s. 2; c. 695, s. 14; 1989, c. 625, s. 22; 1989 (Reg. Sess., 1990), c. 1024, s. 26(d).)

§ 122C-242. Discharges.

(a) Except as provided in subsections (b) through (d) of this section, discharges from facilities for individuals with developmental disabilities are made upon request of the individual authorized in G.S. 122C-241(a) to make application for admission or by the director of the facility.

(b) Any adult who has not been declared incompetent and who is admitted to a 24-hour facility shall be discharged upon his own request, unless the director of the facility has reason to believe that the adult is endangering himself by the discharge. In this case the individual may be held for a period not to exceed five days while the director petitions for the adjudication of incompetency of the individual and the appointment of an interim guardian under Chapter 35A of the General Statutes.

(c) Any individual admitted to a 24-hour facility may be discharged when in the judgment of the director of the facility the individual is no longer in need of care, treatment, habilitation or rehabilitation by the facility or the individual will no longer benefit from the service available. In the case of an area or State facility rules adopted by the Commission or by the Secretary in accordance with G.S. 122C-63 shall be followed.

(d) When the individual to be discharged from an area or State 24-hour facility is a resident of a single portal area, the discharge shall follow the procedures described in the area plan. (1963, c. 1184, s. 6; 1973, c. 476, s. 133; 1983, c. 383, s. 8; 1985, c. 589, s. 2; 1989, c. 625, s.22; 1989 (Reg. Sess., 1990), c. 1024, s. 26(c).)

§§ 122C-243 through 122C-250. Reserved for future codification purposes.

Part 6. Involuntary Commitment - General Provisions.

§ 122C-251. Transportation.

(a) Except as provided in subsections (f) and (g), transportation of a respondent within a county under the involuntary commitment proceedings of this Article, including admission and discharge, shall be provided by the city or county. The city has the duty to provide transportation of a respondent who is a resident of the city or who is taken into custody in the city limits. The county has the duty to provide transportation for a respondent who resides in the county outside city limits or who is taken into custody outside of city limits. However, cities and counties may contract with each other to provide transportation.

(b) Except as provided in subsections (f) and (g) or in G.S. 122C-408(b), transportation between counties under the involuntary commitment proceedings of this Article for admission to a 24-hour facility shall be provided by the county where the respondent is taken into custody. Transportation between counties under the involuntary commitment proceedings of this Article for respondents held in 24-hour facilities who have requested a change of venue for the district court hearing shall be provided by the county where the petition for involuntary commitment was initiated. Transportation between counties under the involuntary commitment proceedings of this Article for discharge of a respondent from a 24-hour facility shall be provided by the county of residence of the respondent. However, a respondent being discharged from a facility may use his own transportation at his own expense.

(c) Transportation of a respondent may be by city-or county-owned vehicles or by private vehicle by contract with the city or county. To the extent feasible, law enforcement officers transporting respondents shall dress in plain clothes and shall travel in unmarked vehicles. Further, law enforcement officers, to the extent possible, shall advise respondents when taking them into custody that they are not under arrest and have not committed a crime, but are being transported to receive treatment and for their own safety and that of others.

(d) In providing transportation of a respondent, a city or county shall provide a driver or attendant who is the same sex as the respondent, unless the law-enforcement officer allows a family member of the respondent to accompany the respondent in lieu of an attendant of the same sex as the respondent.

(e) In providing transportation required by this section, the law-enforcement officer may use reasonable force to restrain the respondent if it appears necessary to protect himself, the respondent, or others. No law-enforcement officer may be held criminally or civilly liable for assault, false imprisonment, or other torts or crimes on account of reasonable measures taken under the authority of this Article.

(f) Notwithstanding the provisions of subsections (a), (b), and (c) of this section, a clerk, a magistrate, or a district court judge, where applicable, may authorize the family or immediate friends of the respondent, if they so request, to transport the respondent in accordance with the procedures of this Article. This authorization shall only be granted in cases where the danger to the public, the family or friends of the respondent, or the respondent himself is not substantial. The family or immediate friends of the respondent shall bear the costs of providing this transportation.

(g) The governing body of a city or county may adopt a plan for transportation of respondents in involuntary commitment proceedings in this Article. Law-enforcement personnel, volunteers, or other public or private agency personnel may be designated to provide all or parts of the transportation required by involuntary commitment proceedings. Persons so designated shall be trained and the plan shall assure adequate safety and protections for both the public and the respondent. Law enforcement, other affected agencies, and the area authority shall participate in the planning. If any person other than a law-enforcement agency is designated by a city or county, the person so designated shall provide the transportation and follow the procedures in this Article. References in this Article to a law-enforcement officer apply to this person.

(h) The cost and expenses of transporting a respondent to or from a 24-hour facility is the responsibility of the county of residence of the respondent. The State (when providing transportation under G.S. 122C-408(b)), a city, or a county is entitled to recover the reasonable cost of transportation from the county of residence of the respondent. The county of residence of the respondent shall reimburse the State, another county, or a city the reasonable transportation costs incurred as authorized by this subsection. The county of residence of the respondent is entitled to recover the reasonable cost of transportation it has paid to the State, a city, or a county. Provided that the county of residence provides the respondent or other individual liable for the respondent's support a reasonable notice and opportunity to object to the reimbursement, the county of residence of the respondent may recover that cost from:

(1) The respondent, if the respondent is not indigent;

(2) Any person or entity that is legally liable for the resident's support and maintenance provided there is sufficient property to pay the cost;

(3) Any person or entity that is contractually responsible for the cost; or

(4) Any person or entity that otherwise is liable under federal, State, or local law for the cost. (1899, c. 1, s. 32; Rev., s. 4555; 1919, c. 326, s. 4; C.S., ss. 6201, 6202; 1945, c. 952, ss. 29, 30; 1953, c. 256, s. 6; 1961, c. 186; 1963, c. 1184, s. 1; 1969, c. 982; 1973, c. 1408, s. 1; 1979, c. 915, ss. 21, 22; 1983, c. 138, ss. 1, 2; 1985, c. 589, s. 2; 1987, c. 268; 1995 (Reg. Sess., 1996), c. 739, s. 4; 1999-201, s. 1; 1999-456, s. 36.)

§ 122C-252. Twenty-four hour facilities for custody and treatment of involuntary clients.

State facilities, 24-hour facilities licensed under this Chapter or hospitals licensed under Chapter 131E may be designated by the Secretary as facilities for the custody and treatment of involuntary clients. Designation of these facilities shall be made in accordance with rules of the Secretary that assure the protection of the client and the general public. Facilities so designated may detain a client under the procedures of Parts 7 and 8 of this Article both before a district court hearing and after commitment of the respondent. (1973, c. 726, s. 1; c. 1408, s. 1; 1977, c. 400, s. 4; c. 679, s. 8; c. 739, s. 1; 1979, c. 358, s. 27; c. 915, s. 4; 1983, c. 380, ss. 4, 10; c. 638, ss. 6, 7, 25.1; c. 864, s. 4; 1985, c. 589, s. 2.)

§ 122C-253. Fees under commitment order.

Nothing contained in Parts 6, 7, or 8 of this Article requires a private physician, private psychologist, or private facility to accept a respondent as a client either before or after commitment. Treatment at a private facility or by a private physician or private psychologist is at the expense of the respondent to the extent that the charges are not disposed of by contract between the area authority and the private facility. An area authority and its contract agencies shall set and recover fees for inpatient or outpatient treatment services provided under a commitment order in accordance with G.S. 122C-146. (1973, c. 726, s. 1; c. 1408, s. 1; 1977, c. 400, s. 8; c. 739, s. 2; 1979, c. 358, s. 26; c. 915, ss. 8, 15, 16; 1981, c. 537, s. 1; 1983, c. 380, s. 8; c. 638, s. 14; c. 864, s. 4; 1985, c. 589, s. 2; c. 695, s. 3.)

§ 122C-254. Housing responsibility for certain clients in or escapees from involuntary commitment.

(a) Any individual who has been involuntarily committed under the provisions of this Article to a 24-hour facility:

(1) Who escapes from or is absent without authorization from the facility before being discharged; and

(2) Who is charged with a criminal offense committed after the escape or during the unauthorized absence; and

(3) Whose involuntary commitment is determined to be still valid by the judge or judicial officer who would make the pretrial release determination regarding the criminal offense under the provisions of G.S. 15A-533 and G.S. 15A-534; or

(4) Who is charged with committing a crime while still residing in the facility and whose commitment is still valid as prescribed by subdivision (3) of this section;

shall be denied pretrial release pursuant to G.S. 15A-533 and G.S. 15A-534. In lieu of pretrial release, and pending the additional proceedings on the criminal offense, the individual shall be returned to the 24-hour facility in which he was residing at the time of the alleged crime or from which he escaped or absented himself for continuation of his commitment.

(b) Absent findings of lack of mental responsibility for his criminal offense or lack of competency to stand trial for the criminal offense, the involuntary commitment of an individual as described in subsection (a) of this section shall not be utilized in lieu of nor shall it constitute a bar to proceeding to trial for the criminal offense. At any time that the district court or the responsible professional of the 24-hour facility finds that the individual should be unconditionally discharged, committed for outpatient treatment, or conditionally released, the facility shall notify the clerk of superior court in the county in which the criminal charge is pending before making the change in status. At this time, a pretrial release determination pursuant to the provisions of G.S. 15A-533 and G.S. 15A-534 shall be made. In this event, arrangements for returning the individual for the pretrial release determination shall be the responsibility of the clerk of superior court.

(c)   An individual who has been processed in accordance with subsections (a) and (b) of this section may not later be returned to a 24-hour facility before trial except pursuant to involuntary commitment proceedings by the district court in accordance with Parts 7 and 8 of this Article or after proceedings in accordance with the provisions of G.S. 15A-1002 or G.S. 15A-1321.

(d)   Other involuntarily committed respondents who escape, but do not meet the additional criteria specified in subsection (a) of this section, are handled in accordance with the provisions of G.S. 122C-205. (1981, c. 936, s. 1; 1985, c. 589, s. 2.)

§ 122C-255. Report required.

Beginning January 1, 2012, each 24-hour residential facility that (i) falls under the category of nonhospital medical detoxification, facility-based crisis service, or inpatient hospital treatment, (ii) is not a State facility under the jurisdiction of the Secretary of Health and Human Services, and (iii) is designated by the Secretary of Health and Human Services as a facility for the custody and treatment of individuals under a petition of involuntary commitment pursuant to G.S. 122C-252 and 10A NCAC 26C .0101 shall submit a written report on involuntary commitments each January 1 and each July 1 to the Department of Health and Human Services, Division of Mental Health, Developmental Disabilities, and Substance Abuse Services. The report shall include all of the following:

(1)   The number and primary presenting conditions of individuals receiving treatment from the facility under a petition of involuntary commitment.

(2)   The number of individuals for whom an involuntary commitment proceeding was initiated at the facility, who were referred to a different facility or program.

(3)   The reason for referring the individuals described in subdivision (2) of this section to a different facility or program, including the need for more intensive medical supervision. (2011-346, s. 2.)

§ 122C-256. Reserved for future codification purposes.

§ 122C-257. Reserved for future codification purposes.

§ 122C-258. Reserved for future codification purposes.

§ 122C-259. Reserved for future codification purposes.

§ 122C-260. Reserved for future codification purposes.

Part 7. Involuntary Commitment of the Mentally Ill; Facilities for the Mentally Ill.

§ 122C-261. Affidavit and petition before clerk or magistrate when immediate hospitalization is not necessary; custody order.

(a) Anyone who has knowledge of an individual who is mentally ill and either (i) dangerous to self, as defined in G.S. 122C-3(11)a., or dangerous to others, as defined in G.S. 122C-3(11)b., or (ii) in need of treatment in order to prevent further disability or deterioration that would predictably result in dangerousness, may appear before a clerk or assistant or deputy clerk of superior court or a magistrate and execute an affidavit to this effect, and petition the clerk or magistrate for issuance of an order to take the respondent into custody for examination by a physician or eligible psychologist. The affidavit shall include the facts on which the affiant's opinion is based. If the affiant has knowledge or reasonably believes that the respondent, in addition to being mentally ill, is also mentally retarded, this fact shall be stated in the affidavit. Jurisdiction under this subsection is in the clerk or magistrate in the county where the respondent resides or is found.

(b) If the clerk or magistrate finds reasonable grounds to believe that the facts alleged in the affidavit are true and that the respondent is probably mentally ill and either (i) dangerous to self, as defined in G.S. 122C-3(11)a., or dangerous to others, as defined in G.S. 122C-3(11)b., or (ii) in need of treatment in order to prevent further disability or deterioration that would predictably result in dangerousness, the clerk or magistrate shall issue an order to a law enforcement officer or any other person authorized under G.S. 122C-251 to take the respondent into custody for examination by a physician or eligible psychologist. If the clerk or magistrate finds that, in addition to probably being mentally ill, the respondent is also probably mentally retarded, the clerk or magistrate shall contact the area authority before issuing a custody order and the area authority shall designate the facility to which the respondent is to be taken for examination by a physician or eligible psychologist. The clerk or magistrate shall provide the petitioner and the respondent, if present, with specific information regarding the next steps that will occur for the respondent.

(c)   If the clerk or magistrate issues a custody order, the clerk or magistrate shall also make inquiry in any reliable way as to whether the respondent is indigent within the meaning of G.S. 7A-450. A magistrate shall report the result of this inquiry to the clerk.

(d)   If the affiant is a physician or eligible psychologist, all of the following apply:

(1)   The affiant may execute the affidavit before any official authorized to administer oaths. This affiant is not required to appear before the clerk or magistrate for this purpose. This affiant shall file the affidavit with the clerk or magistrate by delivering to the clerk or magistrate the original affidavit or a copy in paper form that is printed through the facsimile transmission of the affidavit. If the affidavit is filed through facsimile transmission, the affiant shall mail the original affidavit no later than five days after the facsimile transmission of the affidavit to the clerk or magistrate to be filed by the clerk or magistrate with the facsimile copy of the affidavit.

(2)   This affiant's examination shall comply with the requirements of the initial examination as provided in G.S. 122C-263(c).

(3)   If the physician or eligible psychologist recommends outpatient commitment and the clerk or magistrate finds probable cause to believe that the respondent meets the criteria for outpatient commitment, the clerk or magistrate shall issue an order that a hearing before a district court judge be held to determine whether the respondent will be involuntarily committed. The physician or eligible psychologist shall provide the respondent with written notice of any scheduled appointment and the name, address, and telephone number of the proposed outpatient treatment physician or center. The physician or eligible psychologist shall contact the local management entity that serves the county where the respondent resides or the local management entity that coordinated services for the respondent to inform the local management entity that the respondent has been scheduled for an appointment with an outpatient treatment physician or center.

(4)   If the physician or eligible psychologist recommends inpatient commitment and the clerk or magistrate finds probable cause to believe that the respondent meets the criteria for inpatient commitment, the clerk or magistrate

shall issue an order for transportation to or custody at a 24-hour facility described in G.S. 122C-252, provided that if a 24-hour facility is not immediately available or appropriate to the respondent's medical condition, the respondent may be temporarily detained under appropriate supervision and, upon further examination, released in accordance with G.S. 122C-263(d)(2).

(5)   If the affiant is a physician or eligible psychologist at a 24-hour facility described in G.S. 122C-252 who recommends inpatient commitment; the respondent is physically present on the premises of the same 24-hour facility; and the clerk or magistrate finds probable cause to believe that the respondent meets the criteria for inpatient commitment, then the clerk or magistrate may issue an order by facsimile transmission or may issue an electronically scanned order by electronic transmission to the physician or eligible psychologist at the 24-hour facility, or a designee, to take the respondent into custody at the 24-hour facility and proceed according to G.S. 122C-266. Upon receipt of the custody order, the physician or eligible psychologist at the 24-hour facility, or a designee, shall immediately (i) notify the respondent that the respondent is not under arrest and has not committed a crime but is being taken into custody to receive treatment and for the respondent's own safety and the safety of others, (ii) take the respondent into custody, and (iii) complete and sign the appropriate portion of the custody order and return the order to the clerk or magistrate either by facsimile transmission or by scanning it and sending it by electronic transmission. The physician or eligible psychologist, or a designee, shall mail the original custody order no later than five days after returning it by means of facsimile or electronic transmission to the clerk or magistrate. The clerk or magistrate shall file the original custody order with the copy of the custody order that was electronically returned.

Notwithstanding the provisions of this subdivision, a clerk or magistrate shall not issue a custody order to a physician or eligible psychologist at a 24-hour facility, or a designee, if the physician or eligible psychologist, or a designee, has not completed training in proper service and return of service. As used in this subdivision, the term "designee" includes the 24-hour facility's on-site police security personnel.

The Department of Health and Human Services shall cooperate and collaborate with the Administrative Office of the Courts and the UNC School of Government to develop protocols to implement this section, including a procedure for notifying clerks and magistrates of the names of the physicians, psychologists, and designees who have completed the training. The Secretary of the Department shall oversee implementation of these protocols.

(6) If the clerk or magistrate finds probable cause to believe that the respondent, in addition to being mentally ill, is also mentally retarded, the clerk or magistrate shall contact the area authority before issuing the order and the area authority shall designate the facility to which the respondent is to be transported.

(7) If a physician or eligible psychologist executes an affidavit for inpatient commitment of a respondent, a second physician shall be required to perform the examination required by G.S. 122C-266.

(e) Except as provided in subdivision (5) of subsection (d) of this section, upon receipt of the custody order of the clerk or magistrate or a custody order issued by the court pursuant to G.S. 15A-1003, a law enforcement officer or other person designated in the order shall take the respondent into custody within 24 hours after the order is signed, and proceed according to G.S. 122C-263. The custody order is valid throughout the State.

(f) When a petition is filed for an individual who is a resident of a single portal area, the procedures for examination by a physician or eligible psychologist as set forth in G.S. 122C-263 shall be carried out in accordance with the area plan. Prior to issuance of a custody order for a respondent who resides in an area authority with a single portal plan, the clerk or magistrate shall communicate with the area authority to determine the appropriate 24-hour facility to which the respondent should be admitted according to the area plan or to determine if there are more appropriate resources available through the area authority to assist the petitioner or the respondent. When an individual from a single portal area is presented for commitment at a 24-hour area or State facility directly, the individual may not be accepted for admission until the facility notifies the area authority and the area authority agrees to the admission. If the area authority does not agree to the admission, it shall determine the appropriate 24-hour facility to which the individual should be admitted according to the area plan or determine if there are more appropriate resources available through the area authority to assist the individual. If the area authority agrees to the admission, further planning of treatment for the client is the joint responsibility of the area authority and the facility as prescribed in the area plan.

Notwithstanding the provisions of this section, in no event shall an individual known or reasonably believed to be mentally retarded be admitted to a State psychiatric hospital, except as follows:

(1) Persons described in G.S. 122C-266(b);

(2) Persons admitted pursuant to G.S. 15A-1321;

(3) Respondents who are so extremely dangerous as to pose a serious threat to the community and to other patients committed to non-State hospital psychiatric inpatient units, as determined by the Director of the Division of Mental Health, Developmental Disabilities, and Substance Abuse Services or his designee; and

(4) Respondents who are so gravely disabled by both multiple disorders and medical fragility or multiple disorders and deafness that alternative care is inappropriate, as determined by the Director of the Division of Mental Health, Developmental Disabilities, and Substance Abuse Services or his designee.

Individuals transported to a State facility for the mentally ill who are not admitted by the facility may be transported by law enforcement officers or designated staff of the State facility in State-owned vehicles to an appropriate 24-hour facility that provides psychiatric inpatient care.

No later than 24 hours after the transfer, the responsible professional at the original facility shall notify the petitioner, the clerk of court, and, if consent is granted by the respondent, the next of kin, that the transfer has been completed. (1973, c. 726, s. 1; c. 1408, s. 1; 1977, c. 400, s. 3; 1979, c. 164, s. 2; c. 915, ss. 3, 18; 1983, c. 383, s. 5; c. 638, ss. 3-5; c. 864, s. 4; 1985, c. 589, s. 2; c. 695, ss. 2, 4; 1985 (Reg. Sess., 1986), c. 863, s. 17; 1989 (Reg. Sess., 1990), c. 823, ss. 1, 2; c. 1024, s. 27.1; 1991, c. 37, s. 7; 1995 (Reg. Sess., 1996), c. 739, s. 6; 1997-456, s. 47; 2004-23, s. 1(a); 2005-135, s. 1; 2009-315, s. 1; 2009-340, s. 1; 2013-308, ss. 1, 2.)

§ 122C-262. Special emergency procedure for individuals needing immediate hospitalization.

(a) Anyone, including a law enforcement officer, who has knowledge of an individual who is subject to inpatient commitment according to the criteria of G.S. 122C-261(a) and who requires immediate hospitalization to prevent harm to self or others, may transport the individual directly to an area facility or other place, including a State facility for the mentally ill, for examination by a physician or eligible psychologist in accordance with G.S. 122C-263(c).

(b) Upon examination by the physician or eligible psychologist, if the individual meets the criteria required in G.S. 122C-261(a), the physician or eligible psychologist shall so certify in writing before any official authorized to administer oaths. The certificate shall also state the reason that the individual requires immediate hospitalization. If the physician or eligible psychologist knows or has reason to believe that the individual is mentally retarded, the certificate shall so state.

(c) If the physician or eligible psychologist executes the oath, appearance before a magistrate shall be waived. The physician or eligible psychologist shall send a copy of the certificate to the clerk of superior court by the most reliable and expeditious means. If it cannot be reasonably anticipated that the clerk will receive the copy within 24 hours, excluding Saturday, Sunday, and holidays, of the time that it was signed, the physician or eligible psychologist shall also communicate the findings to the clerk by telephone.

(d) Anyone, including a law enforcement officer if necessary, may transport the individual to a 24-hour facility described in G.S. 122C-252 for examination and treatment pending a district court hearing. If there is no area 24-hour facility and if the respondent is indigent and unable to pay for care at a private 24-hour facility, the law enforcement officer or other designated person providing transportation shall take the respondent to a State facility for the mentally ill designated by the Commission in accordance with G.S. 143B-147(a)(1)a and immediately notify the clerk of superior court of this action. The physician's or eligible psychologist's certificate shall serve as the custody order and the law enforcement officer or other designated person shall provide transportation in accordance with the provisions of G.S. 122C-251.

In the event an individual known or reasonably believed to be mentally retarded is transported to a State facility for the mentally ill, in no event shall that individual be admitted to that facility except as follows:

(1) Persons described in G.S. 122C-266(b);

(2) Persons admitted pursuant to G.S. 15A-1321;

(3) Respondents who are so extremely dangerous as to pose a serious threat to the community and to other patients committed to non-State hospital psychiatric inpatient units, as determined by the Director of the Division of Mental Health, Developmental Disabilities, and Substance Abuse Services or his designee; and

(4) Respondents who are so gravely disabled by both multiple disorders and medical fragility or multiple disorders and deafness that alternative care is inappropriate, as determined by the Director of the Division of Mental Health, Developmental Disabilities, and Substance Abuse Services or his designee.

Individuals transported to a State facility for the mentally ill who are not admitted by the facility may be transported by law enforcement officers or designated staff of the State facility in State-owned vehicles to an appropriate 24-hour facility that provides psychiatric inpatient care.

No later than 24 hours after the transfer, the responsible professional at the original facility shall notify the petitioner, the clerk of court, and, if consent is granted by the respondent, the next of kin, that the transfer has been completed.

(e) Respondents received at a 24-hour facility under the provisions of this section shall be examined by a second physician in accordance with G.S. 122C-266. After receipt of notification that the district court has determined reasonable grounds for the commitment, further proceedings shall be carried out in the same way as for all other respondents under this Part. (1973, c. 726, s. 1; c. 1408, s. 1; 1985, c. 589, s. 2; c. 695, s. 2; 1987, c. 596, s. 1; 1995 (Reg. Sess., 1996), c. 739, s. 7.)

§ 122C-263. Duties of law-enforcement officer; first examination by physician or eligible psychologist.

(a) Without unnecessary delay after assuming custody, the law enforcement officer or the individual designated by the clerk or magistrate under G.S. 122C-251(g) to provide transportation shall take the respondent to an area facility for examination by a physician or eligible psychologist; if a physician or eligible psychologist is not available in the area facility, the person designated to provide transportation shall take the respondent to any physician or eligible psychologist locally available. If a physician or eligible psychologist is not immediately available, the respondent may be temporarily detained in an area facility, if one is available; if an area facility is not available, the respondent may be detained under appropriate supervision in the respondent's home, in a private hospital or a clinic, in a general hospital, or in a State facility for the mentally ill, but not in a jail or other penal facility.

(b) The examination set forth in subsection (a) of this section is not required if:

(1) The affiant who obtained the custody order is a physician or eligible psychologist who recommends inpatient commitment;

(2) The custody order states that the respondent was charged with a violent crime, including a crime involving assault with a deadly weapon, and he was found incapable of proceeding; or

(3) Repealed by Session Laws 1987, c. 596, s. 3.

In any of these cases, the law-enforcement officer shall take the respondent directly to a 24-hour facility described in G.S. 122C-252.

(c) The physician or eligible psychologist described in subsection (a) of this section shall examine the respondent as soon as possible, and in any event within 24 hours, after the respondent is presented for examination. When the examination set forth in subsection (a) of this section is performed by a physician or eligible psychologist the respondent may either be in the physical face-to-face presence of the physician or eligible psychologist or may be examined utilizing telemedicine equipment and procedures. A physician or eligible psychologist who examines a respondent by means of telemedicine must be satisfied to a reasonable medical certainty that the determinations made in accordance with subsection (d) of this section would not be different if the examination had been done in the physical presence of the physician or eligible psychologist. A physician or eligible psychologist who is not so satisfied must note that the examination was not satisfactorily accomplished, and the respondent must be taken for a face-to-face examination in the physical presence of a person authorized to perform examinations under this section. As used in this subsection, "telemedicine" is the use of two-way real-time interactive audio and video between places of lesser and greater medical capability or expertise to provide and support health care when distance separates participants who are in different geographical locations. A recipient is referred by one provider to receive the services of another provider via telemedicine.

The examination shall include but is not limited to an assessment of the respondent's:

(1) Current and previous mental illness and mental retardation including, if available, previous treatment history;

(2) Dangerousness to self, as defined in G.S. 122C-3(11)a. or others, as defined in G.S. 122C-3(11)b.;

(3) Ability to survive safely without inpatient commitment, including the availability of supervision from family, friends or others; and

(4) Capacity to make an informed decision concerning treatment.

(d) After the conclusion of the examination the physician or eligible psychologist shall make the following determinations:

(1) If the physician or eligible psychologist finds that:

a. The respondent is mentally ill;

b. The respondent is capable of surviving safely in the community with available supervision from family, friends, or others;

c. Based on the respondent's psychiatric history, the respondent is in need of treatment in order to prevent further disability or deterioration that would predictably result in dangerousness as defined by G.S. 122C-3(11); and

d. The respondent's current mental status or the nature of the respondent's illness limits or negates the respondent's ability to make an informed decision to seek voluntarily or comply with recommended treatment.

The physician or eligible psychologist shall so show on the examination report and shall recommend outpatient commitment. In addition the examining physician or eligible psychologist shall show the name, address, and telephone number of the proposed outpatient treatment physician or center. The person designated in the order to provide transportation shall return the respondent to the respondent's regular residence or, with the respondent's consent, to the home of a consenting individual located in the originating county, and the respondent shall be released from custody.

(2) If the physician or eligible psychologist finds that the respondent is mentally ill and is dangerous to self, as defined in G.S. 122C-3(11)a., or others, as defined in G.S. 122C-3(11)b., the physician or eligible psychologist shall

recommend inpatient commitment, and shall so show on the examination report. If, in addition to mental illness and dangerousness, the physician or eligible psychologist also finds that the respondent is known or reasonably believed to be mentally retarded, this finding shall be shown on the report. The law enforcement officer or other designated person shall take the respondent to a 24-hour facility described in G.S. 122C-252 pending a district court hearing. If there is no area 24-hour facility and if the respondent is indigent and unable to pay for care at a private 24-hour facility, the law enforcement officer or other designated person shall take the respondent to a State facility for the mentally ill designated by the Commission in accordance with G.S. 143B-147(a)(1)a. for custody, observation, and treatment and immediately notify the clerk of superior court of this action. If a 24-hour facility is not immediately available or appropriate to the respondent's medical condition, the respondent may be temporarily detained under appropriate supervision at the site of the first examination, provided that at anytime that a physician or eligible psychologist determines that the respondent is no longer in need of inpatient commitment, the proceedings shall be terminated and the respondent transported and released in accordance with subdivision (3) of this subsection. However, if the physician or eligible psychologist determines that the respondent meets the criteria for outpatient commitment, as defined in subdivision (1) of this subsection, the physician or eligible psychologist may recommend outpatient commitment, and the respondent shall be transported and released in accordance with subdivision (1) of this subsection. Any decision to terminate the proceedings or to recommend outpatient commitment after an initial recommendation of inpatient commitment shall be documented and reported to the clerk of superior court in accordance with subsection (e) of this section. If the respondent is temporarily detained and a 24-hour facility is not available or medically appropriate seven days after the issuance of the custody order, a physician or psychologist shall report this fact to the clerk of superior court and the proceedings shall be terminated. Termination of proceedings pursuant to this subdivision shall not prohibit or prevent the initiation of new involuntary commitment proceedings when appropriate. Affidavits filed in support of proceedings terminated pursuant to this subdivision may not be submitted in support of any subsequent petitions for involuntary commitment. If the affiant initiating new commitment proceedings is a physician or eligible psychologist, the affiant shall conduct a new examination and may not rely upon examinations conducted as part of proceedings terminated pursuant to this subdivision.

In the event an individual known or reasonably believed to be mentally retarded is transported to a State facility for the mentally ill, in no event shall that individual be admitted to that facility except as follows:

a. Persons described in G.S. 122C-266(b);

b. Persons admitted pursuant to G.S. 15A-1321;

c. Respondents who are so extremely dangerous as to pose a serious threat to the community and to other patients committed to non-State hospital psychiatric inpatient units, as determined by the Director of the Division of Mental Health, Developmental Disabilities, and Substance Abuse Services or his designee; and

d. Respondents who are so gravely disabled by both multiple disorders and medical fragility or multiple disorders and deafness that alternative care is inappropriate, as determined by the Director of the Division of Mental Health, Developmental Disabilities, and Substance Abuse Services or his designee.

Individuals transported to a State facility for the mentally ill who are not admitted by the facility may be transported by law enforcement officers or designated staff of the State facility in State-owned vehicles to an appropriate 24-hour facility that provides psychiatric inpatient care.

No later than 24 hours after the transfer, the responsible professional at the original facility shall notify the petitioner, the clerk of court, and, if consent is granted by the respondent, the next of kin, that the transfer has been completed.

(3) If the physician or eligible psychologist finds that neither condition described in subdivisions (1) or (2) of this subsection exists, the proceedings shall be terminated. The person designated in the order to provide transportation shall return the respondent to the respondent's regular residence or, with the respondent's consent, to the home of a consenting individual located in the originating county and the respondent shall be released from custody.

(e) The findings of the physician or eligible psychologist and the facts on which they are based shall be in writing in all cases. The physician or eligible psychologist shall send a copy of the findings to the clerk of superior court by the most reliable and expeditious means. If it cannot be reasonably anticipated that the clerk will receive the copy within 48 hours of the time that it was signed, the physician or eligible psychologist shall also communicate his findings to the clerk by telephone.

(f) When outpatient commitment is recommended, the examining physician or eligible psychologist, if different from the proposed outpatient treatment physician or center, shall give the respondent a written notice listing the name, address, and telephone number of the proposed outpatient treatment physician or center and directing the respondent to appear at the address at a specified date and time. The examining physician or eligible psychologist before the appointment shall notify by telephone the designated outpatient treatment physician or center and shall send a copy of the notice and his examination report to the physician or center.

(g) The physician or eligible psychologist, at the completion of the examination, shall provide the respondent with specific information regarding the next steps that will occur. (1973, c. 726, s. 1; c. 1408, s. 1; 1977, c. 400, s. 4; c. 679, s. 8; c. 739, s. 1; 1979, c. 358, s. 27; c. 915, s. 4; 1983, c. 380, ss. 4, 10; c. 638, ss. 6, 7, 25.1; c. 864, s. 4; 1985, c. 589, s. 2; c. 695, ss. 2, 5, 6; 1985 (Reg. Sess., 1986), c. 863, s. 18; 1987, c. 596, s. 3; 1989, c. 225, s. 2; c. 770, s. 74; 1989 (Reg. Sess., 1990), c. 823, ss. 3, 4; 1991, c. 37, s. 8; c. 636, s. 2(1); c. 761, s. 49; 1995 (Reg. Sess., 1996), c. 739, s. 8(a)-(d); 2009-315, s. 2; 2009-340, s. 2.)

§ 122C-263.1. Secretary's authority to waive requirement of first examination by physician or eligible psychologist; training of certified providers performing first examinations.

(a) The Secretary of Health and Human Services may, upon request of an LME, waive the requirements of G.S. 122C-261 through G.S. 122C-263 and G.S. 122C-281 through G.S. 122C-283 pertaining to initial (first-level) examinations by a physician or eligible psychologist of individuals meeting the criteria of G.S. 122C-261(a) or G.S. 122C-281(a), as applicable, as follows:

(1) The Secretary has received a request from an LME to substitute for a physician or eligible psychologist, a licensed clinical social worker, a master's level psychiatric nurse, or a master's level certified clinical addictions specialist in accordance with subdivision (8) of this subsection to conduct the initial (first-level) examinations of individuals meeting the criteria of G.S. 122C-261(a) or G.S. 122C-281(a). In making this type of request, the LME shall specifically describe all of the following:

a. How the purpose of the statutory requirement would be better served by waiving the requirement and substituting the proposed change under the waiver.

b. How the waiver will enable the LME to improve the delivery or management of mental health, developmental disabilities, and substance abuse services.

c. How the health, safety, and welfare of individuals will continue to be at least as well protected under the waiver as under the statutory requirement.

(2) The Secretary shall review the request and may approve it upon finding all of the following:

a. The request meets the requirements of this section.

b. The request furthers the purposes of State policy under G.S. 122C-2 and mental health, developmental disabilities, and substance abuse services reform.

c. The request improves the delivery of mental health, developmental disabilities, and substance abuse services in the counties affected by the waiver and also protects the health, safety, and welfare of individuals receiving these services.

(3) The Secretary shall evaluate the effectiveness, quality, and efficiency of mental health, developmental disabilities, and substance abuse services and protection of health, safety, and welfare under the waiver.

(4) A waiver granted by the Secretary under this section shall be in effect for a period of up to three years and may be rescinded at any time within this period if the Secretary finds the LME has failed to meet the requirements of this section.

(5) In no event shall the substitution of a licensed clinical social worker, master's level psychiatric nurse, or master's level certified clinical addictions specialist under a waiver granted under this section be construed as authorization to expand the scope of practice of the licensed clinical social worker, the master's level psychiatric nurse, or the master's level certified clinical addictions specialist.

(6) The Department shall require that individuals performing initial examinations under the waiver have successfully completed the Department's standardized training program and examination. The Department shall maintain a list of these individuals on its Web site.

(7) As part of its waiver request, the LME shall document the availability of a physician to provide backup support.

(8) A master's level certified clinical addiction specialist shall only be authorized to conduct the initial examination of individuals meeting the criteria of G.S. 122C-281(a).

(b) The Division of Mental Health, Developmental Disabilities, and Substance Abuse Services shall expand its standardized certification training program to include refresher training for all certified providers performing initial examinations pursuant to subsection (a) of this section. (2011-346, s. 1.)

§ 122C-263.2. Mental health crisis management: reasonable safety and containment measures.

An acute care hospital licensed under Chapter 131E, a department thereof, or other site of first examination that that uses reasonable safety or containment measures and precautions to manage the population of patients being held under appropriate supervision pending involuntary commitment placement and that does not otherwise operate as a licensable mental health facility shall not be deemed to be acting as a 24-hour facility; operating a psychiatric, substance abuse, or special care unit; offering psychiatric or substance abuse services; or acting as a licensed or unlicensed mental health facility. Actions considered to be reasonable safety or containment measures and precautions shall include the following: (i) altering rooms or removing items to prevent injury; (ii) placing patients in a consolidated location of the hospital; (iii) improvements to security and protection of staff; and (iv) any other reasonable measures that do not violate applicable law.

Reasonable safety or containment measures and precautions shall not be considered a violation of rules regulating acute care hospitals or mental health facilities. Placing patients in a consolidated location of the hospital pursuant to this subsection shall not constitute a special care unit. Nothing in this subsection relieves an acute care hospital or other site of first examination from complying with all other applicable laws or rules. (2012-128, s. 1.)

§ 122C-264. Duties of clerk of superior court and the district attorney.

(a) Upon receipt of a physician's or eligible psychologist's finding that the respondent meets the criteria of G.S. 122C-263(d)(1) and that outpatient commitment is recommended, the clerk of superior court of the county where the petition was initiated, upon direction of a district court judge, shall calendar the matter for hearing and shall notify the respondent, the proposed outpatient treatment physician or center, and the petitioner of the time and place of the hearing. The petitioner may file a written waiver of his right to notice under this subsection with the clerk of court.

(b) Upon receipt of a physician's or eligible psychologist's finding that a respondent meets the criteria of G.S. 122C-263(d)(2) and that inpatient commitment is recommended, the clerk of superior court of the county where the 24-hour facility is located shall, after determination required by G.S. 122C-261(c) and upon direction of a district court judge, assign counsel if necessary, calendar the matter for hearing, and notify the respondent, his counsel, and the petitioner of the time and place of the hearing. The petitioner may file a written waiver of his right to notice under this subsection with the clerk of court.

(b1) Upon receipt of a physician's or eligible psychologist's certificate that a respondent meets the criteria of G.S. 122C-261(a) and that immediate hospitalization is needed pursuant to G.S. 122C-262, the clerk of superior court of the county where the treatment facility is located shall submit the certificate to the Chief District Court Judge. The court shall review the certificate within 24 hours, excluding Saturday, Sunday, and holidays, for a finding of reasonable grounds in accordance with 122C-261(b). The clerk shall notify the treatment facility of the court's findings by telephone and shall proceed as set forth in subsections (b), (c), and (f) of this section.

(c) Notice to the respondent, required by subsections (a) and (b) of this section, shall be given as provided in G.S. 1A-1, Rule 4(j) at least 72 hours before the hearing. Notice to other individuals shall be sent at least 72 hours before the hearing by first-class mail postage prepaid to the individual's last known address. G.S. 1A-1, Rule 6 shall not apply.

(d) In cases described in G.S. 122C-266(b) in addition to notice required in subsections (a) and (b) of this section, the clerk of superior court shall notify the chief district judge and the district attorney in the county in which the defendant was found incapable of proceeding. The notice shall be given in the same way as the notice required by subsection (c) of this section. The judge or the district attorney may file a written waiver of his right to notice under this subsection with the clerk of court.

(d1) For hearings and rehearings pursuant to G.S. 122C-268.1 and G.S. 122C-276.1, the clerk of superior court shall calendar the hearing or rehearing and shall notify the respondent, his counsel, counsel for the State, and the district attorney involved in the original trial. The notice shall be given in the same manner as the notice required by subsection (c) of this section. Upon receipt of the notice, the district attorney shall notify any persons he deems appropriate, including anyone who has filed with his office a written request for notification of any hearing or rehearing concerning discharge or conditional release of a respondent. Notice sent by the district attorney shall be by first-class mail to the person's last known address.

(e) The clerk of superior court of the county where outpatient commitment is to be supervised shall keep a separate list regarding outpatient commitment and shall prepare quarterly reports listing all active cases, the assigned supervisor, and the disposition of all hearings, supplemental hearings, and rehearings.

(f) The clerk of superior court of the county where inpatient commitment hearings and rehearings are held shall provide all notices, send all records and maintain a record of all proceedings as required by this Part; provided that if the respondent has been committed to a 24-hour facility in a county other than his county of residence and the district court hearing is held in the county of the facility, the clerk of superior court in the county of the facility shall forward the record of the proceedings to the clerk of superior court in the county of respondent's residence, where they shall be maintained by receiving clerk. (1973, c. 1408, s. 1; 1977, c. 400, s. 5; c. 414, s. 1; 1979, c. 915, s. 5; 1983, c. 380, s. 9; c. 638, ss. 8, 16; c. 864, s. 4; 1985, c. 589, s. 2; c. 695, s. 7; 1985 (Reg. Sess., 1986), c. 863, s. 19; 1987, c. 596, s. 2; 1991, c. 37, s. 4; 1995 (Reg. Sess., 1996), c. 739, s. 9.)

§ 122C-265. Outpatient commitment; examination and treatment pending hearing.

(a) If a respondent, who has been recommended for outpatient commitment by an examining physician or eligible psychologist different from the proposed outpatient treatment physician or center, fails to appear for examination by the proposed outpatient treatment physician or center at the designated time, the physician or center shall notify the clerk of superior court who shall issue an order to a law-enforcement officer or other person authorized under G.S. 122C-251 to take the respondent into custody and take him immediately to the outpatient treatment physician or center for evaluation. The custody order is valid throughout the State. The law-enforcement officer may wait during the examination and return the respondent to his home after the examination.

(b) The examining physician or the proposed outpatient treatment physician or center may prescribe to the respondent reasonable and appropriate medication and treatment that are consistent with accepted medical standards pending the district court hearing.

(c) In no event may a respondent released on a recommendation that he meets the outpatient commitment criteria be physically forced to take medication or forceably detained for treatment pending a district court hearing.

(d) If at any time pending the district court hearing the outpatient treatment physician or center determines that the respondent does not meet the criteria of G.S. 122C-263(d)(1), he shall release the respondent and notify the clerk of court and the proceedings shall be terminated.

(e) If a respondent becomes dangerous to himself, as defined in G.S. 122C-3(11)a., or others, as defined in G.S. 122C-3(11)b., pending a district court hearing on outpatient commitment, new proceedings for involuntary inpatient commitment may be initiated.

(f) If an inpatient commitment proceeding is initiated pending the hearing for outpatient commitment and the respondent is admitted to a 24-hour facility to be held for an inpatient commitment hearing, notice shall be sent by the clerk of court in the county where the respondent is being held to the clerk of court of the county where the outpatient commitment was initiated and the outpatient commitment proceeding shall be terminated. (1983, c. 638, s. 11; c. 864, s. 4; 1985, c. 589, s. 2; c. 695, s. 6; 1989 (Reg. Sess., 1990), c. 823, s. 5; 1991, c. 636, s. 2(2); c. 761, s. 49; 2004-23, s. 2(a).)

§ 122C-266. Inpatient commitment; second examination and treatment pending hearing.

(a) Except as provided in subsections (b) and (e), within 24 hours of arrival at a 24-hour facility described in G.S. 122C-252, the respondent shall be examined by a physician. This physician shall not be the same physician who completed the certificate or examination under the provisions of G.S. 122C-262 or G.S. 122C-263. The examination shall include but is not limited to the assessment specified in G.S. 122C-263(c).

(1) If the physician finds that the respondent is mentally ill and is dangerous to self, as defined by G.S. 122C-3(11)a., or others, as defined by G.S. 122C-3(11)b., the physician shall hold the respondent at the facility pending the district court hearing.

(2) If the physician finds that the respondent meets the criteria for outpatient commitment under G.S. 122C-263(d)(1), the physician shall show these findings on the physician's examination report, release the respondent pending the district court hearing, and notify the clerk of superior court of the county where the petition was initiated of these findings. In addition, the examining physician shall show on the examination report the name, address, and telephone number of the proposed outpatient treatment physician or center. The physician shall give the respondent a written notice listing the name, address, and telephone number of the proposed outpatient treatment physician or center and directing the respondent to appear at that address at a specified date and time. The examining physician before the appointment shall notify by telephone and shall send a copy of the notice and the examination report to the proposed outpatient treatment physician or center.

(3) If the physician finds that the respondent does not meet the criteria for commitment under either G.S. 122C-263(d)(1) or G.S. 122C-263(d)(2), the physician shall release the respondent and the proceedings shall be terminated.

(4) If the respondent is released under subdivisions (2) or (3) of this subsection, the law enforcement officer or other person designated to provide transportation shall return the respondent to the respondent's residence in the originating county or, if requested by the respondent, to another location in the originating county.

(b) If the custody order states that the respondent was charged with a violent crime, including a crime involving assault with a deadly weapon, and that he was found incapable of proceeding, the physician shall examine him as set forth in subsection (a) of this section. However, the physician may not release him from the facility until ordered to do so following the district court hearing.

(c) The findings of the physician and the facts on which they are based shall be in writing, in all cases. A copy of the findings shall be sent to the clerk of superior court by reliable and expeditious means.

(d)   Pending the district court hearing, the physician attending the respondent may administer to the respondent reasonable and appropriate medication and treatment that is consistent with accepted medical standards. Except as provided in subsection (b) of this section, if at any time pending the district court hearing, the attending physician determines that the respondent no longer meets the criteria of either G.S. 122C-263(d)(1) or (d)(2), he shall release the respondent and notify the clerk of court and the proceedings shall be terminated.

(e)   If the 24-hour facility described in G.S. 122C-252 or G.S. 122C-262 is the facility in which the first examination by a physician or eligible psychologist occurred and is the same facility in which the respondent is held, the second examination shall occur not later than the following regular working day. (1973, c. 726, s. 1; c. 1408, s. 1; 1977, c. 400, s. 6; 1979, c. 915, s. 6; 1983, c. 380, s. 5; c. 638, ss. 9, 10; c. 864, s. 4; 1985, c. 589, s. 2; c. 695, s. 2; 1987, c. 596, s. 4; 1989 (Reg. Sess., 1990), c. 823, s. 6; 1991, c. 37, s. 9; 1995 (Reg. Sess., 1996), c. 739, s. 10(a), (b).)

§ 122C-267. Outpatient commitment; district court hearing.

(a)   A hearing shall be held in district court within 10 days of the day the respondent is taken into custody pursuant to G.S. 122C-261(e). Upon its own motion or upon motion of the proposed outpatient treatment physician or the respondent, the court may grant a continuance of not more than five days.

(b)   The respondent shall be present at the hearing. A subpoena may be issued to compel the respondent's presence at a hearing. The petitioner and the proposed outpatient treatment physician or his designee may be present and may provide testimony.

(c)   Certified copies of reports and findings of physicians and psychologists and medical records of previous and current treatment are admissible in evidence.

(d)   At the hearing to determine the necessity and appropriateness of outpatient commitment, the respondent need not, but may, be represented by counsel. However, if the court determines that the legal or factual issues raised are of such complexity that the assistance of counsel is necessary for an adequate presentation of the merits or that the respondent is unable to speak for himself, the court may continue the case for not more than five days and order the appointment of counsel for an indigent respondent. Appointment of counsel shall be in accordance with rules adopted by the Office of Indigent Defense Services.

(e) Hearings may be held at the area facility in which the respondent is being treated, if it is located within the judge's district court district as defined in G.S. 7A-133, or in the judge's chambers. A hearing may not be held in a regular courtroom, over objection of the respondent, if in the discretion of a judge a more suitable place is available.

(f) The hearing shall be closed to the public unless the respondent requests otherwise.

(g) A copy of all documents admitted into evidence and a transcript of the proceedings shall be furnished to the respondent on request by the clerk upon the direction of a district court judge. If the client is indigent, the copies shall be provided at State expense.

(h) To support an outpatient commitment order, the court is required to find by clear, cogent, and convincing evidence that the respondent meets the criteria specified in G.S. 122C-263(d)(1). The court shall record the facts which support its findings and shall show on the order the center or physician who is responsible for the management and supervision of the respondent's outpatient commitment. (1973, c. 726, s. 1; c. 1408, s. 1; 1975, cc. 322, 459; 1977, c. 400, s. 7; c. 1126, s. 1; 1979, c. 915, ss. 7, 13; 1983, c. 380, s. 6; c. 638, ss. 12, 13; c. 864, s. 4; 1985, c. 589, s. 2; c. 695, s. 8; 1987, c. 282, s. 18; 1987 (Reg. Sess., 1988), c. 1037, s. 113.1; 2000-144, s. 38.)

§ 122C-268. Inpatient commitment; district court hearing.

(a) A hearing shall be held in district court within 10 days of the day the respondent is taken into law enforcement custody pursuant to G.S. 122C-261(e) or G.S. 122C-262. A continuance of not more than five days may be granted upon motion of:

(1) The court;

(2) Respondent's counsel; or

(3) The State, sufficiently in advance to avoid movement of the respondent.

(b) The attorney, who is a member of the staff of the Attorney General assigned to one of the State's facilities for the mentally ill or the psychiatric service of the University of North Carolina Hospitals at Chapel Hill, shall represent the State's interest at commitment hearings, rehearings, and supplemental hearings held for respondents admitted pursuant to this Part or G.S. 15A-1321 at the facility to which he is assigned.

In addition, the Attorney General may, in his discretion, designate an attorney who is a member of his staff to represent the State's interest at any commitment hearing, rehearing, or supplemental hearing held in a place other than at one of the State's facilities for the mentally ill or the psychiatric service of the University of North Carolina Hospitals at Chapel Hill.

(c) If the respondent's custody order indicates that he was charged with a violent crime, including a crime involving an assault with a deadly weapon, and that he was found incapable of proceeding, the clerk shall give notice of the time and place of the hearing as provided in G.S. 122C-264(d). The district attorney in the county in which the respondent was found incapable of proceeding may represent the State's interest at the hearing.

(d) The respondent shall be represented by counsel of his choice; or if he is indigent within the meaning of G.S. 7A-450 or refuses to retain counsel if financially able to do so, he shall be represented by counsel appointed in accordance with rules adopted by the Office of Indigent Defense Services.

(e) With the consent of the court, counsel may in writing waive the presence of the respondent.

(f) Certified copies of reports and findings of physicians and psychologists and previous and current medical records are admissible in evidence, but the respondent's right to confront and cross-examine witnesses may not be denied.

(g) Hearings may be held in an appropriate room not used for treatment of clients at the facility in which the respondent is being treated if it is located within the judge's district court district as defined in G.S. 7A-133 or in the judge's chambers. A hearing may not be held in a regular courtroom, over objection of the respondent, if in the discretion of a judge a more suitable place is available.

(h) The hearing shall be closed to the public unless the respondent requests otherwise.

(i) A copy of all documents admitted into evidence and a transcript of the proceedings shall be furnished to the respondent on request by the clerk upon the direction of a district court judge. If the respondent is indigent, the copies shall be provided at State expense.

(j) To support an inpatient commitment order, the court shall find by clear, cogent, and convincing evidence that the respondent is mentally ill and dangerous to self, as defined in G.S. 122C-3(11)a., or dangerous to others, as defined in G.S. 122C-3(11)b. The court shall record the facts that support its findings. (1985, c. 589, s. 2; c. 695, s. 8; 1985 (Reg. Sess., 1986), c. 1014, s. 195(b); 1987 (Reg. Sess., 1988), c. 1037, s. 114; 1989, c. 141, s. 11; 1989 (Reg. Sess., 1990), c. 823, s. 7; 1991, c. 37, s. 10; c. 257, s. 2; 1995 (Reg. Sess., 1996), c. 739, s. 11(a), (b); 2000-144, s. 39.)

§ 122C-268.1. Inpatient commitment; hearing following automatic commitment.

(a) A respondent who is committed pursuant to G.S. 15A-1321 shall be provided a hearing, unless waived, before the expiration of 50 days from the date of his commitment.

(b) The district attorney in the county in which the respondent was found not guilty by reason of insanity may represent the State's interest at the hearing, rehearings, and supplemental rehearings. Notwithstanding the provisions of G.S. 122C-269, if the district attorney elects to represent the State's interest, upon motion of the district attorney, the venue for the hearing, rehearings, and supplemental rehearings shall be the county in which the respondent was found not guilty by reason of insanity. If the district attorney declines to represent the State's interest, then the representation shall be determined as follows. An attorney, who is a member of the staff of the Attorney General assigned to one of the State's facilities for the mentally ill or the psychiatric service of the University of North Carolina Hospitals at Chapel Hill, may represent the State's interest at commitment hearings, rehearings, and supplemental hearings. Alternatively, the Attorney General may, in his discretion, designate an attorney who is a member of his staff to represent the State's interest at any commitment hearing, rehearing, or supplemental hearing.

(c) The clerk shall give notice of the time and place of the hearing as provided in G.S. 122C-264(d1).

(d) The respondent shall be represented by counsel of his choice, or if he is indigent within the meaning of G.S. 7A-450 or refuses to retain counsel if financially able to do so, he shall be represented by counsel appointed in accordance with rules adopted by the Office of Indigent Defense Services.

(e) With the consent of the court, counsel may in writing waive the presence of the respondent.

(f) Certified copies of reports and findings of physicians and psychologists and previous and current medical records are admissible in evidence, but the respondent's right to confront and cross-examine witnesses may not be denied.

(g) The hearing shall take place in the trial division in which the original trial was held. The hearing shall be open to the public. For purposes of this subsection, "trial division" means either the superior court division or the district court division of the General Court of Justice.

(h) A copy of all documents admitted into evidence and a transcript of the proceedings shall be furnished to the respondent on request by the clerk upon the direction of the presiding judge. If the respondent is indigent, the copies shall be provided at State expense.

(i) The respondent shall bear the burden to prove by a preponderance of the evidence that he (i) no longer has a mental illness as defined in G.S. 122C-3(21), or (ii) is no longer dangerous to others as defined in G.S. 122C-3(11)b. If the court is so satisfied, then the court shall order the respondent discharged and released. If the court finds that the respondent has not met his burden of proof, then the court shall order that inpatient commitment continue at a 24-hour facility designated pursuant to G.S. 122C-252 for a period not to exceed 90 days. The court shall make a written record of the facts that support its findings.

(j) Nothing in this section shall limit the respondent's right to habeas corpus relief. (1991, c. 37, s. 2; 1991 (Reg. Sess., 1992), c. 1034, ss. 2, 3; 1995, c. 140, s. 1; 2000-144, s. 40.)

§ 122C-269. Venue of hearing when respondent held at a 24-hour facility pending hearing.

(a) In all cases where the respondent is held at a 24-hour facility pending hearing as provided in G.S. 122C-268, G.S. 122C-268.1, 122C-276.1, or 122C-277(b1), unless the respondent through counsel objects to the venue, the hearing shall be held in the county in which the facility is located. Upon objection to venue, the hearing shall be held in the county where the petition was initiated, except as otherwise provided in subsection (c) of this section.

(b) An official of the facility shall immediately notify the clerk of superior court of the county in which the facility is located of a determination to hold the respondent pending hearing. That clerk shall request transmittal of all documents pertinent to the proceedings from the clerk of superior court where the proceedings were initiated. The requesting clerk shall assume all duties set forth in G.S. 122C-264. The counsel provided for in G.S. 122C-268(d) shall be appointed in accordance with rules adopted by the Office of Indigent Defense Services.

(c) Upon motion of any interested person, the venue of an initial hearing described in G.S. 122C-268(c) or G.S. 122C-268.1 or a rehearing required by G.S. 122C-276(b), G.S. 122C-276.1, or subsections (b) or (b1) of G.S. 122C-277 shall be moved to the county in which the respondent was found not guilty by reason of insanity or incapable of proceeding when the convenience of witnesses and the ends of justice would be promoted by the change. (1975, 2nd Sess., c. 983, s. 133; 1981, c. 537, s. 6; 1983, c. 380, s. 7; 1985, c. 589, s. 2; 1991, c. 37, ss. 11, 12; 1995, c. 140, s. 2; 2000-144, s. 41; 2001-487, s. 29.)

§ 122C-270. Attorneys to represent the respondent and the State.

(a) In a superior court district or set of districts as defined in G.S. 7A-41.1 in which a State facility for the mentally ill is located, the Commission on Indigent Defense Services shall appoint an attorney licensed to practice in North Carolina as special counsel for indigent respondents who are mentally ill. These special counsel shall serve at the pleasure of the Commission, may not privately practice law, and shall receive annual compensation within the salary range for assistant public defenders as fixed by the Office of Indigent Defense Services. The special counsel shall represent all indigent respondents at all hearings, rehearings, and supplemental hearings held at the State facility. Special counsel shall determine indigency in accordance with G.S. 7A-450(a). Indigency is subject to redetermination by the presiding judge. If the respondent appeals, counsel for the appeal shall be appointed in accordance with rules adopted by the Office of Indigent Defense Services.

(b) The State facility shall provide suitable office space for the counsel to meet privately with respondents. The Office of Indigent Defense Services shall provide secretarial and clerical service and necessary equipment and supplies for the office.

(c) In the event of a vacancy in the office of special counsel, counsel's incapacity, or a conflict of interest, counsel for indigents at hearings or rehearings may be assigned in accordance with rules adopted by the Office of Indigent Defense Services. No mileage or compensation for travel time is paid to a counsel appointed pursuant to this subsection. Counsel may also be so assigned when, in the opinion of the Director of the Office of Indigent Defense Services, the volume of cases warrants.

(d) At hearings held in counties other than those designated in subsection (a) of this section, counsel for indigent respondents shall be appointed in accordance with rules adopted by the Office of Indigent Defense Services.

(e) If the respondent is committed to a non-State 24-hour facility, assigned counsel remains responsible for the respondent's representation at the trial level until discharged by order of district court, until the respondent is unconditionally discharged from the facility, or until the respondent voluntarily admits himself or herself to the facility. If the respondent is transferred to a State facility for the mentally ill, assigned counsel is discharged. If the respondent appeals, counsel for the appeal shall be appointed in accordance with rules adopted by the Office of Indigent Defense Services.

(f) The Attorney General may employ four attorneys, one to be assigned by him full-time to each of the State facilities for the mentally ill, to represent the State's interest at commitment hearings, rehearings and supplemental hearings held under this Article at the State facilities for respondents admitted to those facilities pursuant to Part 3, 4, 7, or 8 of this Article or G.S. 15A-1321 and to provide liaison and consultation services concerning these matters. These attorneys are subject to Chapter 126 of the General Statutes and shall also perform additional duties as may be assigned by the Attorney General. The attorney employed by the Attorney General in accordance with G.S. 114-4.2B shall represent the State's interest at commitment hearings, rehearings and supplemental hearings held for respondents admitted to the University of North Carolina Hospitals at Chapel Hill pursuant to Part 3, 4, 7, or 8 of this Article or G.S. 15A-1321. (1973, c. 47, s. 2; c. 1408, s. 1; 1977, c. 400, s. 11; 1979, c. 915, s. 12; 1983, c. 275, ss. 1, 2; 1985, c. 589, s. 2; 1987 (Reg. Sess., 1988), c. 1037, s. 115; 1989, c. 141, s. 12; 1991, c. 257, s. 1; 1995 (Reg. Sess., 1996), c. 739, s. 12(a); 2000-144, s. 42; 2006-264, s. 61(a).)

§ 122C-271. Disposition.

(a) If an examining physician or eligible psychologist has recommended outpatient commitment and the respondent has been released pending the district court hearing, the court may make one of the following dispositions:

(1) If the court finds by clear, cogent, and convincing evidence that the respondent is mentally ill; that he is capable of surviving safely in the community with available supervision from family, friends, or others; that based on respondent's treatment history, the respondent is in need of treatment in order to prevent further disability or deterioration that would predictably result in dangerousness as defined in G.S. 122C-3(11); and that the respondent's current mental status or the nature of his illness limits or negates his ability to make an informed decision to seek voluntarily or comply with recommended treatment, it may order outpatient commitment for a period not in excess of 90 days.

(2) If the court does not find that the respondent meets the criteria of commitment set out in subdivision (1) of this subsection, the respondent shall be discharged and the facility at which he was last a client so notified.

(b) If the respondent has been held in a 24-hour facility pending the district court hearing pursuant to G.S. 122C-268, the court may make one of the following dispositions:

(1) If the court finds by clear, cogent, and convincing evidence that the respondent is mentally ill; that the respondent is capable of surviving safely in the community with available supervision from family, friends, or others; that based on respondent's psychiatric history, the respondent is in need of treatment in order to prevent further disability or deterioration that would predictably result in dangerousness as defined by G.S. 122C-3(11); and that the respondent's current mental status or the nature of the respondent's illness

limits or negates the respondent's ability to make an informed decision voluntarily to seek or comply with recommended treatment, it may order outpatient commitment for a period not in excess of 90 days. If the commitment proceedings were initiated as the result of the respondent's being charged with a violent crime, including a crime involving an assault with a deadly weapon, and the respondent was found incapable of proceeding, the commitment order shall so show.

(2) If the court finds by clear, cogent, and convincing evidence that the respondent is mentally ill and is dangerous to self, as defined in G.S. 122C-3(11)a., or others, as defined in G.S. 122C-3(11)b., it may order inpatient commitment at a 24-hour facility described in G.S. 122C-252 for a period not in excess of 90 days. However, no respondent found to be both mentally retarded and mentally ill may be committed to a State, area or private facility for the mentally retarded. An individual who is mentally ill and dangerous to self, as defined in G.S. 122C-3(11)a., or others, as defined in G.S. 122C-3(11)b., may also be committed to a combination of inpatient and outpatient commitment at both a 24-hour facility and an outpatient treatment physician or center for a period not in excess of 90 days. If the commitment proceedings were initiated as the result of the respondent's being charged with a violent crime, including a crime involving an assault with a deadly weapon, and the respondent was found incapable of proceeding, the commitment order shall so show. If the court orders inpatient commitment for a respondent who is under an outpatient commitment order, the outpatient commitment is terminated; and the clerk of the superior court of the county where the district court hearing is held shall send a notice of the inpatient commitment to the clerk of superior court where the outpatient commitment was being supervised.

(3) If the court does not find that the respondent meets either of the commitment criteria set out in subdivisions (1) and (2) of this subsection, the respondent shall be discharged, and the facility in which the respondent was last a client so notified.

(4) Before ordering any outpatient commitment, the court shall make findings of fact as to the availability of outpatient treatment. The court shall also show on the order the outpatient treatment physician or center who is to be responsible for the management and supervision of the respondent's outpatient commitment. When an outpatient commitment order is issued for a respondent held in a 24-hour facility, the court may order the respondent held at the facility for no more than 72 hours in order for the facility to notify the designated outpatient treatment physician or center of the treatment needs of the

respondent. The clerk of court in the county where the facility is located shall send a copy of the outpatient commitment order to the designated outpatient treatment physician or center. If the outpatient commitment will be supervised in a county other than the county where the commitment originated, the court shall order venue for further court proceedings to be transferred to the county where the outpatient commitment will be supervised. Upon an order changing venue, the clerk of superior court in the county where the commitment originated shall transfer the file to the clerk of superior court in the county where the outpatient commitment is to be supervised.

(c) If the respondent was found not guilty by reason of insanity and has been held in a 24-hour facility pending the court hearing held pursuant to G.S. 122C-268.1, the court may make one of the following dispositions:

(1) If the court finds that the respondent has not proved by a preponderance of the evidence that he no longer has a mental illness or that he is no longer dangerous to others, it shall order inpatient treatment at a 24-hour facility for a period not to exceed 90 days.

(2) If the court finds that the respondent has proven by a preponderance of the evidence that he no longer has a mental illness or that he is no longer dangerous to others, the court shall order the respondent discharged and released. (1973, c. 726, s. 1; c. 1408, s. 1; 1977, c. 400, s. 8; c. 739, s. 2; 1979, c. 358, s. 26; c. 915, ss. 8, 15, 16; 1981, c. 537, s. 1; 1983, c. 380, s. 8; c. 638, s. 14; c. 864, s. 4; 1985, c. 589, s. 2; c. 695, s. 2; 1985 (Reg. Sess., 1986), c. 863, ss. 20-22; 1989, c. 225, s. 1; c. 770, s. 73; 1989 (Reg. Sess., 1990), c. 823, s. 8; 1991, c. 37, s. 13; 1991 (Reg. Sess., 1992), c. 1034, s. 5; 1995 (Reg. Sess., 1996), c. 739, s. 13.)

§ 122C-272. Appeal.

Judgment of the district court is final. Appeal may be had to the Court of Appeals by the State or by any party on the record as in civil cases. Appeal does not stay the commitment unless so ordered by the Court of Appeals. The Attorney General represents the State's interest on appeal. The district court retains limited jurisdiction for the purpose of hearing all reviews, rehearings, or supplemental hearings allowed or required under this Part. (1973, c. 726, s. 1; c. 1408, s. 1; 1979, c. 915, s. 19; 1985, c. 589, s. 2; 2009-570, s. 27.)

§ 122C-273. Duties for follow-up on commitment order.

(a) Unless prohibited by Chapter 90 of the General Statutes, if the commitment order directs outpatient treatment, the outpatient treatment physician may prescribe or administer, or the center may administer, to the respondent reasonable and appropriate medication and treatment that are consistent with accepted medical standards.

(1) If the respondent fails to comply or clearly refuses to comply with all or part of the prescribed treatment, the physician, the physician's designee, or the center shall make all reasonable effort to solicit the respondent's compliance. These efforts shall be documented and reported to the court with a request for a supplemental hearing.

(2) If the respondent fails to comply, but does not clearly refuse to comply, with all or part of the prescribed treatment after reasonable effort to solicit the respondent's compliance, the physician, the physician's designee, or the center may request the court to order the respondent taken into custody for the purpose of examination. Upon receipt of this request, the clerk shall issue an order to a law-enforcement officer to take the respondent into custody and to take him immediately to the designated outpatient treatment physician or center for examination. The custody order is valid throughout the State. The law-enforcement officer shall turn the respondent over to the custody of the physician or center who shall conduct the examination and then release the respondent. The law-enforcement officer may wait during the examination and return the respondent to his home after the examination. An examination conducted under this subsection in which a physician or eligible psychologist determines that the respondent meets the criteria for inpatient commitment may be substituted for the first examination required by G.S. 122C-263 if the clerk or magistrate issues a custody order within six hours after the examination was performed.

(3) In no case may the respondent be physically forced to take medication or forcibly detained for treatment unless he poses an immediate danger to himself or others. In such cases inpatient commitment proceedings shall be initiated.

(4) At any time that the outpatient treatment physician or center finds that the respondent no longer meets the criteria set out in G.S. 122C-263(d)(1), the physician or center shall so notify the court and the case shall be terminated; provided, however, if the respondent was initially committed as a result of

conduct resulting in his being charged with a violent crime, including a crime involving an assault with a deadly weapon, and the respondent was found incapable of proceeding, the designated outpatient treatment physician or center shall notify the clerk that discharge is recommended. The clerk shall calendar a supplemental hearing as provided in G.S. 122C-274 to determine whether the respondent meets the criteria for outpatient commitment.

(5) Any individual who has knowledge that a respondent on outpatient commitment has become dangerous to himself, as defined by G.S. 122C-3(11)a., and others, as defined in G.S. 122C-3(11)b., may initiate a new petition for inpatient commitment as provided in this Part. If the respondent is committed as an inpatient, the outpatient commitment shall be terminated and notice sent by the clerk of court in the county where the respondent is committed as an inpatient to the clerk of court of the county where the outpatient commitment is being supervised.

(b) If the respondent on outpatient commitment intends to move or moves to another county within the State, the designated outpatient treatment physician or center shall request that the clerk of court in the county where the outpatient commitment is being supervised calendar a supplemental hearing.

(c) If the respondent moves to another state or to an unknown location, the designated outpatient treatment physician or center shall notify the clerk of superior court of the county where the outpatient commitment is supervised and the outpatient commitment shall be terminated.

(d) If the commitment order directs inpatient treatment, the physician attending the respondent may administer to the respondent reasonable and appropriate medication and treatment that are consistent with accepted medical standards. The attending physician shall release or discharge the respondent in accordance with G.S. 122C-277. (1983, c. 638, s. 16; c. 864, s. 4; 1985, c. 589, s. 2; 1985 (Reg. Sess., 1986), c. 863, ss. 23-26; 1989 (Reg. Sess., 1990), c. 823, s. 9; 1991, c. 37, s. 14; 2004-23, s. 2(b).)

§ 122C-274. Supplemental hearings.

(a) Upon receipt of a request for a supplemental hearing, the clerk shall calendar a hearing to be held within 14 days and notify, at least 72 hours before the hearing, the petitioner, the respondent, his attorney, if any, and the designated outpatient treatment physician or center. The respondent shall be notified at least 72 hours before the hearing by personally serving on him an order to appear. Other persons shall be notified as provided in G.S. 122C-264(c).

(b)　The procedures for the hearing shall follow G.S. 122C-267.

(c)　In supplemental hearings for alleged noncompliance, the court shall determine whether the respondent has failed to comply and, if so, the causes for noncompliance. If the court determines that the respondent has failed or refused to comply it may:

(1)　Upon finding probable cause to believe that the respondent is mentally ill and dangerous to himself, as defined in G.S. 122C-3(11)a., or others, as defined in G.S. 122C-3(11)b., order an examination by the same or different physician or eligible psychologist as provided in G.S. 122C-263(c) in order to determine the necessity for continued outpatient or inpatient commitment;

(2)　Reissue or change the outpatient commitment order in accordance with G.S. 122C-271; or

(3)　Discharge the respondent from the order and dismiss the case.

(d)　At the supplemental hearing for a respondent who has moved or intends to move to another county, the court shall determine if the respondent meets the criteria for outpatient commitment set out in G.S. 122C-263(d)(1). If the court determines that the respondent no longer meets the criteria for outpatient commitment, it shall discharge the respondent from the order and dismiss the case. If the court determines that the respondent continues to meet the criteria for outpatient commitment, it shall continue the outpatient commitment but shall designate a physician or center at the respondent's new residence to be responsible for the management or supervision of the respondent's outpatient commitment. The court shall order the respondent to appear for treatment at the address of the newly designated outpatient treatment physician or center and shall order venue for further court proceedings under the outpatient commitment to be transferred to the new county of supervision. Upon an order changing venue, the clerk of court in the county where the outpatient commitment has been supervised shall transfer the records regarding the outpatient commitment to the clerk of court in the county where the commitment will be supervised. Also, the clerk of court in the county where the outpatient commitment has been supervised shall send a copy of the court's order directing the continuation of outpatient treatment under new supervision to the newly designated outpatient treatment physician or center.

(e) At any time during the term of an outpatient commitment order, a respondent may apply to the court for a supplemental hearing for the purpose of discharge from the order. The application shall be made in writing by the respondent to the clerk of superior court of the county where the outpatient commitment is being supervised. At the supplemental hearing the court shall determine whether the respondent continues to meet the criteria specified in G.S. 122C-263(d)(1). The court may either reissue or change the commitment order or discharge the respondent and dismiss the case.

(f) At supplemental hearings requested pursuant to G.S. 122C-277(a) for transfer from inpatient to outpatient commitment, the court shall determine whether the respondent meets the criteria for either inpatient or outpatient commitment. If the court determines that the respondent continues to meet the criteria for inpatient commitment, it shall order the continuation of the original commitment order. If the court determines that the respondent meets the criteria for outpatient commitment, it shall order outpatient commitment for a period of time not in excess of 90 days. If the court finds that the respondent does not meet either criteria, the respondent shall be discharged and the case dismissed. (1983, c. 638, s. 17; c. 864, s. 4; 1985, c. 589, s. 2; c. 695, s. 2; 1989 (Reg. Sess., 1990), c. 823, s. 10.)

§ 122C-275. Outpatient commitment; rehearings.

(a) Fifteen days before the end of the initial or subsequent periods of outpatient commitment if the outpatient treatment physician or center determines that the respondent continues to meet the criteria specified in G.S. 122C-263(d)(1), he shall so notify the clerk of superior court of the county where the outpatient commitment is supervised. If the respondent no longer meets the criteria, the physician shall so notify the clerk who shall dismiss the case; provided, however, if the respondent was initially committed as a result of conduct resulting in his being charged with a violent crime, including a crime involving an assault with a deadly weapon, and the respondent was found incapable of proceeding, the physician or center shall notify the clerk that discharge is recommended. The clerk, at least 10 days before the end of the commitment period, on order of the district court, shall calendar the rehearing.

(b)   Notice and procedures of rehearings are governed by the same procedures as initial hearings, and the respondent has the same rights he had at the initial hearing including the right to appeal.

(c)   If the court finds that the respondent no longer meets the criteria of G.S. 122C-263(d)(1), it shall unconditionally discharge him. A copy of the discharge order shall be furnished by the clerk to the designated outpatient treatment physician or center. If the respondent continues to meet the criteria of G.S. 122C-263(d)(1), the court may order outpatient commitment for an additional period not in excess of 180 days. (1983, c. 638, s. 20; c. 864, s. 4; 1985, c. 589, s. 2; 1991, c. 37, s. 15.)

§ 122C-276. Inpatient commitment; rehearings for respondents other than insanity acquittees.

(a)   Fifteen days before the end of the initial inpatient commitment period if the attending physician determines that commitment of a respondent beyond the initial period will be necessary, he shall so notify the clerk of superior court of the county in which the facility is located. The clerk, at least 10 days before the end of the initial period, on order of a district court judge of the district court district as defined in G.S. 7A-133 in which the facility is located, shall calendar the rehearing. If the respondent was initially committed as the result of conduct resulting in his being charged with a violent crime, including a crime involving an assault with a deadly weapon, and respondent was found incapable of proceeding, the clerk shall also notify the chief district court judge, the clerk of superior court, and the district attorney in the county in which the respondent was found incapable of proceeding of the time and place of the hearing.

(b)   Fifteen days before the end of the initial treatment period of a respondent who was initially committed as a result of conduct resulting in his being charged with a violent crime, including a crime involving an assault with a deadly weapon, having been found incapable of proceeding, if the attending physician determines that commitment of the respondent beyond the initial period will not be necessary, he shall so notify the clerk of superior court who shall schedule a rehearing as provided in subsection (a) of this section.

(c) Subject to the provisions of G.S. 122C-269(c), rehearings shall be held at the facility in which the respondent is receiving treatment. The judge is a judge of the district court of the district court district as defined in G.S. 7A-133 in which the facility is located or a district court judge temporarily assigned to that district.

(d) Notice and proceedings of rehearings are governed by the same procedures as initial hearings and the respondent has the same rights he had at the initial hearing including the right to appeal.

(e) At rehearings the court may make the same dispositions authorized in G.S. 122C-271(b) except a second commitment order may be for an additional period not in excess of 180 days.

(f) Fifteen days before the end of the second commitment period and annually thereafter, the attending physician shall review and evaluate the condition of each respondent; and if he determines that a respondent is in continued need of inpatient commitment or, in the alternative, in need of outpatient commitment, or a combination of both, he shall so notify the respondent, his counsel, and the clerk of superior court of the county, in which the facility is located. Unless the respondent through his counsel files with the clerk a written waiver of his right to a rehearing, the clerk, on order of a district court judge of the district in which the facility is located, shall calendar a rehearing for not later than the end of the current commitment period. The procedures and standards for the rehearing are the same as for the first rehearing. No third or subsequent inpatient recommitment order shall be for a period longer than one year.

(g) At any rehearings the court has the option to order outpatient commitment for a period not in excess of 180 days in accordance with the criteria specified in G.S. 122C-263(d)(1) and following the procedures as specified in this Article. (1973, c. 726, s. 1; c. 1408, s. 1; 1977, c. 400, s. 9; 1979, c. 915, ss. 9, 17; 1981, c. 537, ss. 2-4; 1983, c. 638, ss. 18, 19; c. 864, s. 4; 1985, c. 589, s. 2; 1987 (Reg. Sess., 1988), c. 1037, s. 116; 1991, c. 37, s. 5.)

§ 122C-276.1. Inpatient commitment; rehearings for respondents who are insanity acquittees.

(a) At least 15 days before the end of any inpatient commitment period ordered pursuant to G.S. 122C-268.1, the clerk shall calendar the hearing and notify the parties as specified in G.S. 122C-264(d1), unless the hearing is waived by the respondent.

(b) The proceedings of the rehearing shall be governed by the same procedures provided by G.S. 122C-268.1.

(c) The respondent shall bear the burden to prove by a preponderance of the evidence that he (i) no longer has a mental illness as defined in G.S. 122C-3(21), or (ii) is no longer dangerous to others as defined in G.S. 122C-3(11)b. If the court is so satisfied, then the court shall order the respondent discharged and released. If the court finds that the respondent has not met his burden of proof, then the court shall order inpatient commitment be continued for a period not to exceed 180 days. The court shall make a written record of the facts that support its findings.

(d) At least 15 days before the end of any commitment period ordered pursuant to subsection (c) of this section and annually thereafter, the clerk shall calendar the hearing and notify the parties as specified in G.S. 122C-264(d1). The procedures and standards for the rehearing are the same as under this section. No third or subsequent inpatient recommitment order shall be for a period longer than one year. (1991, c. 37, s. 3; 1991 (Reg. Sess., 1992), c. 1034, s. 4.)

§ 122C-277. Release and conditional release; judicial review.

(a) Except as provided in subsections (b) and (b1) of this section, the attending physician shall discharge a committed respondent unconditionally at any time he determines that the respondent is no longer in need of inpatient commitment. However, if the attending physician determines that the respondent meets the criteria for outpatient commitment as defined in G.S. 122C-263(d)(1), he may request the clerk to calendar a supplemental hearing to determine whether an outpatient commitment order shall be issued. Except as provided in subsections (b) and (b1) of this section, the attending physician may also release a respondent conditionally for periods not in excess of 30 days on specified medically appropriate conditions. Violation of the conditions is grounds for return of the respondent to the releasing facility. A law-enforcement officer, on request of the attending physician, shall take a conditional releasee into custody and return him to the facility in accordance with G.S. 122C-205. Notice of discharge and of conditional release shall be furnished to the clerk of superior court of the county of commitment and of the county in which the facility is located.

(b) If the respondent was initially committed as the result of conduct resulting in his being charged with a violent crime, including a crime involving an assault with a deadly weapon, and respondent was found incapable of proceeding, 15 days before the respondent's discharge or conditional release the attending physician shall notify the clerk of superior court of the county in which the facility is located of his determination regarding the proposed discharge or conditional release. The clerk shall then schedule a rehearing to determine the appropriateness of respondent's release under the standards of commitment set forth in G.S. 122C-271(b). The clerk shall give notice as provided in G.S. 122C-264(d). The district attorney of the district where respondent was found incapable of proceeding may represent the State's interest at the hearing.

(b1) If the respondent was initially committed pursuant to G.S. 15A-1321, 15 days before the respondent's discharge or conditional release the attending physician shall notify the clerk of superior court. The clerk shall calendar a hearing and shall give notice as provided by G.S. 122C-264(d1). The district attorney for the original trial may represent the State's interest at the hearing. The hearing shall be conducted under the standards and procedures set forth in G.S. 122C-268.1. Provided, that in no event shall discharge or conditional release under this section be allowed for a respondent during the period from automatic commitment to hearing under G.S. 122C-268.1.

(c) If a committed respondent under subsections (a), (b), or (b1) of this section is from a single portal area, the attending physician shall plan jointly with the area authority as prescribed in the area plan before discharging or releasing the respondent. (1973, c. 726, s. 1; c. 1408, s. 1; 1981, c. 537, s. 5; 1983, c. 383, s. 6; c. 638, s. 21; c. 864, s. 4; 1985, c. 589, s. 2; 1991, c. 37, s. 6.)

§ 122C-278. Reexamination for capacity to proceed prior to discharge.

Whenever a respondent has been committed to either inpatient or outpatient treatment pursuant to this Chapter after having been found incapable of proceeding and referred by the court for civil commitment proceedings, the respondent shall not be discharged from the custody of the hospital or institution or the outpatient commitment case terminated until the respondent has been examined for capacity to proceed and a report filed with the clerk of court pursuant to G.S. 15A-1002. (2013-18, s. 8.)

§ 122C-279: Reserved for future codification purposes.

§ 122C-280: Reserved for future codification purposes.

Part 8. Involuntary Commitment of Substance Abusers, Facilities for Substance Abusers.

§ 122C-281. Affidavit and petition before clerk or magistrate; custody order.

(a)   Any individual who has knowledge of a substance abuser who is dangerous to himself or others may appear before a clerk or assistant or deputy clerk of superior court or a magistrate, execute an affidavit to this effect, and petition the clerk or magistrate for issuance of an order to take the respondent into custody for examination by a physician or eligible psychologist. The affidavit shall include the facts on which the affiant's opinion is based. Jurisdiction under this subsection is in the clerk or magistrate in the county where the respondent resides or is found.

(b)   If the clerk or magistrate finds reasonable grounds to believe that the facts alleged in the affidavit are true and that the respondent is probably a substance abuser and dangerous to himself or others, he shall issue an order to a law-enforcement officer or any other person authorized by G.S. 122C-251 to take the respondent into custody for examination by a physician or eligible psychologist.

(c)   If the clerk or magistrate issues a custody order, he shall also make inquiry in any reliable way as to whether the respondent is indigent within the meaning of G.S. 7A-450. A magistrate shall report the result of this inquiry to the clerk.

(d)   If the affiant is a physician or eligible psychologist, he may execute the affidavit before any official authorized to administer oaths. He is not required to appear before the clerk or magistrate for this purpose. His examination shall comply with the requirements of the initial examination as provided in G.S. 122C-283(c). If the physician or eligible psychologist recommends commitment and the clerk or magistrate finds probable cause to believe that the respondent meets the criteria for commitment, he shall issue an order for transportation to or custody at a 24-hour facility or release the respondent, pending hearing, as described in G.S. 122C-283(d)(1). If a physician or eligible psychologist executes an affidavit for commitment of a respondent, a second qualified professional shall perform the examination required by G.S. 122C-285.

(e) Upon receipt of the custody order of the clerk or magistrate, a law-enforcement officer or other person designated in the order shall take the respondent into custody within 24 hours after the order is signed. The custody order is valid throughout the State.

(f) When a petition is filed for an individual who is a resident of a single portal area, the procedures for examination by a physician or eligible psychologist as set forth in G.S. 122C-283(c) shall be carried out in accordance with the area plan. When an individual from a single portal area is presented for commitment at a facility directly, he may be accepted for admission in accordance with G.S. 122C-285. The facility shall notify the area authority within 24 hours of admission and further planning of treatment for the individual is the joint responsibility of the area authority and the facility as prescribed in the area plan. (1973, c. 726, s. 1; c. 1408, s. 1; 1977, c. 400, s. 3; 1979, c. 164, s. 2; c. 915, ss. 3, 18; 1983, c. 383, s. 5; c. 638, ss. 3-5; c. 864, s. 4; 1985, c. 589, s. 2; c. 695, ss. 2, 4; 2004-23, s. 1(b).)

§ 122C-282. Special emergency procedure for violent individuals.

When an individual subject to commitment under the provisions of this Part is also violent and requires restraint and when delay in taking him to a physician or eligible psychologist for examination would likely endanger life or property, a law-enforcement officer may take the person into custody and take him immediately before a magistrate or clerk. The law-enforcement officer shall execute the affidavit required by G.S. 122C-281 and in addition shall swear that the respondent is violent and requires restraint and that delay in taking the respondent to a physician or eligible psychologist for an examination would endanger life or property.

If the clerk or magistrate finds by clear, cogent, and convincing evidence that the facts stated in the affidavit are true, that the respondent is in fact violent and requires restraint, and that delay in taking the respondent to a physician or eligible psychologist for an examination would endanger life or property, he shall order the law-enforcement officer to take the respondent directly to a 24-hour facility described in G.S. 122C-252.

Respondents received at a 24-hour facility under the provisions of this section shall be examined and processed thereafter in the same way as all other respondents under this Part. (1973, c. 726, s. 1; c. 1408, s. 1; 1985, c. 589, s. 2; c. 695, s. 2.)

§ 122C-283. Duties of law-enforcement officer; first examination by physician or eligible psychologist.

(a) Without unnecessary delay after assuming custody, the law-enforcement officer or the individual designated by the clerk or magistrate under G.S. 122C-251(g) to provide transportation shall take the respondent to an area facility for examination by a physician or eligible psychologist; if a physician or eligible psychologist is not available in the area facility, he shall take the respondent to any physician or eligible psychologist locally available. If a physician or eligible psychologist is not immediately available, the respondent may be temporarily detained in an area facility if one is available; if an area facility is not available, he may be detained under appropriate supervision, in his home, in a private hospital or a clinic, or in a general hospital, but not in a jail or other penal facility.

(b) The examination set forth in subsection (a) of this section is not required if:

(1) The affiant who obtained the custody order is a physician or eligible psychologist; or

(2) The respondent is in custody under the special emergency procedure described in G.S. 122C-282.

In these cases when it is recommended that the respondent be detained in a 24-hour facility, the law-enforcement officer shall take the respondent directly to a 24-hour facility described in G.S. 122C-252.

(c) The physician or eligible psychologist described in subsection (a) of this section shall examine the respondent as soon as possible, and in any event within 24 hours, after the respondent is presented for examination. The examination shall include but is not limited to an assessment of the respondent's:

(1) Current and previous substance abuse including, if available, previous treatment history; and

(2) Dangerousness to himself or others as defined in G.S. 122C-3(11).

(d) After the conclusion of the examination the physician or eligible psychologist shall make the following determinations:

(1) If the physician or eligible psychologist finds that the respondent is a substance abuser and is dangerous to himself or others, he shall recommend commitment and whether the respondent should be released or be held at a 24-hour facility pending hearing and shall so show on [the] his examination report. Based on the physician's or eligible psychologist's recommendation the law-enforcement officer or other designated individual shall take the respondent to a 24-hour facility described in G.S. 122C-252 or release the respondent.

(2) If the physician or eligible psychologist finds that the condition described in subdivision (1) of this subsection does not exist, the respondent shall be released and the proceedings terminated.

(e) The findings of the physician or eligible psychologist and the facts on which they are based shall be in writing in all cases. A copy of the findings shall be sent to the clerk of superior court by the most reliable and expeditious means. If it cannot be reasonably anticipated that the clerk will receive the copy within 48 hours of the time that it was signed, the physician or eligible psychologist shall also communicate his findings to the clerk by telephone. (1973, c. 726, s. 1; c. 1408, s. 1; 1977, c. 400, s. 4; c. 679, s. 8; c. 739, s. 1; 1979, c. 358, s. 27; c. 915, s. 4; 1983, c. 380, ss. 4, 10; c. 638, ss. 6, 7, 25.1; c. 864, s. 4; 1985, c. 589, s. 2; c. 695, ss. 2, 9.)

§ 122C-284. Duties of clerk of superior court.

(a) Upon receipt of a physician's or eligible psychologist's finding that a respondent is a substance abuser and dangerous to himself or others and that commitment is recommended, the clerk of superior court of the county where the facility is located, if the respondent is held in a 24-hour facility, or the clerk of superior court where the petition was initiated shall upon direction of a district court judge assign counsel, calendar the matter for hearing, and notify the respondent, his counsel, and the petitioner of the time and place of the hearing. The petitioner may file a written waiver of his right to notice under this subsection with the clerk of court.

(b)   Notice to the respondent required by subsection (a) of this section shall be given as provided in G.S. 1A-1, Rule 4(j) at least 72 hours before the hearing. Notice to other individuals shall be given by mailing at least 72 hours before the hearing a copy by first-class mail postage prepaid to the individual at his last known address. G.S. 1A-1, Rule 6 shall not apply.

(c)   Upon receipt of notice that transportation is necessary to take a committed respondent to a 24-hour facility pursuant to G.S. 122C-290(b), the clerk shall issue a custody order for the respondent.

(d)   The clerk of superior court shall upon the direction of a district court judge calendar all hearings, supplemental hearings, and rehearings and provide all notices required by this Part. (1973, c. 1408, s. 1; 1977, c. 400, s. 5; c. 414, s. 1; 1979, c. 915, s. 5; 1983, c. 380, s. 9; c. 638, s. 8; c. 864, s. 4; 1985, c. 589, s. 2; c. 695, s. 10; 1985 (Reg. Sess., 1986), c. 863, s. 27.)

§ 122C-285. Commitment; second examination and treatment pending hearing.

(a)   Within 24 hours of arrival at a 24-hour facility described in G.S. 122C-252, the respondent shall be examined by a qualified professional. This professional shall be a physician if the initial commitment evaluation was conducted by an eligible psychologist. The examination shall include the assessment specified in G.S. 122C-283(c). If the qualified professional finds that the respondent is a substance abuser and is dangerous to himself or others, he shall hold and treat the respondent at the facility or designate other treatment pending the district court hearing. If the qualified professional finds that the respondent does not meet the criteria for commitment under G.S. 122C-283(d)(1), he shall release the respondent and the proceeding shall be terminated. In this case the reasons for the release shall be reported in writing to the clerk of superior court of the county in which the custody order originated. If the respondent is released, the law-enforcement officer or other person designated to provide transportation shall return the respondent to the originating county.

(b) If the 24-hour facility described in G.S. 122C-252 is the facility in which the first examination by a physician or eligible psychologist occurred and is the same facility in which the respondent is held, the second examination must occur not later than the following regular working day. (1973, c. 726, s. 1; c. 1408, s. 1; 1977, c. 400, s. 6; 1979, c. 915, s. 6; 1983, c. 380, s. 5; c. 638, ss. 9, 10; c. 864, s. 4; 1985, c. 589, s. 2; c. 695, s. 11; 1985 (Reg. Sess., 1986), c. 863, s. 28.)

§ 122C-286. Commitment; district court hearing.

(a) A hearing shall be held in district court within 10 days of the day the respondent is taken into custody. Upon its own motion or upon motion of the responsible professional, the respondent, or the State, the court may grant a continuance of not more than five days.

(b) The respondent shall be present at the hearing. A subpoena may be issued to compel the respondent's presence at a hearing. The petitioner and the responsible professional of the area authority or the proposed treating physician or his designee may be present and may provide testimony.

(c) Certified copies of reports and findings of physicians and psychologists and medical records of previous and current treatment are admissible in evidence, but the respondent's right to confront and cross-examine witnesses shall not be denied.

(d) The respondent may be represented by counsel of his choice. If the respondent is indigent within the meaning of G.S. 7A-450, counsel shall be appointed to represent the respondent in accordance with rules adopted by the Office of Indigent Defense Services.

(e) Hearings may be held at a facility if it is located within the judge's district court district as defined in G.S. 7A-133 or in the judge's chambers. A hearing may not be held in a regular courtroom, over objection of the respondent, if in the discretion of a judge a more suitable place is available.

(f) The hearing shall be closed to the public unless the respondent requests otherwise.

(g) A copy of all documents admitted into evidence and a transcript of the proceedings shall be furnished to the respondent on request by the clerk upon the direction of a district court judge. If the respondent is indigent, the copies shall be provided at State expense.

(h) To support a commitment order, the court shall find by clear, cogent, and convincing evidence that the respondent meets the criteria specified in G.S. 122C-283(d)(1). The court shall record the facts that support its findings and shall show on the order the area authority or physician who is responsible for the management and supervision of the respondent's treatment. (1985, c. 589, s. 2; c. 695, s. 8; 1985 (Reg. Sess., 1986), c. 863, ss. 29, 30; 1987 (Reg. Sess., 1988), c. 1037, s. 117; 2000-144, s. 43.)

§ 122C-286.1. Venue of district court hearing when respondent held at a 24-hour facility pending hearing.

(a) In all cases where the respondent is held at a 24-hour facility pending the district court hearing as provided in G.S. 122C-286, unless the respondent through counsel objects to the venue, the hearing shall be held in the county in which the facility is located. Upon objection to venue, the hearing shall be held in the county where the petition was initiated.

(b) An official of the facility shall immediately notify the clerk of superior court of the county in which the facility is located of a determination to hold the respondent pending hearing. That clerk shall request transmittal of all documents pertinent to the proceedings from the clerk of superior court where the proceedings were initiated. The requesting clerk shall assume all duties set forth in G.S. 122C-284. The counsel provided for in G.S. 122C-286(d) shall be appointed in accordance with rules adopted by the Office of Indigent Defense Services. (1985 (Reg. Sess., 1986), c. 863, s. 31; 2000-144, s. 44.)

§ 122C-287. Disposition.

The court may make one of the following dispositions:

(1) If the court finds by clear, cogent, and convincing evidence that the respondent is a substance abuser and is dangerous to himself or others, it shall

order for a period not in excess of 180 days commitment to and treatment by an area authority or physician who is responsible for the management and supervision of the respondent's commitment and treatment.

(2) If the court finds that the respondent does not meet the commitment criteria set out in subdivision (1) of this subsection, the respondent shall be discharged and the facility in which he was last treated so notified. (1973, c. 726, s. 1; c. 1408, s. 1; 1977, c. 400, s. 8; c. 739, s. 2; 1979, c. 358, s. 26; c. 915, ss. 8, 15, 16; 1981, c. 537, s. 1; 1983, c. 380, s. 8; c. 638, s. 14; c. 864, s. 4; 1985, c. 589, s. 2.)

§ 122C-288. Appeal.

Judgment of the district court is final. Appeal may be had to the Court of Appeals by the State or by any party on the record as in civil cases. Appeal does not stay the commitment unless so ordered by the Court of Appeals. The Attorney General shall represent the State's interest on appeal. The district court retains limited jurisdiction for the purpose of hearing all reviews, rehearings, or supplemental hearings allowed or required under this Part. (1973, c. 726, s. 1; c. 1408, s. 1; 1979, c. 915, s. 19; 1985, c. 589, s. 2.)

§ 122C-289. Duty of assigned counsel; discharge.

If the respondent is committed, assigned counsel remains responsible for the respondent's representation at the trial level until discharged by order of district court or until the respondent is otherwise unconditionally discharged. If the respondent appeals, counsel for the appeal shall be appointed in accordance with rules adopted by the Office of Indigent Defense Services. (1973, c. 1408, s. 1; 1985, c. 589, s. 2; 2006-264, s. 61(b).)
§ 122C-290. Duties for follow-up on commitment order.

(a) The area authority or physician responsible for management and supervision of the respondent's commitment and treatment may prescribe or administer to the respondent reasonable and appropriate treatment either on an outpatient basis or in a 24-hour facility.

(b) If the respondent whose treatment is provided on an outpatient basis fails to comply with all or part of the prescribed treatment after reasonable effort to solicit the respondent's compliance or whose treatment is provided on an inpatient basis is discharged in accordance with G.S. 122C-205.1(b), the area authority or physician may request the clerk or magistrate to order the respondent taken into custody for the purpose of examination. Upon receipt of this request, the clerk or magistrate shall issue an order to a law enforcement officer to take the respondent into custody and to take him immediately to the designated area authority or physician for examination. The custody order is valid throughout the State. The law enforcement officer shall turn the respondent over to the custody of the physician or area authority who shall conduct the examination and release the respondent or have the respondent taken to a 24-hour facility upon a determination that treatment in the facility will benefit the respondent. Transportation to the 24-hour facility shall be provided as specified in G.S. 122C-251, upon notice to the clerk or magistrate that transportation is necessary, or as provided in G.S. 122C-408(b). If placement in a 24-hour facility is to exceed 45 consecutive days, the area authority or physician shall notify the clerk of court by the 30th day and request a supplemental hearing as specified in G.S. 122C-291.

(c) If the respondent intends to move or moves to another county within the State, the area authority or physician shall notify the clerk of court in the county where the commitment is being supervised and request that a supplemental hearing be calendared.

(d) If the respondent moves to another state or to an unknown location, the designated area authority or physician shall notify the clerk of superior court of the county where the commitment is supervised and the commitment shall be terminated. (1983, c. 638, s. 16; c. 864, s. 4; 1985, c. 589, s. 2; 1985 (Reg. Sess., 1986), c. 863, s. 32; 1987, c. 674, s. 2; c. 750; 2004-23, s. 2(c).)

§ 122C-291. Supplemental hearings.

(a) Upon receipt of a request for a supplemental hearing, the clerk shall calendar a hearing to be held within 14 days and notify, at least 72 hours before the hearing, the petitioner, the respondent, his attorney, if any, and the designated area authority or physician. Notice shall be provided in accordance with G.S. 122C-284(b). The procedures for the hearing shall follow G.S. 122C-286.

(b) At the supplemental hearing for a respondent who has moved or may move to another county, the court shall determine if the respondent meets the criteria for commitment set out in G.S. 122C-283(d)(1). If the court determines that the respondent no longer meets the criteria for commitment, it shall discharge the respondent from the order and dismiss the case. If the court determines that the respondent continues to meet the criteria for commitment, it shall continue the commitment but shall designate an area authority or physician at the respondent's new residence to be responsible for the management or supervision of the respondent's commitment. The court shall order the respondent to appear for treatment at the address of the newly designated area authority or physician and shall order venue for further court proceedings under the commitment to be transferred to the new county of supervision. Upon an order changing venue, the clerk of court in the county where the commitment has been supervised shall transfer the records regarding the commitment to the clerk of court in the county where the commitment will be supervised. Also, the clerk of court in the county where the commitment has been supervised shall send a copy of the court's order directing the continuation of treatment under new supervision to the newly designated area authority or physician.

(c) At a supplemental hearing for a respondent to be held longer than 45 consecutive days in a 24-hour facility, the court shall determine if the respondent meets the criteria for commitment set out in G.S. 122C-283(d)(1). If the court determines that the respondent continues to meet the criteria and that further treatment in the 24-hour facility is necessary, the court may authorize continued care in the facility for not more than 90 days, after which a rehearing for the purpose of determining the need for continued care in the 24-hour facility shall be held, or the court may order the respondent released from the 24-hour facility and continued on the commitment on an outpatient basis. If the court determines that the respondent no longer meets the criteria for commitment the respondent shall be released and his case dismissed.

(d) At any time during the term of commitment order, a respondent may apply to the court for a supplemental hearing for the purpose of discharge from the order. The application shall be made in writing to the clerk of superior court. At the supplemental hearing the court shall determine whether the respondent continues to meet the criteria for commitment. The court may reissue or change the commitment order or discharge the respondent and dismiss the case. (1985, c. 589, s. 2.)

§ 122C-292. Rehearings.

(a) Fifteen days before the end of the initial or subsequent periods of commitment if the area authority or physician determines that the respondent continues to meet the criteria specified in G.S. 122C-283(d)(1), the clerk of superior court of the county where commitment is supervised shall be notified. The clerk, at least 10 days before the end of the commitment period, on order of the district court, shall calendar the rehearing. If the respondent no longer meets the criteria, the area authority or physician shall so notify the clerk who shall dismiss the case.

(b) Rehearings are governed by the same notice and procedures as initial hearings, and the respondent has the same rights he had at the initial hearing including the right to appeal.

(c) If the court finds that the respondent no longer meets the criteria of G.S. 122C-283(d)(1), it shall unconditionally discharge him. A copy of the discharge order shall be furnished by the clerk to the designated area authority or physician. If the respondent continues to meet the criteria of G.S. 122C-283(d)(1), the court may order commitment for additional periods not in excess of 365 days each. (1973, c. 726, s. 1; c. 1408, s. 1; 1977, c. 400, s. 9; 1979, c. 915, ss. 9, 17; 1981, c. 537, ss. 2-4; 1983, c. 638, ss. 18-19; 864, s. 4; 1985, c. 589, s. 2.)

§ 122C-293. Release by area authority or physician.

The area authority or physician as designated in the order shall discharge a committed respondent unconditionally at any time he determines that the respondent no longer meets the criteria of G.S. 122C-283(d)(1). Notice of discharge and the reasons for the release shall be reported in writing to the clerk of superior court of the county in which the commitment was ordered. (1973, c. 726, s. 1; c. 1408, s. 1; 1981, c. 537, s. 5; 1983, c. 383, s. 6; c. 638, s. 21; c. 864, s. 4; 1985, c. 589, s. 2.)

§ 122C-294. Local plan.

Each area authority shall develop a local plan with local law-enforcement agencies, local courts, local hospitals, and local medical societies necessary to facilitate implementation of this Part. (1973, c. 1408, s. 1; 1977, c. 679, s. 8; 1979, c. 358, ss. 26, 27; 1985, c. 589, s. 2.)

§§ 122C-295 through 122C-300. Reserved for future codification purposes.

Part 9. Public Intoxication.

§ 122C-301. Assistance to an individual who is intoxicated in public; procedure for commitment to shelter or facility.

(a) An officer may assist an individual found intoxicated in a public place by taking any of the following actions:

(1) The officer may direct or transport the intoxicated individual home;

(2) The officer may direct or transport the intoxicated individual to the residence of another individual willing to accept him;

(3) If the intoxicated individual is apparently in need of and apparently unable to provide for himself food, clothing, or shelter but is not apparently in need of immediate medical care, the officer may direct or transport him to an appropriate public or private shelter facility;

(4) If the intoxicated individual is apparently in need of but apparently unable to provide for himself immediate medical care, the officer may direct or transport him to an area facility, hospital, or physician's office; or the officer may direct or transport the individual to any other appropriate health care facility; or

(5) If the intoxicated individual is apparently a substance abuser and is apparently dangerous to himself or others, the officer may proceed as provided in Part 8 of this Article.

(b) In providing the assistance authorized by subsection (a) of this section, the officer may use reasonable force to restrain the intoxicated individual if it appears necessary to protect himself, the intoxicated individual, or others. No officer may be held criminally or civilly liable for assault, false imprisonment, or other torts or crimes on account of reasonable measures taken under authority of this Part.

(c) If the officer takes the action described in either subdivision (a)(3) or (a)(4) of this section, the facility to which the intoxicated individual is taken may detain him only until he becomes sober or a maximum of 24 hours. The individual may stay a longer period if he wishes to do so and the facility is able to accommodate him.

(d) Any individual who has knowledge that a person assisted to a shelter or other facility under subdivisions (a)(3) or (a)(4) of this section is a substance abuser and is dangerous to himself or others may proceed as provided in Part 8 of this Article. (1977, 2nd Sess., c. 1134, s. 2; 1981, c. 519, s. 5; 1985, c. 589, s. 2.)

§ 122C-302. Cities and counties may employ officers to assist intoxicated individuals.

A city or county may employ officers to assist individuals who are intoxicated in public. Officers employed for this purpose shall be trained to give assistance to those who are intoxicated in public including the administration of first aid. An officer employed by a city or county to assist intoxicated individuals has the powers and duties set out in G.S. 122C-301 within the same territory in which criminal laws are enforced by law-enforcement officers of that city or county. (1977, 2nd Sess., c. 1134, s. 2; 1985, c. 589, s. 2.)

§ 122C-303. Use of jail for care for intoxicated individual.

In addition to the actions authorized by G.S. 122C-301(a), an officer may assist an individual found intoxicated in a public place by directing or transporting that individual to a city or county jail. That action may be taken only if the intoxicated individual is apparently in need of and apparently unable to provide for himself food, clothing, or shelter but is not apparently in need of immediate medical care and if no other facility is readily available to receive him. The officer and employees of the jail are exempt from liability as provided in G.S. 122C-301(b). The intoxicated individual may be detained at the jail only until he becomes sober or a maximum of 24 hours and may be released at any time to a relative or other individual willing to be responsible for his care. (1977, 2nd Sess., c. 1134, s. 3; 1985, c. 589, s. 2.)

§§ 122C-304 through 122C-310. Reserved for future codification purposes.

Part 10. Voluntary Admissions, Involuntary Commitments and Discharges, Inmates and Parolees, Division of Adult Correction of the Department of Public Safety.

§ 122C-311. Individuals on parole.

Any individual who has been released from any correctional facility on parole is admitted, committed and discharged from facilities in accordance with the procedures specified in this Article for other individuals. (1959, c. 1002, s. 24; 1963, c. 1184, s. 28; 1973, c. 253, s. 4; 1985, c. 589, s. 2.)

§ 122C-312. Voluntary admissions and discharges of inmates of the Division of Adult Correction of the Department of Public Safety.

Inmates in the custody of the Division of Adult Correction of the Department of Public Safety may seek voluntary admission to State facilities for the mentally ill or substance abusers. The provisions of Part 2 of this Article shall apply except that an admission may be accomplished only when the Secretary and the Secretary of Public Safety jointly agree to the inmate's request. When an inmate is admitted he shall be discharged in accordance with the provisions of Part 2 of this Article except that an inmate who is ready for discharge, but still under a term of incarceration, shall be discharged only to an official of the Division of Adult Correction of the Department of Public Safety. The Division of Adult Correction of the Department of Public Safety is responsible for the security and cost of transporting inmates to and from facilities under the provisions of this section. (1979, c. 547; 1985, c. 589, s. 2; 2011-145, s. 19.1(h), (i).)

§ 122C-313. Inmate becoming mentally ill and dangerous to himself or others.

(a) An inmate who becomes mentally ill and dangerous to himself or others after incarceration in any facility operated by the Division of Adult Correction of the Department of Public Safety in the State is processed in accordance with Part 7 of this Article, as modified by this section, except when the provisions of Part 7 are manifestly inappropriate. A staff psychiatrist or eligible psychologist of the correctional facility shall execute the affidavit required by G.S. 122C-261 and send it to the clerk of superior court of the county in which the correctional facility is located. Upon receipt of the affidavit, the clerk shall calendar a district court hearing and notify the respondent and his counsel as required by G.S. 122C-284(a). The hearing is conducted in a district courtroom. If the judge finds by clear, cogent, and convincing evidence that the respondent is mentally ill and dangerous to himself or others, he shall order him transferred for treatment to a State facility designated by the Secretary. The judge shall not order outpatient commitment for an inmate-respondent.

(b) If the sentence of an inmate-respondent expires while he is committed to a State facility, he is considered in all respects as if he had been initially committed under Part 7 of this Article.

(c) If the sentence of an inmate-respondent has not expired, and if in the opinion of the attending physician of the State facility an inmate-respondent ceases to be mentally ill and dangerous to himself or others, he shall notify the Division of Adult Correction of the Department of Public Safety which shall arrange for the inmate-respondent's return to a correctional facility.

(d) Special counsel at a State facility shall represent any inmate who becomes mentally ill and dangerous to himself or others while confined in a correctional facility in the same county, otherwise counsel is assigned in accordance with G.S. 122C-270(d).

(e) The Division of Adult Correction of the Department of Public Safety is responsible for the security and cost of transporting inmates to and from State facilities under the provisions of this section. (1899, c. 1, s. 66; Rev., s. 4619; C.S., s. 6238; 1923, c. 165, s. 55; 1945, c. 952, s. 55; 1955, c. 887, s. 14; 1957, c. 1232, s. 26; 1963, c. 1184, s. 27; 1965, c. 800, s. 13; 1973, c. 253, s. 3; c. 1433; 1977, c. 679, s. 8; 1979, c. 358, s. 27; c. 915, s. 11; 1985, c. 589, s. 2; c. 695, s. 2; 2011-145, s. 19.1(h).)

§§ 122C-314 through 122C-320: Reserved for future codification purposes.

Part 11. Voluntary Admissions, Involuntary Commitments and Discharges, the Psychiatric Service of the University of North Carolina Hospitals at Chapel Hill.

§ 122C-321. Voluntary admissions and discharges.

Any individual in need of treatment for mental illness or substance abuse may seek voluntary admission to the psychiatric service of the University of North Carolina Hospitals at Chapel Hill. Procedures for admission and discharge shall be made in accordance with Parts 2 through 4 of this Article. The applicant may be admitted only upon the approval of the director of the psychiatric service or his designee. (1955, c. 1274, s. 2; 1963, c. 1184, s. 2; 1973, c. 723, s. 3; c. 1084; 1985, c. 589, s. 2; 1989, c. 141, s. 14.)

§ 122C-322. Involuntary commitments.

(a) Except as otherwise specifically provided in this section references in Parts 6 through 8 of this Article to 24-hour facilities, outpatient treatment centers, or area authorities, or private facilities shall include the psychiatric service of the University of North Carolina Hospitals at Chapel Hill. The psychiatric service may be used for temporary detention pending a district court hearing, for commitment of the respondent after the hearing, or as the manager and supervisor of outpatient commitment. However, no individual may be held at or committed to the psychiatric service without the prior approval of the director of the psychiatric service or his designee.

(b) Initial hearings, supplemental hearings, and rehearings may be held at the psychiatric service facility or at any place in Orange County where district court can be held under G.S. 7A-133. Legal counsel for the respondent at all hearings and rehearings shall be assigned from among the members of the bar of the same county in accordance with G.S. 122C-270(d). (1977, c. 738, s. 1; 1981, c. 442; 1985, c. 589, s. 2; 1989, c. 141, s. 15.)

§§ 122C-323 through 122C-330. Reserved for future codification purposes.

Part 12. Voluntary Admissions, Involuntary Commitments and Discharges, Veterans Administration Facilities.

§ 122C-331. Voluntary admissions and discharges.

Veterans in need of treatment for mental illness or substance abuse may seek voluntary admission to a facility operated by the Veterans Administration. Procedures for admission and discharge shall be made in accordance with Parts 2 and 4 of this Article. The Veterans Administration may require additional procedures not inconsistent with these Parts. (1973, c. 1408, s. 1; 1985, c. 589, s. 2.)

§ 122C-332. Involuntary commitments.

(a) Except as otherwise specifically provided in this section, references in Parts 6 through 8 of this Article to 24-hour facilities, outpatient treatment centers, or area authorities, or private facilities shall include the facilities operated by the Veterans Administration. Veterans Administration facilities may be used for temporary detention pending a district court hearing, for commitment of the respondent after the hearing, or as the manager and supervisor of outpatient commitment. Eligibility of the veteran-respondent for treatment at a Veterans Administration facility and the availability of space shall be determined by the Veterans Administration in all cases before sending or committing a veteran-respondent.

(b) Initial hearings, supplemental hearings, and rehearings for veteran-respondents may be held at the facility or at the county courthouse in the county in which the facility is located, and counsel shall be assigned from among the members of the bar of the same county in accordance with G.S. 122C-270(d). (1985, c. 589, s. 2.)

§ 122C-333. Order of another state.

The judgment or order of commitment by a court of competent jurisdiction of another state, committing a person to the Veterans Administration or another federal agency that is located in this State shall have the same force and effect on the committed person while in this State as in the jurisdiction of the court entering the judgment or making the order. The courts of the committing state shall retain jurisdiction of the person so committed for the purpose of inquiring into the mental condition of the person, and for determining the necessity for continuance of his restraint. Consent is given to the application of the law of the committing state on the authority of the chief officer of any facility of the Veterans Administration or of any institution operated in this State by any other federal agency to retain custody, transfer, parole, or discharge the committed person. (1985, c. 589, s. 2.)

§§ 122C-334 through 122C-340. Reserved for future codification purposes.

Part 13. Voluntary Admissions, Involuntary Commitment and Discharge of Non-State Residents and the Return of North Carolina Resident Clients.

§ 122C-341. Determination of residence.

It is the responsibility of the facility to determine if a client is not a resident of the State. (1899, c. 1, s. 18; Rev., ss. 3591, 4587, 4588; C.S., ss. 6187, 6188; 1945, c. 952, ss. 16, 17; 1947, c. 537, s. 11; 1953, c. 256, s. 3; 1957, c. 1386; 1963, c. 1184, s. 1; 1973, c. 673, s. 13; 1985, c. 589, s. 2.)

§ 122C-342. Voluntary admissions and discharges.

A non-State resident may be admitted to and discharged from a facility on a voluntary basis in accordance with Parts 2 through 5 of this Article at his own expense. If the facility determines that the client should be returned to his own state the provisions of G.S. 122C-345 or G.S. 122C-361, as appropriate, shall apply. (1899, c. 1, s. 16; Rev., s. 4584; C.S., s. 6210; 1945, c. 952, s. 33; 1947, c. 537, s. 18; 1963, c. 1184, s. 1; 1971, c. 1140; 1973, c. 476, s. 133; c. 673, s. 13; 1985, c. 589, s. 2.)

§ 122C-343. Involuntary commitments.

Involuntary commitments of non-State residents are made under the provisions of Parts 6 through 8 of this Article. If after commitment to a 24-hour facility the facility determines that the respondent needs long-term care and should be returned to his state of residence, the provisions of G.S. 122C-345 or G.S. 122C-361, as appropriate, shall apply. (1899, c. 1, s. 16; Rev., s. 4584; C.S., s. 6210; 1945, c. 952, s. 33; 1947, c. 537, s. 18; 1963, c. 1184, s. 1; 1971, c. 1140; 1973, c. 476, s. 133; c. 673, s. 13; 1985, c. 589, s. 2.)

§ 122C-344. Citizens of other countries.

In addition to the provisions of G.S. 122C-341 through G.S. 122C-343, if a 24-hour facility determines that a client is not a citizen of the United States, the facility shall notify the Governor of this State of the name of the client, the country and place of his residence in the country and other facts in the case as can be obtained, together with a copy of pertinent medical records. The Governor shall send the information to the nearest consular office of the committed foreign national, with the request that the consular office tell the minister resident or plenipotentiary of the country of which the client is alleged to be a citizen. (1899, c. 1, s. 16; Rev., s. 4585; C.S., s. 6211; 1963, c. 1184, s. 1; 1985, c. 589, s. 2; 1993, c. 561, s. 86(a).)

§ 122C-345. Return of a non-State resident client to his resident state.

(a)   Except as provided in subsection (c) of this section, it is the responsibility of the director of a facility to arrange for the transfer of a client to his resident state. The cost of returning the client to his resident state is the responsibility of the client or his family.

(b)   A non-State resident client of an area 24-hour facility may be transferred to a State facility in accordance with G.S. 122C-206 in order for the client to be returned to his resident state.

(c)   A non-State resident client of a State facility may be returned to his resident state under procedures established under G.S. 122C-346 or G.S. 122C-361. The cost of returning a client to his resident state under this subsection shall be the responsibility of the State. (1899, c. 1, s. 16; Rev., s. 4584; C.S., s. 6210; 1945, c. 952, s. 33; 1947, c. 537, ss. 18, 20; 1955, c. 887, s. 13; 1959, c. 1002, s. 22; 1963, c. 1184, s. 1; 1971, c. 1140; 1973, c. 476, s. 133; c. 673, s. 13; 1977, c. 679, s. 7; 1981, c. 51, s. 3; 1985, c. 589, s. 2.)

§ 122C-346. Authority of the Secretary to enter reciprocal agreements.

The Secretary may enter agreements with other states for the return of non-State resident clients to their resident state and for the return of North Carolina residents to North Carolina when under treatment in another state. (1947, c. 537, s. 20; 1955, c. 887, s. 13; 1959, c. 1002, s. 22; 1963, c. 1184, s. 1; 1973, c. 476, s. 133; 1977, c. 679, s. 7; 1981, c. 51, s. 3; 1985, c. 589, s. 2.)

§ 122C-347. Return of North Carolina resident clients from other states.

North Carolina residents who are in treatment in another state may be returned to North Carolina either under an agreement authorized in G.S. 122C-346 or under the provisions of G.S. 122C-361. The cost of returning a North Carolina resident to this State is the responsibility of the sending state. Within 72 hours after admission in a State facility, a returned resident shall be evaluated. The returned resident may agree to a voluntary admission or may be released, or proceedings for an involuntary commitment under this Article may be initiated as necessary by the responsible professional in the facility. (1945, c. 952, s. 34; 1947, c. 537, s. 19; 1959, c. 1002, ss. 20, 21; 1963, c. 1184, s. 1; 1965, c. 800, s. 9; 1969, c. 982; 1973, c. 476, ss. 133, 138; c. 673, s. 13; 1985, c. 589, s. 2.)

§ 122C-348. Residency not affected.

(a) A nonresident of this State who is under care in a 24-hour facility in this State is not considered a resident. No length of time spent in this State while a client in a 24-hour facility is sufficient to make a nonresident a resident or entitled to care or treatment.

(b) A North Carolina resident who is under care and treatment in a 24-hour facility in another state shall retain his residency in North Carolina. (1899, c. 1,

s. 18; Rev., ss. 3591, 4587, 4588; C.S., ss. 6187, 6188; 1945, c. 952, ss. 16, 17; 1947, c. 537, ss. 11, 20; 1953, c. 256, s. 3; 1955, c. 887, s. 13; 1957, c. 1386; 1959, c. 1002, s. 22; 1963, c. 1184, s. 1; 1973, c. 476, s. 133; c. 673, s. 13; 1977, c. 679, s. 7; 1981, c. 51, s. 3; 1985, c. 589, s. 2.)

§§ 122C-349 through 122C-360. Reserved for future codification purposes.

Part 14. Interstate Compact on Mental Health.

§ 122C-361. Compact entered into; form of Compact.

The Interstate Compact on Mental Health is hereby enacted into law and entered into by this State with all other states legally joining therein in the form substantially as follows: The contracting states solemnly agree that:

Article I.

The party states find that the proper and expeditious treatment of the mentally ill and mentally deficient can be facilitated by cooperative action, to the benefit of the patients, their families, and society as a whole. Further, the party states find that the necessity of and desirability for furnishing such care and treatment bears no primary relation to the residence or citizenship of the patient but, that, on the contrary, the controlling factors of community safety and humanitarianism require that facilities and services be made available for all who are in need of them. Consequently, it is the purpose of this Compact and of the party states to provide the necessary legal basis for the institutionalization or other appropriate care and treatment of the mentally ill and mentally deficient under a system that recognizes the paramount importance of patient welfare and to establish the responsibilities of the party states in term of such welfare.

Article II.

As used in this Compact:

(a) "Sending state" shall mean a party state from which a patient is transported pursuant to the provisions of the Compact or from which it is contemplated that a patient may be so sent.

(b) "Receiving state" shall mean a party state to which a patient is transported pursuant to the provisions of the Compact or to which it is contemplated that a patient may be so sent.

(c) "Institution" shall mean any hospital or other facility maintained by a party state or political subdivision thereof for the care and treatment of mental illness or mental deficiency.

(d) "Patient" shall mean any person subject to or eligible as determined by the laws of the sending state, for institutionalization or other care, treatment, or supervision pursuant to the provisions of this Compact.

(e) "Aftercare" shall mean care, treatment and services provided a patient, as defined herein, on convalescent status or conditional release.

(f) "Mental illness" shall mean mental disease to such extent that a person so afflicted requires care and treatment for his own welfare, or the welfare of others, or of the community.

(g) "Mental deficiency" shall mean mental deficiency as defined by appropriate clinical authorities to such extent that a person so afflicted is incapable of managing himself and his affairs, but shall not include mental illness as defined herein.

(h) "State" shall mean any state, territory or possession of the United States, the District of Columbia, and the Commonwealth of Puerto Rico.

Article III.

(a) Whenever a person physically present in any party state shall be in need of institutionalization by reason of mental illness or mental deficiency, he shall be eligible for care and treatment in an institution in that state irrespective of his residence, settlement or citizenship qualifications.

(b) The provisions of paragraph (a) of this Article to the contrary notwithstanding, any patient may be transferred to an institution in another state whenever there are factors based upon clinical determinations indicating that the care and treatment of said patient would be facilitated or improved thereby. Any such institutionalization may be for the entire period of care and treatment or for any portion or portions thereof. The factors referred to in this paragraph shall include the patient's full record with due regard for the location of the patient's family, character of the illness and probable duration thereof, and such other factors as shall be considered appropriate.

(c) No state shall be obliged to receive any patient pursuant to the provisions of paragraph (b) of this Article unless the sending state has given advance notice of its intention to send the patient; furnished all available medical and other pertinent records concerning the patient; given the qualified medical or other appropriate clinical authorities of the receiving state an opportunity to examine the patient if said authorities so wish; and unless the receiving state shall agree to accept the patient.

(d) In the event that the laws of the receiving state establish a system of priorities for the admission of patients, an interstate patient under this Compact shall receive the same priority as a local patient and shall be taken in the same order and at the same time that it would be taken if he were a local patient.

(e) Pursuant to this Compact, the determination as to the suitable place of institutionalization for a patient may be reviewed at any time and such further transfer of the patient may be made as seems likely to be in the best interest of the patient.

Article IV.

(a) Whenever, pursuant to the laws of the state in which a patient is physically present, it shall be determined that the patient should receive aftercare or supervision, such care or supervision may be provided in a receiving state. If the medical or other appropriate clinical authorities have responsibility for the care and treatment of the patient in the sending state shall have reason to believe that aftercare in another state would be in the best interest of the patient and would not jeopardize the public safety, they shall request the appropriate authorities in the receiving state to investigate the desirability of affording the patient such aftercare in said receiving state, and such investigation shall be made with all reasonable speed. The request for investigation shall be accompanied by complete information concerning the patient's intended place of residence and the identity of the person in whose charge it is proposed to place the patient, the complete medical history of the patient, and such other documents as may be pertinent.

(b) If the medical or other appropriate clinical authorities having responsibility for the care and treatment of the patient in the sending state and the appropriate authorities in the receiving state find that the best interest of the patient would be served thereby, and if the public safety would not be jeopardized thereby, the patient may receive aftercare or supervision in the receiving state.

(c) In supervising, treating, or caring for a patient on aftercare pursuant to the terms of this Article, a receiving state shall employ the same standards of visitation, examination, care, and treatment that it employs for similar local patients.

Article V.

Whenever a dangerous or potentially dangerous patient escapes from an institution in any party state, that state shall promptly notify all appropriate authorities within and without the jurisdiction of the escape in a way reasonably calculated to facilitate the speedy apprehension of the escapee. Immediately upon the apprehension and identification of any such dangerous or potentially dangerous patient, he shall be detained in the state where found pending disposition in accordance with law.

Article VI.

The duly accredited officers of any state party to this Compact, upon the establishment of their authority and the identity of the patient, shall be permitted to transport any patient being moved pursuant to this Compact through any and all states party to this Compact, without inferference.

Article VII.

(a) No person shall be deemed a patient of more than one institution at any given time. Completion of transfer of any patient to an institution in a receiving state shall have the effect of making the person a patient of the institution in the receiving state.

(b) The sending state shall pay all costs of and incidental to the transportation of any patient pursuant to this Compact, but any two or more party states may, by making a specific agreement for that purpose, arrange for a different allocation of costs as among themselves.

(c) No provision of this Compact shall be construed to alter or affect any internal relationships among the departments, agencies and officers of and in the government of a party state, or between a party state and its subdivisions, as to the payment of costs, or responsibilities therefor.

(d) Nothing in this Compact shall be construed to prevent any party state or subdivision thereof from asserting any right against any person, agency or other entity in regard to costs for which such party state or subdivision thereof may be responsible pursuant to any provision of this Compact.

(e) Nothing in this Compact shall be construed to invalidate any reciprocal agreement between a party state and a nonparty state relating to institutionalization, care or treatment of the mentally ill or mentally deficient, or any statutory authority pursuant to which such agreements may be made.

Article VIII.

(a) Nothing in this Compact shall be construed to abridge, diminish, or in any way impair the rights, duties, and responsibilities of any patient's guardian on his own behalf or in respect of any patient for whom he may serve, except that where the transfer of any patient to another jurisdiction makes advisable the appointment of a supplemental or substitute guardian, any court of competent jurisdiction in the receiving state may make such supplemental or substitute appointment and the court which appointed the previous guardian shall upon being duly advised of the new appointment, and upon the satisfactory completion of such accounting and other acts as such court may by law require, relieve the previous guardian of power and responsibility to whatever extent shall be appropriate in the circumstances; provided, however, that in the case of any patient having settlement in the sending state, the court of competent jurisdiction in the sending state shall have the sole discretion to relieve a guardian appointed by it or continue his power and responsibility, whichever it shall deem advisable. The court in the receiving state may, in its discretion, confirm or reappoint the person or persons previously serving as guardian in the sending state in lieu of making a supplemental or substitute appointment.

(b)   The term "guardian" as used in paragraph (a) of this Article shall include any guardian, trustee, legal committee, conservator, or other person or agency however denominated who is charged by law with power to act for or responsibility for the person or property of a patient.

Article IX.

(a)   No provision of this Compact except Article V shall apply to any person institutionalized while under sentence in a penal or correctional institution or while subject to trial on a criminal charge, or whose institutionalization is due to the commission of an offense for which, in the absence of mental illness or mental deficiency, said person would be subject to incarceration in a penal or correctional institution.

(b)   To every extent possible, it shall be the policy of states party to this Compact that no patient shall be placed or detained in any prison, jail or lockup, but such patient shall, with all expedition, be taken to a suitable institutional facility for mental illness or mental deficiency.

Article X.

(a)   Each party state shall appoint a "Compact Administrator" who, on behalf of his state, shall act as general coordinator of activities under the Compact in his state and who shall receive copies of all reports, correspondence, and other documents relating to any patient processed under the Compact by his state either in the capacity of sending or receiving state. The Compact Administrator or his duly designated representative shall be the official with whom other party states shall deal in any matter relating to the Compact or any patient processed thereunder.

(b) The Compact Administrators of the respective party states shall have power to promulgate reasonable rules and regulations to carry out more effectively the terms and provisions of this Compact.

Article XI.

The duly constituted administrative authorities of any two or more party states may enter into supplementary agreements for the provision of any service or facility or for the maintenance of any institution on a joint or cooperative basis whenever the states concerned shall find that such agreements will improve services, facilities, or institutional care and treatment in the fields of mental illness or mental deficiency. No such supplementary agreement shall be construed so as to relieve any party state of any obligation which it otherwise would have under other provisions of this Compact.

Article XII.

This Compact shall enter into full force and effect as to any state when enacted by it into law and such state shall thereafter be a party thereto with any and all states legally joining therein.

Article XIII.

(a) A state party to this Compact may withdraw therefrom by enacting a statute repealing the same. Such withdrawal shall take effect one year after notice thereof has been communicated officially and in writing to the governors and Compact administrators of all other party states. However, the withdrawal of any state shall not change the status of any patient who has been sent to said state or sent out of said state pursuant to the provisions of the Compact.

(b) Withdrawal from any agreement permitted by Article VII(b) as to costs or from any supplementary agreement made pursuant to Article XI shall be in accordance with the terms of such agreement.

Article XIV.

This Compact shall be liberally construed so as to effectuate the purposes thereof. The provisions of this Compact shall be severable and if any phrase, clause, sentence or provision of this Compact is declared to be contrary to the constitution of any party state or of the United States or the applicability thereof to any government, agency, person or circumstance is held invalid, the validity of the remainder of this Compact and the applicability thereof to any government, agency, person or circumstance shall not be affected thereby. If this Compact shall be held contrary to the constitution of any state party thereto, the Compact shall remain in full force and effect as to the remaining states and in full force and effect as to the state affected as to all severable matters. (1959, c. 1003, s. 1; 1963, c. 1184, s. 12; 1985, c. 589, s. 2.)

§ 122C-362. Compact Administrator.

Pursuant to the Compact, the Secretary is the Compact Administrator and, acting jointly with like officers of other party states, may adopt rules to carry out more effectively the terms of the Compact. The Compact Administrator shall cooperate with all departments, agencies and officers of and in the government of this State and its subdivisions in facilitating the proper administration of the Compact, of any supplementary agreement, or agreements entered into by this State. (1959, c. 1003, s. 2; 1963, c. 1184, s. 12; 1973, c. 476, s. 133; 1985, c. 589, s. 2.)

§ 122C-363. Supplementary agreements.

The Compact Administrator may enter into supplementary agreements with appropriate officials of other states pursuant to Articles VII and XI of the Compact. In the event that these supplementary agreements shall require or contemplate the use of any institution or facility of this State or require or contemplate the provision of any service by this State, no such agreement shall be effective until approved by the head of the department or agency under whose jurisdiction the institution or facility is operated or whose department or agency will be charged with the rendering of this service. (1959, c. 1003, s. 3; 1963, c. 1184, s. 12; 1985, c. 589, s. 2.)

§ 122C-364. Financial arrangements.

The Compact Administrator, with the approval of the Director of the Budget, may make or arrange for any payments necessary to discharge any financial obligations imposed upon this State by the Compact or by any supplementary agreement entered into under it. (1959, c. 1003, s. 4; 1963, c. 1184, s. 12; 1985, c. 589, s. 2.)

§ 122C-365. Transfer of clients.

The Compact Administrator is directed to consult with the immediate family or legally responsible person of any proposed transferee. (1959, c. 1003, s. 5; 1963, c. 1184, ss. 12, 38; 1985, c. 589, s. 2.)

§ 122C-366. Transmittal of copies of Part.

Copies of this Part shall, upon its approval, be transmitted by the Compact Administrator to the governor of each state, the attorney general of each state, the Administrator of General Services of the United States, and the Council of State Governments. (1959, c. 1003, s. 6; 1963, c. 1184, s. 12; 1985, c. 589, s. 2.)

§§ 122C-367 through 122C-400. Reserved for future codification purposes.

Article 6.

Special Provisions.

Part 1. Camp Butner and Community of Butner.

§ 122C-401. Use of Camp Butner Hospital authorized.

The State may use the Camp Butner Hospital, including buildings, equipment, and land necessary for the operation of modern up-to-date facilities for the care and treatment of citizens of this State. (1947, c. 789, s. 2; 1963, c. 1166, s. 10; 1973, c. 476, s. 133; 1985, c. 589, s. 2.)

§ 122C-402. Application of State highway and motor vehicle laws at State institutions on Camp Butner reservation.

The provisions of Chapter 20 of the General Statutes relating to the use of the highways of the State and the operation of motor vehicles thereon are made applicable to the streets, alleys, and driveways on the Camp Butner reservation that are on the grounds of any State facility or any State institution operated by the Department or by the Division of Adult Correction of the Department of Public Safety. Any person violating any of the provisions of Chapter 20 of the General Statutes in or on these streets, alleys, or driveways shall upon conviction be punished as prescribed in that Chapter. This section does not interfere with the ownership and control of the streets, alleys, and driveways on the grounds as is now vested by law in the Department. (1949, c. 71, s. 2; 1955, c. 887, s. 1; 1959, c. 1028, s. 4; 1963, c. 1166, s. 10; 1973, c. 476, s. 133; 1985, c. 589, s. 2; 2011-145, s. 19.1(h).)

§ 122C-403. Secretary's authority over Camp Butner reservation.

The Secretary shall administer the Camp Butner reservation except (i) those areas within the municipal boundaries of the Town of Butner and (ii) that portion of the Town of Butner's extraterritorial jurisdiction consisting of lands not owned by the State of North Carolina. In performing this duty, the Secretary has the powers listed below. In exercising these powers the Secretary has the same authority and is subject to the same restrictions that the governing body of a city would have and would be subject to if the reservation was a city, unless this section provides to the contrary. The Secretary may:

(1) Regulate airports on the reservation in accordance with the powers granted in Article 4 of Chapter 63 of the General Statutes.

(2) Take actions in accordance with the general police power granted in Article 8 of Chapter 160A of the General Statutes.

(3) Regulate the development of the reservation in accordance with the powers granted in Article 19, Parts 2, 3, 3C, 5, 6, and 7, of Chapter 160A of the General Statutes. The Secretary may not, however, grant a special use permit, a conditional use permit, or a special exception under Part 3 of that Article. In addition, the Secretary is not required to notify landowners of zoning classification actions under G.S. 160A-384, and the protest petition requirements in G.S. 160A-385, and 160A-386 do not apply, but the Secretary shall give the mayor of the Town of Butner at least 14 days' advance written notice of any proposed zoning change. The Secretary may designate Advisory establish a board to act like a Board of Adjustment to make recommendations to the Secretary concerning implementation of plans for the development of the reservation. When acting as a Board of Adjustment, Advisory that board shall be subject to subsections (b), (c), (d), (f), and (g) of G.S. 160A-388.

(4) Establish one or more planning agencies in accordance with the power granted in G.S. 160A-361.

(5) Regulate streets, traffic, and parking on the reservation in accordance with the powers granted in Article 15 of Chapter 160A of the General Statutes.

(6) Control erosion and sedimentation on the reservation in accordance with the powers granted in G.S. 160A-458 and Article 4 of Chapter 113A of the General Statutes.

(7) Contract with and undertake agreements with units of local government in accordance with the powers granted in G.S. 160A-413 and Article 20, Part 1, of Chapter 160A of the General Statutes.

(8) Regulate floodways on the reservation in accordance with the powers granted in G.S. 160A-458.1 and Article 21, Part 6, of Chapter 143 of the General Statutes.

(8a) Repealed by Session Laws 2007-269, s. 4. For effective date, see editor's note.

(9) Assign duties given by the statutes listed in the preceding subdivisions to a local official to the Secretary's designee.

(9a) Repealed by Session Laws 2007-269, s. 4. For effective date, see editor's note.

(10) Adopt rules to carry out the purposes of this Article. (1949, c. 71, s. 3; 1955, c. 887, s. 1; 1959, c. 1028, s. 4; 1963, c. 1166, s. 10; 1965, c. 933; 1973, c. 476, s. 133; 1985, c. 589, s. 2; 1987, c. 536, s. 2; 1995 (Reg. Sess., 1996), c. 667, s. 3; 1997-59, s. 5; 1997-443, s. 11A.118(a); 1999-140, s. 4; 2007-269, s. 4.)

§ 122C-404: Repealed by Session Laws 1995 (Regular Session, 1996), c. 667, s. 4.

§ 122C-405. Procedure applicable to rules.

Rules adopted by the Secretary under this Article shall be adopted in accordance with the procedures for adopting a city ordinance on the same subject, shall be subject to review in the manner provided for a city ordinance adopted on the same subject, and shall be enforceable in accordance with the procedures for enforcing a city ordinance on the same subject. Violation of a rule adopted under this Article is punishable as provided in G.S. 122C-406.

Rules adopted under this Article may apply to part or all of the Camp Butner Reservation, except those areas within the municipal boundaries of the Town of Butner and that portion of the Town of Butner's extraterritorial jurisdiction consisting of lands not owned by the State of North Carolina. If a public hearing is required before the adoption of a rule, Advisory the Secretary shall designate one or more employees of the Department to conduct the hearing. The Butner Town Council shall receive at least 14 days' advance written notice of any public hearing with all correspondence concerning such public hearings to be directed to the mayor of the Town of Butner and sent by certified mail, return receipt requested, or equivalent delivery service to Butner Town Hall. (1949, c. 71, s. 4; 1963, c. 1166, s. 10; 1973, c. 476, s. 133; 1981, c. 614, s. 6; 1985, c. 589, s. 2; 1987, c. 536, s. 4; c. 720, s. 3; 1995 (Reg. Sess., 1996), c. 667, s. 5; 1997-59, s. 6; 1999-140, s. 5; 2007-269, s. 5.)

§ 122C-406. Violations made misdemeanor.

A person who violates an ordinance or rule adopted under this Part is guilty of a Class 3 misdemeanor. (1949, c. 71, s. 5; 1985, c. 589, s. 2; 1993, c. 539, s. 927; 1994, Ex. Sess., c. 24, s. 14(c).)

§ 122C-407. Water and sewer system.

(a) The Department may acquire, construct, establish, enlarge, maintain, operate, and contract for the operation of a water supply and distribution system and a sewage collection and disposal system for the Camp Butner Reservation, and may enter into such contracts, memoranda of understanding, and other agreements with other persons or entities, including, but not limited to, local governments, authorities, and private enterprises, reasonably necessary to extend or otherwise provide water and sewer service to any portion of the Camp Butner Reservation.

(b) Those things authorized by subsection (a) of this section may be operated for the benefit of persons and property within the Camp Butner reservation and areas outside the reservation within reasonable limitations specifically including any sanitary district, water and sewer authority, county water and sewer district, or municipality in Durham or Granville Counties.

(c) The Secretary may fix and enforce water and sewer rates and charges in accordance with G.S. 160A-314 as if it were a city. (1985, c. 589, s. 2; 2007-269, s. 6.)

§ 122C-408. Former Butner Public Safety Authority; jurisdiction; fire and police protection.

(a) Police and Fire Protection. - The Town of Butner may contract with the State of North Carolina or any state agency for the provision of special police officers or fire protection or both to any State or federal institution or lands within the territory of the Camp Butner Reservation. The territorial jurisdiction of these officers shall consist of the property shown on a map produced May 20, 2003, by the Information Systems Division of the North Carolina General Assembly and kept on file in the office of the Butner Town Manager and such additional areas which are within the incorporated limits of the Town of Butner as shown on a map to be kept in the office of the Butner Town Manager.

(b) Authority of Special Police Officers. - In order to assist the Town of Butner in providing contractual services to State agencies and facilities within the territorial jurisdiction set out in subsection (a) of this section, the officers providing police services to the Town of Butner shall have the additional authority set out in this subsection. After taking the oath of office required for law-enforcement officers, the special police officers authorized by this section shall have the authority of deputy sheriffs of Durham and Granville Counties in those counties respectively. Within the territorial jurisdiction stated in subsection (a) of this section, the special police officers have the authority to enforce the laws of North Carolina, the ordinances of the Town of Butner, and any rule applicable to the Camp Butner Reservation adopted under authority of this Part or under G.S. 143-116.6 or G.S. 143-116.7 or under the authority granted any other agency of the State and also have the powers set forth for firemen in Articles 80, 82, and 83 of Chapter 58 of the General Statutes. Notwithstanding the foregoing, the Town of Butner has no obligation or responsibility to provide law enforcement or fire protection services outside of the corporate limits of the Town of Butner except pursuant to a contract with a State agency or facility, a federal entity, or a private person or entity. In the event that any State agency contracts with the Town of Butner for police services at any facility within the territorial jurisdiction described in subsection (a) of this section, any civil or criminal process to be served on any individual confined at any such State facility may be forwarded by the sheriff of the county in which the process originated to the director or chief of the Town of Butner's law enforcement department or that officer's designee. (1949, c. 71, s. 6; 1955, c. 887, s. 1; 1959, c. 35; c. 1028, s. 4; 1963, c. 1166, s. 10; 1973, c. 476, s. 133; 1981, c. 491, s. 1; c. 964, s. 19; c. 1127, s. 49; 1983, c. 761, s. 165; 1985, c. 589, s. 2; 1987, c. 827, s. 246; 1989, c. 141, s. 16; 2003-346, s. 2; 2007-269, s. 7; 2011-145, ss. 19.1(g), (jj), 19.3(b); 2011-260, ss. 1, 6(a), (b); 2011-391, s. 43(m); 2012-50, ss. 1-3; 2013-360, s. 16B.4(b).)

§ 122C-409. Community of Butner comprehensive emergency management plan.

The Department of Public Safety shall establish an emergency management agency as defined in G.S. 166A-19.3(9) for the Camp Butner Reservation, and the Town of Butner. (1985, c. 589, s. 2; 2007-269, s. 8; 2011-145, s. 19.1(g); 2012-12, s. 2(r).)

§ 122C-410. Authority of county or city over Camp Butner Reservation; zoning jurisdiction by Town of Butner over State lands.

(a) A municipality other than the Town of Butner may not annex territory extending into or extend its extraterritorial jurisdiction into the Camp Butner reservation without written approval from the Secretary and the Butner Town Council of each proposed annexation or extension. The Town of Butner may not annex territory extending into or extend its extraterritorial jurisdiction into those portions of the Camp Butner Reservation owned by the State of North Carolina without written approval from the Secretary of each proposed annexation or extension. The procedures, if any, for withdrawing approval granted by the Secretary to an annexation or extension of extraterritorial jurisdiction shall be stated in the notice of approval.

(b) A county ordinance may apply in part or all of the Camp Butner reservation (other than areas within the Town of Butner) if the Secretary gives written approval of the ordinance, except that ordinances adopted by a county under Article 18 of Chapter 153A of the General Statutes may not apply in the extraterritorial jurisdiction of the Town of Butner without approval of the Butner Town Council. The Secretary may withdraw approval of a county ordinance by giving written notification, by certified mail, return receipt requested, to the county. A county ordinance ceases to be effective in the Camp Butner reservation 30 days after the county receives the written notice of the withdrawal of approval. This section does not enhance or diminish the authority of a county to enact ordinances applicable to the Town of Butner and its extraterritorial jurisdiction.

(c) Notwithstanding any other provision of this Article, no portion of the lands owned by the State as of September 1, 2007, which are located in the extraterritorial jurisdiction or the incorporated limits of the Town of Butner shall be subject to any of the powers granted to the Town of Butner pursuant to Article 19 of Chapter 160A of the General Statutes except as to property no longer owned by the State. If any portion of such property owned by the State of North Carolina as of September 1, 2007, is no longer owned by the State, the Town of Butner may exercise all legal authority granted to the Town pursuant to the terms of its charter or by Article 19 of Chapter 160A of the General Statutes and may do so by ordinances adopted prior to the actual date of transfer. Before the State shall dispose of any property inside the incorporated limits of the Town of Butner or any of that property currently under the control of the North Carolina Department of Health and Human Services or the North Carolina Department of Agriculture and Consumer Services within the extraterritorial jurisdiction of the

Town of Butner, southeast of Old Highway 75, northeast of Central Avenue, southwest of 33rd Street, and northwest of "G" Street, by sale or lease for any use not directly associated with a State function, the Town of Butner shall first be given the right of first refusal to purchase said property at fair market value as determined by the average of the value of said property as determined by a qualified appraiser selected by the Secretary and a qualified appraiser selected by the Town of Butner. (1987, c. 536, s. 5; 2007-269, s. 9.)

§ 122C-411: Repealed by Session Laws 2011-260, s. 2, effective June 23, 2011.

§ 122C-411.1: Repealed by Session Laws 1996, Second Extra Session, c. 18, s. 21.4.

Part 1A. Butner Planning Council.

§ 122C-412. Repealed.

§ 122C-412.1. Repealed.

§ 122C-412.2. Repealed.

§ 122C-413: Repealed by Session Laws 2007-269, s. 10. For effective date, see Editor's note.

§ 122C-413.1: Repealed by Session Laws 2007-269, s. 10. For effective date, see Editor's note.

Part 1D. Butner Commissions.

§ 122C-414: Repealed by Session Laws 2011-260, s. 2, effective June 23, 2011.

§ 122C-415: Repealed by Session Laws 2011-266, s. 1.5, effective July 1, 2011.

§ 122C-416. Reserved for future codification purposes.

§ 122C-417. Reserved for future codification purposes.

§ 122C-418. Reserved for future codification purposes.

§ 122C-419. Reserved for future codification purposes.

§ 122C-420. Reserved for future codification purposes.

Part 2. Black Mountain Joint Security Force.

§ 122C-421. Joint security force.

(a) The Secretary may designate one or more special police officers who shall make up a joint security force to enforce the law of North Carolina and any ordinance or regulation adopted pursuant to G.S. 143-116.6 or G.S. 143-116.7 or pursuant to the authority granted the Department by any other law on the territory of the Black Mountain Center, the Alcohol Rehabilitation Center, and the Juvenile Evaluation Center, all in Buncombe County. After taking the oath of office for law enforcement officers as set out in G.S. 11-11, these special police officers have the same powers as peace officers now vested in sheriffs within the territory embraced by the named centers. These special police officers shall also have the power prescribed by G.S. 7B-1900 outside the territory embraced by the named centers but within the confines of Buncombe County. These special police officers may arrest persons outside the territory of the named centers but within the confines of Buncombe County when the person arrested has committed a criminal offense within that territory, for which the officers could have arrested the person within that territory, and the arrest is made during the person's immediate and continuous flight from that territory.

(b) These special police officers may exercise any and all of the powers enumerated in this Part upon or in pursuit from the property formerly occupied by the Black Mountain Center and transferred to the Division of Adult Correction of the Department of Public Safety by Senate Bill 388 and House Bill 709 of the 1985 Session of the General Assembly. These special police officers shall exercise said powers upon the property transferred to the Division of Adult Correction of the Department of Public Safety only by agreement of the Division of Adult Correction of the Department of Public Safety and the Department of Health and Human Services. (1983 (Reg. Sess., 1984), c. 1116, s. 30; 1985, c.

408, ss. 3, 5; c. 589, s. 2; 1995, c. 391, s. 3; 1997-320, s. 2; 1997-443, s. 11A.118(a); 1998-202, s. 13(gg); 2011-145, s. 19.1(h).)

§§ 122C-422 through 122C-429. Reserved for future codification purposes.

Part 2A. Broughton Hospital Joint Security Force.

§ 122C-430. Joint security force.

The Secretary may designate one or more special police officers who shall make up a joint security force to enforce the law of North Carolina and any ordinance or regulation adopted pursuant to G.S. 143-116.6 or G.S. 143-116.7 or pursuant to the authority granted the Department by any other law on the territory of the Broughton Hospital, North Carolina School for the Deaf at Morganton (K-12), Western Regional Vocational Rehabilitation Facility, J. Iverson Riddle Developmental Center, and the surrounding grounds and land adjacent to Broughton Hospital allocated to the Department of Agriculture and Consumer Services, all in Burke County. After taking the oath of office for law enforcement officers as set out in G.S. 11-11, these special police officers have the same powers as peace officers now vested in sheriffs within the territory embraced by the named facilities. These special police officers may arrest persons outside the territory of the named institutions but within the confines of Burke County when the person arrested has committed a criminal offense within that territory for which the officers could have arrested the person within that territory, and the arrest is made during the person's immediate and continuous flight from that territory. (1997-320, s. 1; 2007-177, s. 3; 2008-187, s. 30.)

Part 2B. Cherry Hospital Joint Security Force.

§ 122C-430.10. Joint security force.

The Secretary may designate one or more special police officers who shall make up a joint security force to enforce the law of North Carolina and any ordinance or regulation adopted pursuant to G.S. 143-116.6 or G.S. 143-116.7 or pursuant to the authority granted the Department by any other law on the territory of the Cherry Hospital in Wayne County. After taking the oath of office for law enforcement officers as set out in G.S. 11-11, these special police officers have the same powers as peace officers now vested in sheriffs within the territory of the Cherry Hospital. These special police officers shall also have the power prescribed by G.S. 122C-205 outside the territory of the Cherry Hospital but within the confines of Wayne County. These special police officers may arrest persons outside the territory of the Cherry Hospital but within the confines of Wayne County, when the person arrested has committed a criminal offense within the territory of the Cherry Hospital, for which the officers could have arrested the person within that territory, and the arrest is made during the person's immediate and continuous flight from that territory. (2001-125, s. 1.)

Part 2C. Dorothea Dix Hospital Joint Security Force.

§ 122C-430.20. Joint security force.

The Secretary may designate one or more special police officers who shall make up a joint security force to enforce the law of North Carolina and any ordinance or regulation adopted pursuant to G.S. 143-116.6 or G.S. 143-116.7 or pursuant to the authority granted the Department by any other law on the territory of the Dorothea Dix Hospital in Wake County. After taking the oath of office for law enforcement officers as set out in G.S. 11-11, these special police officers have the same powers as peace officers now vested in sheriffs within the territory of the Dorothea Dix Hospital. These special police officers shall also have the power prescribed by G.S. 122C-205 outside the territory of the Dorothea Dix Hospital but within the confines of Wake County. These special police officers may arrest persons outside the territory of the Dorothea Dix Hospital but within the confines of Wake County, when the person arrested has committed a criminal offense within the territory of the Dorothea Dix Hospital, for which the officers could have arrested the person within that territory, and the arrest is made during the person's immediate and continuous flight from that territory. (2001-125, s. 1.)

Part 2D. Long Leaf Neuro-Medical Treatment Center and Eastern North Carolina School for the Deaf Joint Security Force.

§ 122C-430.30. Joint security force.

The Secretary may designate one or more special police officers who shall make up a joint security force to enforce the law of North Carolina and any ordinance or regulation adopted pursuant to G.S. 143-116.6 or G.S. 143-116.7 or pursuant to the authority granted the Department by any other law on the territory of the Long Leaf Neuro-Medical Treatment Center and the Eastern North Carolina School for the Deaf in Wilson County. After taking the oath of office for law enforcement officers as set out in G.S. 11-11, these special police officers have the same powers as peace officers now vested in sheriffs within the territory embraced by the named facilities. These special police officers may arrest persons outside the territory of the named institutions but within the confines of Wilson County when the person arrested has committed a criminal offense within that territory for which the officers could have arrested the person within that territory, and the arrest is made during the person's immediate and continuous flight from that territory. (2009-315, s. 3.)

Part 3. North Carolina Alcoholism Research Authority.

§ 122C-431. North Carolina Alcoholism Research Authority created.

(a) The North Carolina Alcoholism Research Authority is created and shall consist of and be governed by a nine-member board to be appointed by the Governor. Three of the members shall be appointed for a two-year term, three shall be appointed for a four-year term and three shall be appointed for a six-year term; thereafter all appointments shall be for terms of six years. Any vacancy occurring in the membership of the board shall be filled by the Governor for the unexpired term.

(b) The board shall elect one of its members as chairman and one as vice-chairman. The director of the Center for Alcohol Studies of The University of North Carolina at Chapel Hill shall serve ex officio as executive secretary to the Authority. Board members shall receive the same per diem, subsistence, and travel allowances as members of similar State boards and commissions, provided funds are available in the "Alcoholism Research Fund" for this purpose. (1973, c. 682, ss. 1, 2; 1985, c. 589, s. 2.)

§ 122C-432. Authorized to receive and spend funds.

The Authority may receive funds from State, federal, private, or other sources. These funds shall be held separately and designated as the "Alcoholism Research Fund". The Authority shall spend the Fund on research as to the causes and effects of alcohol abuse and alcoholism and for the training of alcohol research personnel. Expenditures for the purposes specified in this section shall be made as grants to nonprofit corporations, organizations, agencies, or institutions engaging in such research or training. The Authority may also pay necessary administrative expenses from the Fund. (1973, c. 682, s. 3; 1985, c. 589, s. 2.)

§ 122C-433. Applications for grants; promulgation of rules.

(a) Applications for grants are processed by the Center for Alcohol Studies. All applications shall be reviewed by scientific consultants to the Center; and the Center, after review and study, shall make recommendations to the Authority as to the awarding of grants. The Center shall also furnish to the Authority clerical assistance as may be required.

(b) The Authority shall adopt rules relative to applications for grants, the reviewing of grants and awarding of grants. (1973, c. 682, ss. 4, 5; 1985, c. 589, s. 2.)

Chapter 122D.

North Carolina Agricultural Finance Act.

§ 122D-1. Short title.

This chapter shall be known and may be cited as the "North Carolina Agricultural Finance Act." (1983, c. 789, s. 1; 1985 (Reg. Sess., 1986), c. 1011, s. 1; 1989, c. 500, s. 109(e); 1989 (Reg. Sess., 1990), c. 1074, s. 32(b).)

§ 122D-2. Legislative findings and purposes.

(a) The General Assembly hereby finds and declares that there exists in the State of North Carolina a serious shortage of capital and credit available for investment in agriculture, for domestic and export purposes, at interest rates within the financial means of persons engaged in agricultural production and agricultural exports. This shortage of available capital and credit is severe throughout the State, has persisted for a number of years, and constitutes a grave threat to the agricultural industry and to the health, welfare, safety and prosperity of all residents of the State.

(b) The General Assembly hereby finds and declares further that private enterprise and existing federal and state governmental programs have not adequately alleviated the severe shortage of capital and credit available at affordable interest rates for investment in agriculture.

(c) The General Assembly hereby finds and declares that it is a matter of grave public necessity that the North Carolina Agricultural Finance Authority be created and empowered to alleviate the severe shortage of capital and credit available at affordable interest rates for investment in agriculture and for the export of agricultural products, commodities and services by providing such capital and credit at interest rates within the financial means of persons and businesses engaged in agriculture and agricultural exports. (1983, c. 789, s. 1; 1985 (Reg. Sess., 1986), c. 1011, s. 1; 1989, c. 500, s. 109(e); 1989 (Reg. Sess., 1990), c. 1074, s. 32(b).)

§ 122D-3. Definitions.

As used in this Chapter, the following terms, unless the context clearly indicates a different meaning, shall have the following meanings:

(1) "Agricultural Loan" means a loan made by a lending institution or by the Authority to any person for the purpose of financing or refinancing land acquisition or improvement; soil conservation; irrigation; construction, renovation or expansion of buildings and facilities; purchase of farm fixtures, livestock, poultry, and fish of any kind; seeds; fertilizers; pesticides; feeds; machinery; equipment; containers or supplies or any other products employed in the production, cultivation, harvesting, storage, marketing, distribution or export of agricultural products.

(2) "Agriculture" means the commercial production, storage, processing, marketing, distribution or export of any agronomic, floricultural, horticultural, viticultural, silvicultural or aquacultural crop including, but not limited to, farm products, livestock and livestock products, poultry and poultry products, milk

and dairy products, fruit and other horticultural products, and seafood and aquacultural products.

(3)   "Authority" means the North Carolina Agricultural Finance Authority created by this Chapter.

(4)   "Bonds" or "notes" means the bonds, notes, renewal notes, refunding bonds, interim certificates, certificates of indebtedness, debentures, warrants, commercial paper, or other obligations or evidences of indebtedness authorized to be issued by the Authority pursuant to the provisions of this Chapter.

(5)   "Commissioner" means the North Carolina Commissioner of Agriculture.

(6)   "Department" means the North Carolina Department of Agriculture and Consumer Services.

(7)   "Federal government" means the United States of America and any agency or instrumentality, corporate or otherwise, of the United States of America.

(8)   "Lending institution" means any bank, bank or trust company, federal land bank, production credit association, bank for cooperatives, building and loan association, homestead, insurance company, investment banker, mortgage banker or company, pension or retirement fund, savings bank or savings and loan association, small business investment company, credit union, the federal government or any other financial institution authorized to do business in North Carolina or operating under the supervision of any federal agency or any corporation organized or operating pursuant to Section 25 of the Federal Reserve Act.

(9)   "Persons" means any individual, partnership, firm, corporation, company, cooperative, association, society, trust or any other business unit or entity, including any state or federal agency.

(10)   "State" means the State of North Carolina or any agency or instrumentality thereof. (1983, c. 789, s. 1; 1985 (Reg. Sess., 1986), c. 1011, s. 1; 1987, c. 112, s. 3; 1989 (Reg. Sess., 1990), c. 1074, s. 32(b); 1997-261, s. 85.)

§ 122D-4. North Carolina Agricultural Finance Authority.

(a)   The North Carolina Agricultural Finance Authority, a body politic and corporate, is hereby created within the Department of Agriculture and Consumer Services. The Authority shall be constituted a public agency and an instrumentality of the State for the performance of essential public functions.

(b)   The Authority shall be composed of 10 members appointed to three-year terms as follows:

(1)   One member appointed by the Governor to a term that expires on 1 July of years that precede by one year those years that are evenly divisible by three.

(2)   One member appointed by the Governor to a term that expires on 1 July of years that are evenly divisible by three.

(3)   One member appointed by the Governor to a term that expires on 1 July of years that follow by one year those years that are evenly divisible by three.

(4)   One member appointed by the General Assembly upon the recommendation of the President Pro Tempore of the Senate to a term that expires on 1 July of years that precede by one year those years that are evenly divisible by three.

(5)   One member appointed by the General Assembly upon the recommendation of the President Pro Tempore of the Senate to a term that expires on 1 July of years that are evenly divisible by three.

(6)   One member appointed by the General Assembly upon the recommendation of the President Pro Tempore of the Senate to a term that expires on 1 July of years that follow by one year those years that are evenly divisible by three.

(7)   One member appointed by the General Assembly upon the recommendation of the Speaker of the House of Representatives to a term that expires on 1 July of years that precede by one year those years that are evenly divisible by three.

(8)   One member appointed by the General Assembly upon the recommendation of the Speaker of the House of Representatives to a term that expires on 1 July of years that are evenly divisible by three.

(9) One member appointed by the General Assembly upon the recommendation of the Speaker of the House of Representatives to a term that expires on 1 July of years that follow by one year those years that are evenly divisible by three.

(10) The Commissioner or the Commissioner's designee shall serve ex officio, with the same rights and privileges, including voting rights, as other members.

(c) A member appointed under subdivisions (1) through (9) of subsection (b) of this section may be reappointed to no more than two successive three-year terms. Upon the expiration of a three-year term, a member shall continue to serve until a successor is appointed and duly qualified as provided by G.S. 128-7.

(d) Vacancies in the offices of any appointed members of the Authority shall be filled in accordance with G.S. 120-122 for the remainder of the unexpired term. No vacant office shall be included in the determination of a quorum. No vacancy in office shall impair the rights of the members to exercise all rights and to conduct official business of the Authority.

(e) The domicile of the Authority shall be the City of Raleigh.

(f) A majority of the members shall constitute a quorum for the transaction of official business. All official actions of the Authority shall require an affirmative vote of a majority of the members present and voting at any meeting.

(g) Members of the Authority shall not receive any salary for the performance of their duties as members. Appointed members may receive per diem and necessary travel and subsistence expenses in accordance with the provisions of G.S. 138-5.

(h) The Authority shall meet quarterly and may meet more frequently upon call.

(i) The Authority may delegate to one or more of its members, officers, employees or agents such powers and duties as it may deem proper. (1983, c. 789, s. 1; 1985, c. 583, s. 2; 1985 (Reg. Sess., 1986), c. 1011, s. 1; 1989, c. 500, s. 109(e); 1989 (Reg. Sess., 1990), c. 1074, s. 32(b); 1995, c. 490, s. 4; 1997-261, s. 109; 2004-195, s. 5.1.)

§ 122D-5. Officers and employees; administration of Chapter.

(a)   The Authority shall annually elect a chairman and vice-chairman from its members.

(b)   The Authority may appoint an Executive Director. The salary of the Executive Director shall be set by the General Assembly in the Current Operations Appropriations Act.

(c)   The Executive Director shall administer and enforce this Chapter in accordance with rules promulgated by the Authority. The Executive Director may employ such personnel as may be necessary to administer and enforce the provisions of this Chapter, subject to the approval of the Authority. All employees other than the Executive Director shall be compensated in accordance with the salary schedules adopted pursuant to the North Carolina Human Resources Act. All employees shall be under the supervision of the Executive Director.

(d)   The Authority may employ legal, financial and technical experts and consultants as it deems necessary on a contractual basis. (1983, c. 789, s. 1; 1985, c. 583, s. 2; 1985 (Reg. Sess., 1986), c. 1011, s. 1; 1989, c. 500, s. 109(e); 1989 (Reg. Sess., 1990), c. 1074, s. 32(b); 2013-382, s. 9.1(c).)

§ 122D-6. General powers of Authority.

The Authority shall have all the powers necessary to give effect to and carry out the purposes and provisions of this Chapter, including the following powers in addition to all other powers granted by other provisions of this Chapter, to:

(1)   Sue and be sued in its own name and in the name of any subsidiary corporation or entity which may be created pursuant to paragraph (19) of this section;

(2)   Have a seal and alter the same at its pleasure;

(3)   Adopt bylaws for the internal organization and government of the Authority;

(4) Adopt, promulgate and amend rules for the administration of the Chapter;

(4a) Limit the definition of agricultural loan under G.S. 122D-3(1);

(5) Make and execute contracts and all other instruments necessary or convenient for the exercise of its powers and functions under this Chapter with any federal or State governmental agency, public or private corporation, lending institution or other entity or person, and each and any North Carolina governmental agency is hereby authorized to enter into contracts and otherwise cooperate with the agency to facilitate the purposes of this Chapter;

(6) Accept, administer and expend donations of movable or immovable property from any source, and receive, administer and expend appropriations from the legislature and financial assistance, guarantees, insurance or subsidies from the federal or State government;

(7) Subject to the rights of holders of bonds of the Authority, to renegotiate, refinance or foreclose on any mortgage, security interest or lien; or commence any action to protect or enforce any right or benefit conferred upon the Authority by any law, mortgage, security interest, lien, contract or other agreement; and bid for and purchase property at any foreclosure or at any other sale or otherwise acquire or take possession of any property; and in any such event, the Authority may complete, administer, pay the principal of and interest on any obligation incurred in connection with such property, dispose of and otherwise deal with such property in such manner as may be necessary or desirable to protect the interest of the Authority or of holders of its bonds therein;

(8) Procure or provide for the procurement of insurance or reinsurance against any loss in connection with its property or operations, including but not limited to insurance, reinsurance or other guarantees from any federal or State governmental agency or private insurance company for the payment of any bonds issued by the Authority, or bond, notes or any other obligations or evidences of indebtedness issued or made by any subsidiary corporation or entity created pursuant to subdivision (19) of this section or by any lending institution or other entity or person, or insurance or reinsurance against loss with respect to agricultural loans, mortgages or mortgage loans, or any other type of loans, including the power to pay premiums on such insurance or reinsurance;

(9) Make, insure, coinsure, reinsure, or cause to be insured, coinsured or reinsured, agricultural loans, mortgage loans or mortgages, or any other type of

loans and pay or receive premiums on such insurance, coinsurance or reinsurance, and establish reserves for losses, and participate in the insurance, coinsurance or reinsurance of agricultural loans, mortgage loans or mortgages, or any other type of loans with the federal or State government or any private insurance company;

(10) Undertake and carry out or authorize the completion of studies and analyses of agricultural conditions and needs within the State and needs relating to the promotion of agricultural exports and ways of meeting such needs, and make such studies and analyses available to the public and to the agricultural industry, and to engage in research or disseminate information on agriculture and agricultural exports;

(11) Accept federal, State or private financial or technical assistance and comply with any conditions for such assistance, provided such conditions are not in conflict with the intent of this Chapter;

(12) Establish, pay and collect fees and charge in connection with its loans, deposits, insurance commitments and services, including but not limited to, reimbursement of costs of issuing bonds, origination and servicing fees, and insurance premiums;

(13) Make loans to or deposits with lending institutions and purchase or sell agricultural loans;

(14) Acquire or contract to acquire from any person, firm, corporation, municipality, federal or State agency, by grant, purchase or otherwise, movable or immovable property or any interest therein; own, hold, clear, improve, lease, construct or rehabilitate, and sell, invest, assign, exchange, transfer, convey, lease, mortgage or otherwise dispose of or encumber the same, subject to the rights of holders of the bonds of the Authority, at public or private sale, with or without public bidding;

(15) Borrow money, issue bonds, and provide for the rights of the lenders or holders thereof and purchase, discount, sell, negotiate and guarantee, insure, coinsure and reinsure note, drafts, checks, bills of exchange, acceptances, bankers acceptances, cable transfers, letters of credit and other evidence of indebtedness with or without credit enhancement devices;

(16) Subject to the rights of holders of the bonds of the Authority, consent to any modification with respect to the rate of interest, time, payment of any

installment of principal or interest, security or any other term or condition of any loan, contract, mortgage, mortgage loan or commitment therefor or agreement of any kind to which the Authority is a party or beneficiary;

(17) Maintain an office at such place or places as the Authority shall determine;

(18) Serve as the beneficiary of any public trust;

(19) After reporting to the agriculture committees of the House of Representatives and the Senate, to create such subsidiary corporations or entities as may be necessary to borrow money, insure or reinsure agricultural loans, or issue bonds in the international financial market; and

(20) Purchase or participate in the purchase and enter into commitments by itself or together with others for the purchase of federally issued securities; provided that the proceeds of such securities will be utilized in accordance with the provisions of this Chapter. (1983, c. 789, s. 1; 1985 (Reg. Sess., 1986), c. 1011, s. 1; 1987, c. 112, s. 4; 1989, c. 500, s. 109(e); 1989 (Reg. Sess., 1990), c. 1000, s. 1, c. 1074, s. 32(b); 1993, c. 553, ss. 37, 38.)

§ 122D-7. Purchases and sales of agricultural loans.

The Authority may purchase or contract to purchase and sell or contract to sell agricultural loans made by lending institutions. All lending institutions are hereby authorized to purchase and sell agricultural loans to the Authority in accordance with the provisions of this Chapter and the rules and regulations of the Authority. To the extent that any provisions of this section may be inconsistent with any provision of law governing lending institutions, the provisions of this section shall control. (1985 (Reg. Sess., 1986), c. 1011, s. 1; 1989, c. 500, s. 109(e); 1989 (Reg. Sess., 1990), c. 1074, s. 32(b).)

§ 122D-8. Loans to and deposits with lending institutions.

The Authority may make, or contract to make, loans to and deposits with lending institutions. All lending institutions may borrow funds and accept deposits from the Authority in accordance with the provisions of this Chapter and the rules and regulations of the Authority. The Authority shall require that all proceeds of its loans to or deposits with lending institutions, or an equivalent amount, shall be used by such lending institutions to make agricultural loans, subject to such terms and conditions as the Authority may prescribe. To the extent that any provisions of this section may be inconsistent with any provision of the law governing lending institutions, the provisions of this section shall control. (1983, c. 789, s. 1; 1985 (Reg. Sess., 1986), c. 1011, s. 1; 1989, c. 500, s. 109(e); 1989 (Reg. Sess., 1990), c. 1074, s. 32(b).)

§ 122D-9. Insurance of agricultural loans.

(a)   The Authority may insure and reinsure agricultural loans made by lending institutions, subject to the terms, conditions, limitations, collateral and security provisions, and reserve requirements as shall be determined by the Authority in accordance with the rules adopted by the Authority.

(b)   Unless otherwise determined by the Authority, insurance of agricultural loans shall be in the amount of one hundred percent (100%) of the unpaid principal and interest on each loan.

(c)   An insured agricultural loan shall be in default when the holder of such loan makes application to the Authority for payment of insurance on such loan stating that such loan is in default in accordance with the terms of any agreement with respect to such insurance executed pursuant to this section.

(d)   The Authority may enter into agreements with any person, lending institution or holder of an insured agricultural loan upon such terms as may be agreed upon between the Authority and such person, lending institution, or holder, to provide for the administration, applications therefor, repayment thereof, and to establish the conditions for payment of insurance by the Authority, and the servicing, suit upon, or foreclosure of insured agricultural loans.

(e)   The aggregate value of all agricultural loans insured by the Authority and outstanding at any one time shall not exceed 20 times the total value of funds, investments, properties and other assets of the Authority except that this insurance may be further expanded by use of federal, state or private loan insurance, reinsurance, or guarantees of which the Authority is or shall become the beneficiary. (1985 (Reg. Sess., 1986), c. 1011, s. 1; 1989, c. 500, s. 109(e); 1989 (Reg. Sess., 1990), c. 1074, s. 32(b).)

§ 122D-10. Bonds of the Authority.

(a) The Authority may issue from time to time bonds, notes, bond anticipation notes, renewal notes, refunding bonds, interim certificates, certificates of indebtedness, debentures, warrants, commercial paper or other obligations or evidences of indebtedness, hereinafter collectively referred to as "bonds", to provide funds for and to fulfill and achieve its authorized public functions or corporate purposes, as set forth in this Chapter, including, but not limited to, the purchase of agricultural loans from lending institutions, the making of loans to or deposits with lending institutions, the payment of interest on bonds of the Authority, the establishment of reserves to secure such bonds, the establishment of reserves with respect to the insurance of agricultural loans, and all other purposes and expenditures of the Authority incident to and necessary or convenient to carry out its public functions or corporate purposes.

(b) Except as may otherwise be provided by the Authority, all bonds issued by the Authority shall be negotiable instruments and may be general obligations of the Authority, secured by the full faith and credit of the Authority and payable out of any money, assets or revenues of the Authority or from any other sources whatsoever that may be available to the Authority. Obligations issued under the provisions of this Chapter shall not be deemed to constitute a debt, liability or obligation of the State or of any political subdivision thereof or a pledge of the faith and credit of the State or of any such political subdivision, but shall be payable solely from the revenues or assets of the Authority. Each obligation issued under this Chapter shall contain on the face thereof a statement to the effect that the Authority shall not be obligated to pay the same nor the interest thereon except from the revenues or assets pledged therefor and that neither the faith and credit nor the taxing power of the State or of any political subdivision thereof is pledged to the payment of the principal of or the interest on such obligation.

(c) Bonds shall be authorized, issued and sold by a resolution or resolutions of the Authority adopted as provided in this Chapter. Such bonds may be of such series, bear such date or dates, mature at such time or times, bear interest at such rate or rates including variable, adjustable or zero interest rates, be payable at such time or times, be in such denominations, be sold at such price or prices, at public or private negotiated sale, be in such form, carry such registration and exchangeability privileges, be payable at such place or places, be subject to such terms of redemption, and be entitled to such priorities on the income, revenue and receipts of, or available to, the Authority as may be provided by the Authority in the resolution or resolutions providing for the issuance and sale of the bonds of the Authority.

(d) The bonds of the Authority shall be signed by such members or officers of the Authority, by either manual or facsimile signatures, as shall be determined by resolution or resolutions of the Authority, and shall have impressed or imprinted thereon the seal of the Authority, or a facsimile thereof. The coupons attached to coupon bonds of the Authority shall bear the facsimile signature of such member or officer of the Authority as shall be determined by resolution or resolutions of the Authority. The Authority may also provide for the authentication of the bonds, notes or coupons by a trustee or fiscal agent.

(e) Any bonds of the Authority may be validly issued, sold and delivered, notwithstanding that one or more of the members or officers of the Authority signing such bonds, or whose facsimile signature or signatures may be on the bonds or on coupons, shall have ceased to be such member or officer of the Authority at the time such bonds shall actually have been delivered.

(f) Bonds of the Authority may be sold for such price in such manner and from time to time as may be determined by the Authority to be most beneficial, and the Authority may pay all expenses, premiums, fees or commissions which it may deem necessary or advantageous in connection with the issuance and sale thereof, subject to the provisions of this Chapter.

(g) The bonds or notes may be issued in coupon or in registered form, or both, as the Agency may determine, and provision may be made for the registration of any coupon bonds or notes as to principal alone and also as to both principal and interest, and for the reconversion into coupon bonds or notes of any bonds or notes registered as to both principal and interest, and for the interchange of registered and coupon bonds or notes.

(h) Prior to the preparation of definitive bonds, the Authority may, under like restrictions, issue interim receipts or temporary bonds, with or without coupons, exchangeable for definitive bonds when such bonds shall have been executed and are available for delivery. The Authority may also provide for the replacement of any bonds or notes which shall become mutilated or shall be destroyed or lost.

(i) Bonds or notes may be issued under the provisions of this Chapter without obtaining, except as otherwise expressly provided in this Chapter, the consent of any department, division, commission, board, body, bureau or agency of the State, and without any other proceedings or the happening of any conditions or things other than those proceedings, conditions or things which are specifically required by this Chapter and the provisions of the resolution authorizing the issuance of such bonds or notes or the trust agreement securing the same. (1983, c. 789, s. 1; 1985 (Reg. Sess., 1986), c. 1011, s. 1; 1989, c. 500, s. 109(e); 1989 (Reg. Sess., 1990), c. 1000, s. 1.)

§ 122D-11. Statutory pledge.

Any pledge made by the Authority shall be valid and binding from time to time when the pledge is made. The money, assets or revenues of the Authority so pledged and thereafter received by the Authority shall immediately be subject to the lien of such pledge without any physical delivery thereof or further act, and the lien of any pledge shall be valid and binding as against all parties having claims of any kind in tort, contract or otherwise against the Authority, irrespective of whether such parties have notice thereof. Neither the resolution nor any other instrument by which a pledge is created need be recorded or filed in order to establish and perfect a lien or security interest in the property so pledged by the Authority. Nothing herein shall be construed to prohibit the Authority from selling any assets subject to any such pledge except to the extent that any such sale may be restricted by the trust agreement or resolution providing for the issuance of such obligations. (1983, c. 789, s. 1; 1985 (Reg. Sess., 1986), c. 1011, s. 1; 1989, c. 500, s. 109(e); 1989 (Reg. Sess., 1990), c. 1074, s. 32(b).)

§ 122D-12. Refunding bonds.

Subject to the rights of the holders of the bonds of the Authority, the Authority may issue from time to time its bonds for the purpose of refunding any bonds of the Authority then outstanding, together with the payment of any redemption premiums thereon and interest accrued or to accrue to the date of redemption of such outstanding bonds. All such refunding bonds of the Authority shall be issued, sold or exchanged, and delivered, shall be secured, and shall be subject to the provisions of this Chapter in the same manner and to the same extent as any other bonds issued by the Authority pursuant to this Chapter, unless otherwise determined by resolution of the Authority. Refunding bonds issued by the Authority as herein provided may be sold or exchanged for outstanding bonds of the Authority and, if sold, the proceeds thereof may be applied, in addition to any other authorized purposes, to the purchase, redemption or payment of such outstanding bonds.

Pending the application of the proceeds of any such refunding obligations, with any other available funds, to the payment of the principal, accrued interest and any redemption premium on the obligations being refunded, and, if so provided or permitted in the resolution authorizing the issuance of such refunding obligations or in the trust agreement securing the same, to the payment of any interest on such refunding obligations and any expenses in connection with such refunding, such proceeds may be invested in direct obligations of, or obligations the principal of and the interest on which are unconditionally guaranteed by, the United States of America which shall mature or which shall be subject to redemption by the holders thereof, at the option of such holders, not later than the respective dates when the proceeds, together with the interest accruing thereon, will be required for the purposes intended. (1983, c. 789, s. 1; 1985 (Reg. Sess., 1986), c. 1011, s. 1; 1989, c. 500, s. 109(e); 1989 (Reg. Sess., 1990), c. 1000, s. 1.)

§ 122D-13. Purchase of bonds by Authority.

Subject to the rights of holders of bonds, the Authority shall have the power out of any funds available therefor, to purchase bonds of the Authority, which shall thereupon be cancelled, at a price not exceeding:

(1) If the bonds are then subject to optional redemption, the optional redemption price then applicable plus accrued interest to the next interest payment date thereon; or

(2) If the bonds are not then subject to optional redemption, the optional redemption price applicable on the first date after such purchase upon which the notes or bonds become subject to optional redemption plus accrued interest to such date. (1985 (Reg. Sess., 1986), c. 1011, s. 1; 1989, c. 500, s. 109(e); 1989 (Reg. Sess., 1990), c. 1074, s. 32(b).)

§ 122D-14. Exemption from taxes.

The exercise of the powers granted by this Chapter will be in all respects for the benefit of the people of the State, for their well-being and prosperity and for the improvement of their social and economic conditions, and the Authority shall not be required to pay any tax or assessment on any property owned by the Authority under the provisions of this Chapter or upon the income therefrom.

Any obligations issued by the Authority under the provisions of this Chapter shall at all times be free from taxation by the State or any local unit or political subdivision or other instrumentality of the State, excepting inheritance or gift taxes, income taxes on the gain from the transfer of the obligations, and franchise taxes. The interest on the obligations is not subject to taxation as income. (1985 (Reg. Sess., 1986), c. 1011, s. 1; 1989 (Reg. Sess., 1990), c. 1000, s. 1; 1995, c. 46, s. 11.)

§ 122D-15. Covenant of State.

In consideration of the acceptance of and payment for the bonds of the Authority by the holders thereof, the State does hereby pledge to and agree with the holders of any bonds of the Authority issued pursuant to the provisions of this Chapter, that the State will not impair, limit or alter the rights hereby vested in the Authority to fulfill the terms of any agreements made with the holders of the bonds of the Authority, or in any way impair the rights or remedies of such holders thereof, until such bonds, together with the interest thereon, with interest on any unpaid installments of interest, and all costs and expenses in connection with any action or proceedings by or on behalf of such holders, are fully met and discharged. The Authority is authorized to include this pledge and agreement of the State in any agreement with the holders of bonds of the Authority. (1983, c. 789, s. 1; 1985 (Reg. Sess., 1986), c. 1011, s. 1; 1989, c. 500, s. 109(e); 1989 (Reg. Sess., 1990), c. 1000, s. 1.)

§ 122D-16. Trust funds.

(a) Notwithstanding any other provisions of law to the contrary, all moneys received pursuant to the authority of this Chapter shall be deemed to be trust funds to be held and applied solely as provided in this Chapter. Interest earned from these moneys and interest received from loans made from these moneys may be used for any purpose set out in this Chapter and for the costs of administering this Chapter. The resolution authorizing any obligations or the trust agreement securing any obligations may provide that any of these moneys may be temporarily invested pending the disbursement of the moneys and shall provide that any officer with whom, or any bank or trust company with which, such moneys shall be deposited, shall act as trustee of the moneys and shall hold and apply the moneys for the purposes under this Chapter, subject to any rules adopted pursuant to this Chapter and any provisions in the provision or trust agreement.

(b) All moneys of the Authority may be invested in the following:

(1) Bonds, notes or treasury bills of the United States;

(2) Non-convertible debt securities of the following issuers:

a. The Federal Home Loan Bank Board;

b. Fannie Mae;

c. The Federal Farm Credit Bank; and

d. The Student Loan Marketing Association;

(3) Any other obligations not listed above which are guaranteed as to principal and interest by the United States or any of its agencies;

(4) Certificates of deposit and other evidences of deposit at state and federal chartered banks and savings and loan associations; provided that any principal amount of such certificate in excess of the amount insured by the federal government or any agency thereof be fully collateralized;

(5) Obligations of the United States or its agencies under a repurchase agreement for a shorter time than the maturity date of the security itself if the market value of the security itself is more than the amount of funds invested;

(6) Money market funds whose portfolios consist of any of the foregoing investments;

(7) A guaranteed investment or similar contract, which provides for the investment of funds at a guaranteed rate of return, with an insurance company or depository financial institution with a claim paying rating of no less than either of the two highest grades given by a nationally recognized rating agency; and

(8) Any other investment authorized by law for the investment of funds by a unit of local government. (1983, c. 789, s. 1; 1985 (Reg. Sess., 1986), c. 1011, s. 1; 1987, c. 112, s. 1; 1989, c. 500, s. 109(e); 1989 (Reg. Sess., 1990), c. 1074, s. 32(b); 1997-443, s. 14.5; 2001-487, s. 14(k).)

§ 122D-17. Bonds as legal investment and security for public deposits.

Obligations issued under the provisions of this Chapter are hereby made securities in which all public officers and public bodies of the State and its political subdivisions, all insurance companies, trust companies, banking associations, investment companies, executors, administrators, trustees and other fiduciaries may properly and legally invest funds, including capital in their control or belonging to them. Such obligations are hereby made securities which may properly and legally be deposited with and received by any State or municipal officer or any agency or political subdivision of the State for any purpose for which the deposit of bonds, notes or obligations of the State is now or may hereafter be authorized by law. (1983, c. 789, s. 1; 1985 (Reg. Sess., 1986), c. 1011, s. 1; 1989, c. 500, s. 109(e); 1989 (Reg. Sess., 1990), c. 1000, s. 1.)

§ 122D-18. Account and audits.

(a) Subject to the provisions of any contract with the holders of its bonds, the Authority shall establish a system of accounts.

(b) The Authority may cause an independent audit of its books and accounts to be prepared annually and the cost thereof may be paid from any available moneys of the Authority.

(c) Within six months after the end of each fiscal year, the Authority shall submit to the Governor and to the General Assembly an annual report on the operations of the Authority. Within 60 days after receipt thereof, the Authority shall submit to the Governor and to the General Assembly a copy of the report of every audit of the books and accounts of the Authority. (1983, c. 789, s. 1; 1985 (Reg. Sess., 1986), c. 1011, s. 1; 1989, c. 500, s. 109(e); 1989 (Reg. Sess., 1990), c. 1074, s. 32(b).)

§ 122D-19. Cooperation of State agencies.

All State officers and agencies may render such services to the Authority within their respective functions as may be requested by the Authority. (1985 (Reg. Sess., 1986), c. 1011, s. 1; 1989, c. 500, s. 109(e); 1989 (Reg. Sess., 1990), c. 1074. s. 32(b).)

§ 122D-20. Construction of Chapter.

This Chapter, being necessary for the welfare of the State and its residents, shall be liberally construed to effect the purposes thereof. (1983, c. 789, s. 1; 1985 (Reg. Sess., 1986), c. 1011, s. 1; 1989, c. 500, s. 109(e); 1989 (Reg. Sess., 1990), c. 1074, s. 32(b).)

§ 122D-21. Termination of the Authority.

In the event of the termination of the Authority, all of its rights, money, assets and revenues in excess of its obligations shall be deposited in the general fund. (1985 (Reg. Sess., 1986), c. 1011, s. 1; 1989, c. 500, s. 109(e); 1989 (Reg. Sess., 1990), c. 1074, s. 32(b).)

§ 122D-22. Severability.

The provisions of this Chapter are severable, and if any provision of this Chapter is held invalid by a court of competent jurisdiction, the invalidity shall not affect other provisions of this Chapter which can be given effect without the invalid provision. (1983, c. 789, s. 1; 1985 (Reg. Sess., 1986), c. 1011, s. 1; 1989, c. 500, s. 109(e); 1989 (Reg. Sess., 1990), c. 1074, s. 32(b).)

§ 122D-23. Immunity.

There shall be no liability on the part of and no cause of action of any nature may arise against the members of the Authority for any acts or omission to act by them in the performance of their powers and duties under this Chapter. The immunity established by this section shall not extend to willful neglect or malfeasance that would otherwise be actionable. The immunity established by this section further shall not extend to any act or omission occurring or arising out of the operation of a motor vehicle. The immunity established herein is waived to the extent of any indemnification by insurance for the liability of the members of the authority for which this act otherwise provides immunity. (1987, c. 335, s. 1; 1989, c. 500, s. 109(e); 1989 (Reg. Sess., 1990), c. 1074, s. 32(b).)

Chapter 122E.

North Carolina Housing Trust and Oil Overcharge Act.

§ 122E-1. Short title.

This Chapter shall be known and may be cited as the "North Carolina Housing Trust and Oil Overcharge Act." (1987, c. 841, s. 1.)

§ 122E-2. Definitions.

As used in this Chapter:

(1) The term "substandard unit" means a housing unit which, by reason of dilapidation, deterioration, age or obsolescence, inadequate provision for ventilation, light, air, sanitation, or open spaces, high density of population and overcrowding, unsanitary or unsafe conditions, or the existence of conditions which endanger life or property by fire and other causes, or any combination of such factors, is conducive to ill health, transmission of disease, or has an adverse effect upon the public health, safety, morals or welfare of its inhabitants.

(2) The term "Partnership" means the North Carolina Housing Partnership.

(3) The term "Agency" means the North Carolina Housing Finance agency.

(4) The term "Fund" means the North Carolina Housing Trust Fund.

(5) The term "Treasurer" means the North Carolina State Treasurer.

(6) The term "affordable housing unit" means a unit for which an occupant is paying no more than thirty percent (30%) of gross monthly household income for rent and utilities.

(7) The term "Stripper Well Litigation Funds" means funds received by North Carolina, and all interest and other income generated by such funds, pursuant to the Settlement Agreement that was approved by Order of the Court, dated July 7, 1986, in In re: The Department of Energy Stripper Well Exemption Litigation M.D.L. No. 378 (D. Kan.).

(8) The term "Diamond Shamrock Litigation Funds" means funds received by North Carolina, and all interest and other income generated by such funds, pursuant to the Order of the Court, dated June 6, 1986, in Diamond Shamrock Refining and Marketing Co. v. Standard Oil Co., Civil Action No. C2-84-1432 (S.D. Ohio). (1987, c. 841, s. 1.)

§ 122E-3. North Carolina Housing Trust Fund.

(a) There is established a North Carolina Housing Trust Fund, separate and distinct from the General Fund.

(b) The Fund shall consist of monies received under this act and any other sources of revenue, public or private, dedicated for inclusion in the Fund.

(c) The State Treasurer shall serve as trustee for the Fund. The Treasurer shall invest the North Carolina Housing Trust Fund revenues he receives as provided in G.S. 147-69.2(b). The Treasurer shall provide the Agency with quarterly and annual reports of Fund revenues and interest earnings. (1987, c. 841, s. 1.)

§ 122E-3.1. Community Living Housing Fund.

(a) Definitions. - The following definitions apply in this section:

(1) Catchment area. - As defined in G.S. 122C-3.

(2) Targeted units. - Units within Low Income Housing Tax Credit developments that are specifically designed to facilitate the inclusion of individuals with disabilities.

(b) Creation and Source of Funds. - The Community Living Housing Fund is established within the Housing Finance Agency to pay for the transition of individuals diagnosed with severe mental illness or severe and persistent mental illness as defined in G.S. 122C-20.5 from institutional settings to integrated, community-based supported housing and to increase the percentage of targeted housing units available to individuals with disabilities for use in the North Carolina Supportive Housing Program under Article 1B of Chapter 122C of the General Statutes. Beginning with fiscal year 2013-2014, any unexpended, unencumbered balance of the amount appropriated to the Transitions to Community Living Fund established pursuant to Section 10.23A(d) of S.L. 2012-142 at the end of each fiscal year shall not revert but shall be transferred and made available to the Community Living Housing Fund.

(c) Use of Funds. - The North Carolina Housing Finance Agency, in consultation with the Department of Health and Human Services, shall be responsible for administering the Community Living Housing Fund. The monies in the Fund shall be available for expenditure only upon an act of appropriation by the General Assembly and only for the following purposes:

(1) To provide permanent community-based housing in integrated settings appropriate for individuals with severe mental illness and severe and persistent mental illness.

(2) To support an increase in the number of targeted units for individuals with disabilities located in housing projects funded by the Housing Finance Agency from ten percent (10%) to fifteen percent (15%). The additional targeted units funded shall be made available to the Department of Health and Human Services for use in the North Carolina Supportive Housing Program under Article 1B of Chapter 122C of the General Statutes. Priority for funding of the additional targeted units shall be given to units to be located in catchment areas identified by the Department of Health and Human Services, in consultation with the North Carolina Housing Finance Agency and LMECOs, as having the greatest need for targeted units. (2013-397, s. 8.)

§ 122E-4. North Carolina Housing Partnership created; compensation; organization.

(a) The North Carolina Housing Partnership is hereby created within the North Carolina Housing Finance Agency to establish policy, promulgate rules and regulations, and oversee the operation of the Fund. The Partnership shall be constituted to coordinate private enterprise and investment with public efforts to address the serious shortage of decent, safe, and affordable housing for low and moderate income citizens of this State.

(b) The Partnership shall consist of 13 members as follows:

(1) The Executive Director of the North Carolina Housing Finance Agency shall serve ex officio;

(2) The Secretary of the Department of Commerce or his designee shall serve ex officio;

(3) The State Treasurer or his designee shall serve ex officio;

(4) In accordance with G.S. 120-121, five members shall be appointed by the General Assembly upon the recommendation of the President Pro Tempore of the Senate, provided that one member shall be a representative of the homebuilding industry, one member shall be a low income housing advocate, and one member shall be a representative of the League of Municipalities;

(5) In accordance with G.S. 120-121, five members shall be appointed by the General Assembly upon the recommendation of the Speaker of the House of Representatives, provided that one member shall be a representative of the real estate lending industry; one member shall be a representative of a non-profit housing development corporation; and one member shall be a resident of low income housing.

The members of the Partnership shall elect one of their members to serve as Chairman for a term of one year. Seven members of the Partnership shall constitute a quorum. All members shall have the right to vote on all issues before the Partnership.

(c) Members of the Partnership shall serve for three year terms. Initial terms shall begin on September 1, 1987. Appointed members shall serve until their successors are appointed and qualify.

(d)   Vacancies in the offices of any appointed members shall be filled in accordance with G.S. 120-122 for the remainder of the unexpired term. No vacant office shall be included in the determination of a quorum. No vacancy in office shall impair the rights of the members to exercise all rights and conduct the official business of the Partnership.

(e)   Members of the Partnership shall receive as compensation for each day spent on work for the Partnership such actual expenses as may be incurred for such travel and subsistence in the performance of official duties and such per diem as is allowed by law for other such State boards and commissions. Members shall not receive a salary for the performance of their duties as members.

(f)   The Partnership shall have the following powers and duties:

(1)   To promulgate rules and regulations governing all policy matters relating to the implementation of all programs for uses of the Fund and the Partnership's oversight of the Agency's administration of the Fund.

(2)   To promote the development of a coordinated State low income housing plan.

(3)   To obtain necessary information from other State agencies concerning housing; and

(4)   To allocate monies contained in the Fund.

(g)   The Partnership may appoint an Executive Director. The Executive Director shall be empowered to employ such additional professional and clerical assistance as the Partnership may deem necessary to administer the provisions of this Chapter. All employees of the Partnership, other than the Executive Director, shall be compensated in accordance with the salary schedules adopted pursuant to the North Carolina Human Resources Act. The Partnership and the Agency may enter into agreements for the use of Agency staff to assist the Partnership and the provision of administrative support for the Partnership by the Agency.

(h)   The Partnership shall meet quarterly and can meet more regularly upon the call of the Chairman or upon written request of four members.

(i) Members of the Partnership may not receive any direct benefit from, or participate in, the programs of the Fund. Members of the Partnership may be employed by, or serve as a board member of, a nonprofit entity participating in a program of the Fund if the member discloses the employment or the membership in the minutes of the Partnership and does not vote on any matter pertaining to the entity's participation. This policy applies to:

(1) Individual members of the Partnership;

(2) Businesses, corporations, or partnerships owned in whole or in part by members of the Partnership; and

(3) The immediate family members of the members of the Partnership. (1987, c. 841, s. 1; 1989, c. 727, ss. 218(84), 223(c); c. 751, ss. 7(12), 9(c), 16; c. 754, s. 53; 1991 (Reg. Sess., 1992), c. 959, s. 31; 1995, c. 490, s. 25; 2013-382, s. 9.1(c).)

§ 122E-5. Administration.

(a) The North Carolina Housing Finance Agency shall administer the Fund in accordance with the policies, rules and regulations promulgated by the Partnership.

(b) The Agency's responsibilities shall include:

(1) The Management of the overall program for the use of the fund;

(2) Development of program design in accordance with policies established by the Partnership;

(3) Development and management of a selection system in accordance with policies established by the Partnership;

(4) Provision of technical assistance to prospective applicants; and

(5) Monitoring of projects to ensure compliance with applicable State and federal laws and regulations and relevant court decisions.

(6) The Agency shall promulgate rules and regulations governing the administration of the Fund and its overall program for use of the Fund in accordance with the policies, rules and regulations promulgated by the Partnership.

(c) In administering the Fund, the Agency shall maintain a separate account for and shall keep separate records regarding the principal and expenditures made from the Stripper Well Litigation funds and the Diamond Shamrock Litigation funds in order to assure the proper expenditure and reporting of these funds to the respective courts and to the United States Department of Energy.

(d) The Agency shall file all required reports with the appropriate courts in the Stripper Well Litigation and in the Diamond Shamrock Litigation, and otherwise shall fully comply with all relevant court orders. The Agency also shall file the report of planned expenditures which is required under Paragraph II. B. 3. f. iv of the Final Settlement Agreement in the Stripper Well Litigation prior to its first expenditure of Stripper Well Litigation Funds. (1987, c. 841, s. 1.)

§ 122E-6. Uses of funds.

Funds from the Fund shall be used to increase the supply of decent, affordable and energy-efficient housing for low, very low, and moderate income residents of the State as defined in G.S. 122E-2. Such funds shall be used to finance, in whole or in part, projects and activities eligible under this section. The Agency shall make available loans, grants, interest reduction payments, or other comparable forms of assistance to eligible applicants. Provided, however, that with regard to those funds of the Fund which are Stripper Well Litigation Funds or Diamond Shamrock Funds, grants shall be from both the principal and income generated by the principal of such Funds so that all such Funds will be expended within a reasonable period of time. Provided, further, that with regard to that portion of the Fund which is derived from the appropriation of State funds, the amount of grants to be made in any fiscal year shall be limited to the amount of income generated by the principal of that portion of the Fund.

(a) Beneficiaries.

(1) The Partnership shall ensure that the Agency's program for uses of monies from the Fund directly benefit low, very low and moderate income persons and families as set forth in subsections (2), (3), and (4) below.

(2) The Partnership shall ensure that at least thirty percent (30%) of the total funds from the Fund eligible for expenditure by the Agency in any fiscal year directly benefit persons and families whose incomes do not exceed thirty percent (30%) of the median family income for the local area, with adjustments for family size, according to the latest figures available from the U.S. Department of Housing and Urban Development.

(3) The Partnership shall be authorized to allocate up to thirty percent (30%) of the total funds from the Fund for the benefit of persons and families whose incomes do not exceed fifty percent (50%) of the median family income for the local area, with adjustments for family size, according to the latest figures available from the U.S. Department of Housing and Urban Development; provided, however, these funds may also be directed for the benefit of the persons and families defined in subsection (2).

(4) The Partnership shall ensure that no more than forty percent (40%) of the total funds from the fund eligible for expenditure by the Agency in any fiscal year directly benefit persons and families whose incomes do not exceed eighty percent (80%) of the median family income for the local area, with adjustments for family size, according to the latest figures available from the U.S. Department of Housing and Urban Development.

(b) Eligible Projects.

(1) An eligible project consists of one or more residential buildings containing similarly constructed units, the site on which the building(s) is located and any functionally related facilities. Multiple buildings may constitute a project only if bounded together as a result of proximate location, or common ownership and financing.

(2) Projects which provide for the construction or rehabilitation of rental projects must contain contractual guarantees to ensure that at least twenty percent (20%) of the units are occupied by persons and families defined in G.S. 122E-6(a) (2) and (3) for a period of time following the award of grants or loan funds from the Fund, said period to be not less than 10 years, and shall be established by the rules and regulations promulgated by the Partnership and are affordable housing units as defined in G.S. 122E-2(9) [G.S. 122E-2(6)].

(c) Eligible Uses for State Appropriated Funds.

Eligible activities include, but are not limited to the following:

(1) Rehabilitation, including weatherization, of sub-standard housing units;

(2) Assistance for costs of necessary studies, surveys, plans and permits, engineering, legal and architectural and other technical services;

(3) new construction, including costs of land acquisition and site preparation;

(4) Assistance for the construction or rehabilitation of shelters for the homeless;

(5) Assistance in the development of manufactured housing sites which constitute eligible projects as defined in subsection (b) of this section. The Agency may contract with outside organizations to provide such assistance; and

(6) Such other programs which increase the supply of decent and affordable housing for low, very low, and moderate income persons which the Partnership shall deem appropriate to meet the purposes stated in this section.

(d) Eligible Uses for Stripper Well Litigation Funds and Diamond Shamrock Litigation Funds.

(1) Eligible uses for the Stripper Well Litigation funds shall be those uses permitted under Paragraph II.B.3.f.ii. of the Settlement Agreement that was approved by Order of the Court, dated July 7, 1986, including, but not limited to, those residential energy-related uses which are identified in Exhibit J to said Settlement Agreement.

(2) Eligible uses for the Diamond Shamrock Litigation funds shall be those uses permitted under Exhibit B to the Order of the Court, dated June 6, 1986, including but no [not] limited to those residential energy-related uses which are identified in Attachment C to Exhibit B to said Order. (1987, c. 841, s. 1.)

§ 122E-7. Eligible applicants.

Eligible applicants shall include units of State and local governments including municipal corporations, for profit and nonprofit housing developers. Provided, however, that the Partnership's rules and regulations shall ensure an equitable distribution of Fund funds based upon population and low and moderate income housing needs across the State. (1987, c. 841, s. 1.)

§ 122E-8. Allocation of funds.

(a) Monies within the Fund shall be allocated to eligible applicants under this Chapter by the Agency, in accordance with funding cycles established at least annually. The Partnership shall establish rules and regulations with full public input, including at least one public hearing for which adequate notice is provided in a timely manner. These rules and regulations shall establish general policies governing the eligibility of applicants, application procedures, project eligibility requirements, and the criteria and standards for awarding grants and loans. Such rules and regulations shall be adopted within 270 days from the effective date of this Chapter.

(b) The Agency shall promulgate rules and regulations governing the review of applications for assistance and the awarding of grants or loans under this Chapter in accordance with the rules and regulations adopted pursuant to subsection (a) above. The rules and regulations shall provide that if an application is rejected, the Agency shall detail in writing the reasons for the rejection.

(c) The Agency shall give priority to applications providing for:

(1) The improvement of existing housing stock which is affordable for low and very low income families;

(2) The construction of housing units for very low income families; and

(3) The leveraging of Fund monies by combination with other private or governmental loan grant or bond financing programs.

(d) The Agency shall also give priority to applications which include provisions such as:

(1) Interest rates and loan terms more favorable than those conventionally offered;

(2) Developer contributions to project costs;

(3) Local government contributions to project costs, including infrastructure improvements, contributions of publicly owned land for housing development, and the provision of funds for such services as child care and job training;

(4) Coordination with other housing and/or infrastructure investments in the community;

(5) Provision of housing to the disabled, single parent households, or rurally isolated households; or

(6) Provision of housing to persons whose current housing fails to meet basic standards of health and safety and who have little prospect of improving the condition of their housing except by residing in an eligible project receiving assistance under this Chapter. (1987, c. 841, s. 1; 1997-506, s. 44.)

§ 122E-9. Displacement.

In establishing criteria for G.S. 122E-8(a), the Agency shall give special attention to designing protections to provide that any lawful occupants who live in a project as defined in G.S. 122E-6(b) prior to rehabilitation or demolition shall not be displaced as a result of such activity, other than temporarily, in which case suitable relocation arrangements shall be provided. The Agency shall promulgate rules concerning acquisition of property and relocation. (1987, c. 841, s. 1.)

Vision Books Order Form

Fax Orders:	1-980-299-5965
Phone Orders:	1-704-898-0770
E-mail Orders:	www.visionbooks.org
Mail Orders:	Vision Books, LLC P.O. Box 42406 Charlotte, NC 28215

Shipp To:
Name_____
Address_____
City_____State_____Zip_____
Phone_____Fax_____
Email_____@_____

Bill To: We can bill a third party on your behalf.
Name_____
Address_____
City_____State_____Zip_____
Phone____(_____)_____Fax_____
Email_____@_____

Pamphlet Number ($15.00 Each)	Qty	Total Cost
_____	_____	_____
_____	_____	_____
_____	_____	_____
_____	_____	_____
_____	_____	_____
_____	_____	_____
_____	_____	_____
_____	_____	_____
Full Volume Set 1-92	92 Pamphlets	1,380.00

Free Shipping Shipping & Handling on Full Volume Orders
Add $1.00 Shipping & Handling per pamphlet $_____

Total Cost $_____

Thank you for your support. Management!

DID YOU ENJOY THIS BOOK?

Vision Books, LLC would like to hear from you! If you or someone you know has been fasely imprisoned, we would like to hear your story. If the 'North Carolina Criminal Law and Procedure' has had an effect in your life or if you have suggestions, we would like to hear from you. Send your letters to:

Vision Books, LLC
Attn: Staff Writers
P.O. Box 42406
Charlotte, NC 28215
Email: staff@visionbooks.org

Order Additional Copies:

Fax Orders:	1-980-299-5965
Phone Orders:	1-704-898-0770
E-mail Orders:	www.visionbooks.org
Mail Orders:	Vision Books, LLC P.O. Box 42406 Charlotte, NC 28215